HRD
RADICALISM IN THE SERVICE SECTOR

HRD
RADICALISM IN THE SERVICE SECTOR

M.P. Srivastava

GYAN

GYAN PUBLISHING HOUSE

NEW DELHI - 110002

HRD
RADICALISM IN THE SERVICE SECTOR
(Human Rights)

ISBN : 81-212-0722-3

Published in 2000 in India by
Gyan Publishing House
5, Ansari Road
New Delhi 110 002
Phone : 3282060, 3261060 Fax : 3285914
E-mail : gyanbook@del2.vsnl.net.in
Visit Our Website At http:\\www.gyanbooks.com

Laser Typesetting: Grow Computers, Delhi
Printed at: Mehra Offset Press, New Delhi

Contents

PREFACE

Human Resource Development (HRD) has relevance both at micro and macro level. At micro level, it is concerned with improving the quality of work. At macro level, it encompasses a number of inter-related elements which are the pivot of development. These elements among others include the development of individual (physical, mental and cultural) and the organization.

There is a growing awareness about the importance of HRD both in the public and private sector organizations. The concept of HRD has been taken as a main theme in many organizations but the concept is not being implemented and practised as the organizations have proved inadequate to meet the challenges of change.

It is in this context, that I conceptualized the present work which deals with HRD Radicalism in the Service Sector and particularly in service sub-sectors like Telecommunication, Banking and Railways. The purpose of this book is to help HRD planners to develop and strengthen the HRD system for each category of worker within the organization. The issues covered are expected to contribute to the formulation of actual HRD plans as they provide a set of suggestions which the organizations may like to follow for the growth and development of their employees. Similarly, to bring about the required changes systematic integrated HRD plans has been identified which inter alia takes into account the knowledge, skills, attitudes, ethos and environment, of the employees.

This work particularly, assumes importance at this moment when a number of HRD strategies/initiatives are under way to develop willingness to learn, work hard, dedication, integrity, ability to get along with others, positive attitude and confidence within the employees. It is a moment of hope and anxiety both for the worker and the organization as old uncertainties and dogmas are giving way to an open minded quest for policies that can work to improve the working conditions and environment of the organization.

In the same wake, the volume reviews the existing HRD practices, and deliberates on the new HRD needs and on the role that HRD can play in moving the organization and the worker towards greater efficiency and effectiveness.

The book also attempts to translate the various concerns of the HRD planners into operational terms by means of appropriate policies, plans and programmes; building and strengthening of the necessary institutions like education and training, information systems, monitoring and evaluation.

Chapter I of the book starts with International Scenario of HRD that includes policies and programmes relating HRD. ILO standards on Human Resource Development have also been broadly explained.

The chapter II deals with policies that exist for HRD, impact of economic reforms on the organization and employee and the major HRD interventions required for the development of the sector.

Chapter III of the book stresses on the "Management and Development of Human Resources: Indian scenario" - Besides dealing with the mechanism, scope and future role of HRD, the chapter also looks at the planning and utilization pattern of employees in the Government, Public and Private Sector. Issues like growth of HRD, personnel policies and evolution of human resource management have also been covered.

Chapter IV deals with HRD at organizational level. Various aspects like need for HRD in the organization, role of HRD in the organization and also the need for developing HRD perspective within the organization have been covered. Evaluation of employees performance component of evaluation as a tool of HRD also forms an integral part of this chapter.

Chapter V : Education : Retrospect and Prospect deals with the development of Educational Programmes of two levels : physical resources and human resources and further identifies that it is not education per-se but a broad concept encompassing health, nutrition, employment, science and technology.

Chapter VI deals with the HRD issues in various sub-sectors of the service sector. The sub-sectors dealt with include Telecommunications, Banking Industry and Railways. Issues dealt in this chapter provide details on HRD activities, such as training and development, recruitment and promotion, human resource information system and their impact on the development of the organization and the employee. It also provides an insight into the HRD policy issues and how these policies strengthen the organization, what are the existing weaknesses and how can they be overcome. It also provides details about the training programmes organized by these organization for the development of their employees.

Chapter VII identifies the need for introspection in HRD issues and goes on to stress the importance of 'knowledge' as well as its applications to meet the coming challenges of this millennium. The chapter concludes by suggesting the following six sets of assumptions which are relevant for the growth and development of the organization and the employee, if practised and adopted. These are:

- An employee does not necessarily dislike work.
- External controls are not essential for performance.
- Commitment to objectives is associated with the satisfaction of ego and self-realization.
- Average employee learns to seek responsibility.
- The capacity to be creative in solving organizational problems is widely distributed within the organization.
- Under modern industrial life only a part of the intellectual potential of the employees is being utilized.

July 2000 **M. P. Srivastava**

ACKNOWLEDGEMENTS

The author acknowledges with gratitude the valuable contributions made by a number of persons towards the completion of this book. Special mention may be made of the encouragement and moral support given by Professor Ashoka Chandra, Director, Institute of Applied Manpower Research, New Delhi.

I am grateful to Smt. Ruby Dhar, Research Associate for her valuable assistance in the preparation of this book. I would also like to express my gratitude to Miss Chatali Pal and Dr. Indu Sekhar, Research Associates for providing assistance in the bibliographical research. My thanks are also due to Shri S.J. Khera, who has provided secretarial service in the preparation of the book.

The responsibility of the comments made and the suggestions given in this book is solely that of the author in his personal capacity. Inspite of his close association to the IAMR since its inception, it must be clearly made that the Institute is in no way responsible for the views expressed by the author.

INTRODUCTION

Resources-material and human and technology are the basic determinants of development. The availability of physical capital is an essential but not a sufficient condition for increase in output. Therefore, W. Schultz observes, "Some growth, of course, can be had from the increase in more conventional capital even though the labour that is available, is lacking both in skill and knowledge". But the rate of growth will be seriously limited. It simply is not possible to have fruits of modern agriculture and the abundance of modern industry without making large investments in human beings.

The demographic profile and perspective of a country determine the quantitative aspects of potential and actual human resources including labour supplies, and investments required for fulfilling the demand for goods and services.

Human capital is a 'lever' which engineers productive activities. The speed of economic reconstruction of Japan and countries of Western Europe was facilitated by their already having the prerequisite foundation of human capital. The 'Korean Miracle' may be described as 'human resource based' since human resources development preceded physical capital accumulation.

However, this emphasis on human resources is not a new concern for human development and well-being is as old as the human being himself. Its integration with development policies, especially in relation to the evaluation of their effectiveness, is of recent origin. Human development issues have admittedly strong regional and global dimensions, but they fall mainly in the domain of national policies.

Human resource development, universally known as HRD at macro level, is a comprehensive and composite concept. It embraces social development as in the field of population, education and health. It calls for the participation of all sections of the population, both rich and poor in the process of development.

Development of human resources is of paramount importance for the economic development and also for enhancing the quality of life of the people.

The importance of human resource development cannot be overemphasized. There should be a sense of priority so far as the development of human resource is concerned. Though there are many dimensions of human resource development, the most important is when you seek to motivate human beings to perform to their full capacity.

Gunner Myrdal has listed eight components of HRD. They are: (a) Food and Nutrition, (B) Clothing, (c) Housing and Sanitation, (d) Health, (e) Education, (f) Information, (g) Energy consumption, and (h) Transport. The World Bank, however, takes into consideration only three components, which go to make an HRD package viz., Nutrition, Health and Education. The ILO includes employment to be the strongest component of HRD. The ESCAP definition of HRD does not include culture but that of UNESCO does. In many developing countries HRD has been conceived as an economy measure, a poverty-alleviation measure.

It must be remembered that HRD is not a sector of economy, although it boosts economic forces. HRD means optimum utilization of existing human capabilities. These cababilities include intellectual, technological and creative ones taken in their totality. HRD is value-based. The core of HRD is equity, equality and distributive justice.

In the organizational sense HRD is a process by which employees of an organization are helped in a planned way to acquire capabilities required to perform various tasks as individuals and to develop organizational culture. In the national context, HRD is a process by which people in various groups are helped to acquire new competencies for self-reliance, self-confidence and self-support. HRD is not a welfare activity. It raises the quality of life. Training is the ladder among others by which HRD is accomplished and nurtured. Training alone can improve the existing capabilities of human resources and help them to acquire new capabilities needed for the fulfillment of growth in different sectors of economy.

The Problem

Four decades ago, studies in development planning concentrated largely on optimizing the use of capital, however during 1960's and 70's there grew a trend towards emphasizing shortages of skills and the role played by technical progress in economic growth. Leadership in this direction certainly came from the industrialized countries which pioneered in the field of human resources planning and development.

During 1980's the contribution of industrialization was analyzed, and it was examined whether the advanced skills necessary for the application of modern industrial technology could bring down the technological gap between the industrialized and underdeveloped economies.

Although, increasing recognition is being given to the fact that industrialization involves the adoption of advanced technologies, this adoption poses several problems. These technologies have evolved within the framework of a resource endowment pattern which, though common to the developed countries, is alien to the developing countries.

A crucial problem for the developing economies is to take into account the present and likely future pattern of skills and to plan ahead for the changes in skill requirements, which have resulted from the inception of new industrial programmes using advanced technology. It is, therefore, necessary that developing economies must make such decisions that would be most conducive to rapid and sustained growth of the economy on the basis of the optimal utilization of their available skills and facilities for the development of new skills. Once due consideration is given to these factors, developing economies will perhaps shift some of the emphasis from education as a general "infrastructure" type of requirement to the demand for skills emanating from the productive side.

Keeping in line with the requirement of developing economies, an attempt has been made here to deal with the issues of skill development at three different levels, i.e. theory, planning and policy. These levels are fundamental in relation to the analysis of future requirements for skills. In his work on educational requirements of the British economy, Vaizey has considered five separate sub-sectors within services and manufacturing sector of the economy with five different characteristics: (i) capital intensive industries which use limited skill and limited research, e.g. railways; (ii) skill intensive industries, with limited capital and research e.g. education (iii) skill and research intensive industries, e.g. pharmaceuticals; (iv) skill intensive, capital intensive and research intensive industries, e.g. aerospace (v) industries that require limited skill, limited capital and limited research e.g. retail trade.

The employees of individual industries have a characteristic structure of educational levels and occupational composition. This structure is determined primarily by the technology used in the sector, and more precisely by the homogeneous or heterogeneous character of the products and production process, the diversity of the product mix and the rate of change of the products, the batch size of production, the amount of work necessary for product development and by the mechanical or chemical character of the technology in the production process.

This method makes the importance of the more qualified labour force perceptible. Differences in the complexity of labour in the sectors are characteristic of the sectors, showing the same pattern at very dissimilar levels of development. This fact can be traced back to the influence of technology on the composition of labour in the industrial sectors.

Human Resource Development (HRD) planning has both a static aspect—concerning accounting identities and a dynamic aspect, dealing with qualitative changes in particular with changes in productivity, and with change in the quality of the labour force—usually measured by the skill composition of its human resource.

The main factors, or rather groups of factors, influencing productivity are: (i) the quantity and quality of capital equipment, (ii) the use made of available capacities, (iii) the skills of the workers (quality of the labour force), (iv) welfare and social factors, and (v) natural factors.

There is also a need to determine the different combinations of knowledge, ability and practice that go into every skilled blue collar occupation independent of traditional ways and obsolete customs. Regretfully, little is known about this because educators are mostly interested in formal education while a large proportion of those employed in skilled occupations acquire the training for their job informally.

The role of HRD is a subject on which the current body of knowledge is so deficient that policy conclusions could, of necessity, be largely tentative only. Perhaps the biggest gap in this important area is the lack of empirical research in fields closely related to policy.

"Why HRD is needed?"

What is really at stake is the problem of choice of techniques for HRD. What quality of skills and in what quantity are required? How could these skills be efficiently formed? What are the present observable imbalances of supply and demand of skills? How should planning for skilled human resource be organized? What are the needs of data to permit efficient planning of skilled human resource? What are the observed and necessary relationships between formal education and other forms of skills formations?

This leads us to the question of the measurement and classification of skills. There are two main methods. One is to take the occupational distribution as the basis for measurement and classification—a work of enormous complexity—but giving a very high degree of specificity. It is then possible to take specific requirements for specific skills and train specifically for them as Z. Slawinski argues. This is the approach of "education for use" employed in the socialist countries. The second approach is to measure skill by educational background. This approach is widely advocated, and is used in almost all the work of the Organization for Economic Cooperation and Development (OECD). This points to the necessity of (further) research in a vital area, i.e. that of inquiring into the different ways or paths of skill acquisition especially at the level of the blue-collar skilled worker and that of obtaining better data on the human functions, involved in production.

Of all the human resource variables, education has a catalytic role affecting as it does the other proximate human resource variables and thereby to the ultimate output variables. Basic education has interlinkages with other social policy variables like family size, health, life expectancy, nutrition and social awareness as it increases productivity, reduces fertility and improves longevity and leads to more integrated or sectoral development activities. Returns to educational investment in general and in rural areas in particular have remained comparable to these, from other types of physical capital investment, specially in developing countries, although investment in education complemented with investments in capital make them more productive.

In view of the simultaneity of relationship between human resource variables and economic development, the question is whether the strategy for development should be one of viewing HRD as a derivative of the growth process or one of deriving economic development as a consequence of human resource development and efficient utilization of human resources. In view of this, what is needed is an integrated approach to HRD encompassing population planning, planning for a better educational and health status of the labour force, planning for a more competitive functioning of the labour market, and planning for better training and delivery systems.

HRD in India

A balanced and integrated approach to development links the supply and demand aspects of HRD through participation in economic activity. It is essential that education and training programmes be integrated with employment programmes so that the quality of human capital is enhanced. Such an integrated approach also implies a multi-sectoral strategy for the implementation of HRD.

The HRD approach is essentially dynamic, that is, it calls continuous innovation and adjustment in an effort to organize and develop its own resources. Organizations grow when they exploit unutilised human capabilities and also their underemployed human resource. In fact, the growth pressure emanates from within as the organization develops its capability to take on new tasks. An organization that continues to adopt the conservative posture cannot claim to be well managed.

There has been a tremendous interest in developing human resource through a variety of programmes in the different areas of HRD immediately after independence. However, these programmes have restricted themselves to training as training and education are important components of Human Resource Development.

In late 1940's, the All India Council of Technical Education (AICTE) appointed a committee on management and later in 1953 formed an All-India Board of Technical Studies in Management to coordinate management studies in the country.

In 1950's, the Government of India invited foreign specialists like Mrs. Mary Cushing Niles, Col. Urwick, and Mr. Andrew Brown to help in developing management training institutions and programmes appropriate to the requirements of the country. On the initiative of the All-India Board of Technical Education in Management, the government also sent teams like the Fazalbhoy Committee to the US and other developed countries.

By late 1950's, the Administrative Staff College of India, the Indian Institute of Public Administration, the National Productivity Council and the All India Management Association had begun their work on HRD issues.

In early 1960's the two Indian Institutes of Management (IIMS) were established as an expression of the general concern for management education and training while institutes like Small Industry Extension Training Institute (SIETI) and National

Institute for Training in Industrial Engineering (NITIE) began to function as an expression of the concern for training the existing work force both in government and public and private sectors of the economy.

The Administrative Reforms Commission (ARC) of India had made comprehensive recommendations for training in 1969, but only a partial adoption of the training policy has been followed. In most of departments, formal statements of training policy probably do not exist. Guidelines on training generally seems to have evolved over time, and policy decisions, if any, had been taken only on some aspects of policy. One likely consequence of this approach was that ad-hoc decisions tended to prevail and long-term planning that was essential in human resources development got low priority.

This concern led the Government of India and some state governments to take up, from time to time, several exercises for going into causes of this lag and to find remedial measures for removing it. The most notable and comprehensive of these initiatives was the work of Administrative Reforms Commission which went into all broad aspects of refining the administration, and the civil services, to the requirements of their responsibilities. Its recommendations on the subject of training of civil services specifically, were accepted by the government and implemented substantially.

In fact, the gap between these recommendations and their implementations called for a fresh initiative for studying the training situation and led to several other exercises being initiated by the Government of India, notable among them being the Economic Administration Reforms Commission (EARC) of the early eighties. The training objectives of the civil services, articulated from this exercise, as well as several other less comprehensive exercises, led to the designing and implementation of a fresh package of training programme with their focus on the responsiveness of the administration to the hopes and aspirations of the employees.

However, the steps taken since the mid-1980s have predominantly covered the All India Services and several Group

'A' Central Services, but not so much the other Group 'A' Services, much less, other level of the civil service system.

Apart from these practical, operational steps, much work has been done since the days of the ARC, to articulate a National Training Policy covering the training requirements of the whole gamut of public administration and public management. However, this has not led to the articulation of a clear and compact policy-package at one palace, still it is undisputable that underlying the training efforts of Government, the design of training programmes and their contents, there is perceivable feature of an emerging training policy.

The typical problems of a developing country like ours, which has a planned economy with emphasis on accelerated growth and development of different sectors of the economy (primary, secondary and services), have given a new significance to the issue of human resource development. For each sector of economy a continuous supply of workforce is a vital necessity for economic growth. Be it agriculture, manufacturing or service sector or privately operated or state managed, the processes for human resource development are followed more or less on a pattern similar in concepts, objectives and techniques.

Organizations whether governmental, private or public have a large number of professionals, who work under different conditions with different work assignments, sometimes with different designations but responsible for 'results' in a particular activity. They are professional with different educational backgrounds, with varying periods and types of experience and perhaps also with different loyalties. This class of professional group should receive a course or courses on various aspects of HRD to make themselves realize the responsibilities and demands of their jobs. The best tool that attempts to bring about this much-needed change is a well-designed and well-directed programme of professional training on general awareness and as well as specified discipline.

In the current phase of the interface between globalization and the spread of new technologies, new opportunities continuously arise which can be effectively tapped by an organization with the right skills and the right products at the right time. In a global corporate planning the cost is the loss of the enormous development benefit which could be gained by taking advantage of new emerging 'niches'.

Training systems are under pressure. As the demand for skills shifts, it is not only 'higher' skills but 'different' skills which are required to meet the demands of the organization. Training systems need to react quickly and flexibly.

It is of fundamental importance that training systems be based on social partnership between the employers who are the end-users of the skills, the workers who receive them and the government, and public and private sector organizations that provide the framework.

HRD specialists in various organizations hold particular views, assumptions, values and preferences about how to manage and develop professionals in order to attain organizational as well as individual goals. Such views, assumptions, values and preferences need to be translated into formal policies, practices and procedures of managing and developing professionals within the organization.

A very frequent concern expressed by the employees in organizations in which new HRD systems are being introduced is: "To what extent are these systems applicable to Indian organizations? Are these HRD systems not based on foreign experiences?"

Such questions reflect a long-standing controversy among HRD practitioners as well as academicians and researchers about the applicability of HRD practices for developing the personnel in the organization.

One school of thought has held that "Management is management, wherever practised, a universal profession whose principles can be applied in every form of organized activity." Such a view has found support in some well known research findings. A classic study is that of Harbison and Myers who studied management practices in 23 countries and concluded that managements did not differ fundamentally from country to country.

One of the best known is JBP Sinha who suggested that Indians, because of our social and cultural background, have a strong need for a tough but 'nuturant' style of management which is authoritarian but also benevolent. Translated into HRD practices, this would suggest that we require fairly well structured system and procedures of HRD with strong linkages with reward and punishment systems.

Organizational management includes various basic functions. (1) it has to procure people for the organization, (2) it has to retain people by adequately rewarding them through a compensation system, (3) the organization has to satisfy the psychological and social needs of people by providing facilities and systems which maintain good quality of work-life, (4) the organization has to ensure that its professionals like its physical, financial and operational resources, gain in value over time. Therefore, it has to provide for continual planning and development as well as create organizational conditions which ensure the utilization and promotion of potential of professional and the resources within the organization.

These basic functions of planning and development are common to all or most organizations regardless of their location, size, type and nature of activity. However, different organizations may emphasize one or the other function differently. Such differences in emphasis largely contribute to differences in professional development policies and practices.

The major factors which account for differences in practices are:

Cultural Dimensions

In his well known study, Geert Hofstede identified four basic cultural dimensions which may account for differences in management and HRD practices across cultures. These are:

- the extent to which a society emphasizes collective rather than individual activity.
- the extent of social inequality;
- the extent of acceptance of uncertainty, and

- the extent to which a society emphasizes "masculine" values and behaviours such as assertiveness, ambitiousness, domination, etc.

India, for instance, has been identified as a country in which there is a moderate extent of collectivism, a high tolerance of social inequality, general acceptance of uncertainty and a moderately masculine orientation. Such cultural differences would need to be reflected in the kinds of professional management the organizations are prepared to adopt. For example, in cultures like ours where there is moderate collectivism and a tolerance of uncertainty, Organization Development (OD) and team building activities may be more acceptable and effective. Contrastingly, in a culture with a high degree of individualism and an intolerance for uncertainty like the USA, systems such as performance appraisal, feedback and counseling may be more acceptable and effective.

Economic Dimensions

In a mixed socialist economy like ours, corporate policies and strategies are influenced by government regulations, social policies of the government regarding employment and development of disadvantaged social groups, competition from other public and private sector organizations, etc. These factors need to be reflected in the professional management policies and practices too.

The level of industrialization already achieved in an economy also influences professional management of the organizations. Other things being equal, it appears that higher level of industrialization results in the development of a professional and organized workforce, whose needs are different from the managerial, technical and skilled workforce and also from informal workforce in non-industrialized societies.

The sensitive industrial relations climate due to political affiliations of trade unions have made many organizations cautious about applying to workers the same professional development policies which they apply to the non-unionized managers and supervisors.

The level of technological sophistication in a resource based organization will affect a number of organizational related matters such as employees training, transferability and job rotation, inflow and outflow in and out of the organization, even the type of climate and interpersonal relationships prevailing in the organization.

Training for Skill Development

On the above basis, if we consider central or state government department with a small enclave of an advanced sector (including modern manufacturing industry) and a traditional sector or sectors around it, we may be able to say a little about the place of skill development in the services and manufacturing sector particularly in modernising the economy as a whole. In the first place, the spread of colonial education leads mainly to social unrest, drift to the towns, educated unemployment, etc. rather than to the creation of reservoir of skills. Secondly, experience suggests that many skills necessary in the manufacturing industry are fairly easily acquired, and that immigrants from the rural areas will acquire them with minimal formal education and training. Thirdly, advanced managerial skills and professional skills will often be provided by nationals trained abroad. It is perhaps fair to say that there is a tendency to identify the need for skills of a very high degree at the managerial and scientific level to meet the need for lower level skills. It has also been observed that a number of countries appear to be training human resource of high levels to fill jobs of the middle levels.

We may conclude by asking certain questions: Is it correct to train aspirants for specific skills, or to educate generally to a high level? Is there (in any serious sense) a skill bottleneck? Is there a managerial bottleneck? Further, how far is it possible to predict technological change, and how far is high-level scientific and technological human resource necessary for the development of advanced technological sectors? This takes us straight back to the classical problem in development economics as whether a developing economy can or should make a technological leap into the very latest modes of production. It is quite clear that, as far as training is concerned, it is feasible to a greater extent than it is for physical capital, since advanced education and training (if confined to a narrow class, who are not permitted to emigrate) is far cheaper than the physical capital which the advanced skills complement. Suppose the view is taken that such a leap should be made. Then a number of important questions arise: How many skills should be produced, at what cost and how far in advance of assessed needs? Is it not likely that, if the skills are produced in advance in a developing economy, pressures to emigrate and social unrest will arise, as a result of white-collar unemployment?

At a lower level also a number of problems arise: what is the appropriate relationship between high-level and middle-level human resources, under the circumstances where the relationships are not technologically determined, but where there is some degree of flexibility? And how far is learning on-the-job susceptible to high-level advance planning?

The purpose in reviewing about training is not to pronounce a verdict on the records of the government. In fact, it is to highlight the lessons learnt from experience, which are presented below. The first three lessons offer guidelines which are largely within the capacity of training institutions to realize and apply. The remaining three call for intervention by the government in terms of policy decisions and support to institutions.

If the training needs and training programmes are evaluated skillfully, considerable improvement in the efficiency and effectiveness of training can be achieved.

Increased attention to the problems of client and greater willingness to facilitate learning rather than teaching tend to augment the impact of training.

A long-term perspective on the development of training capacity is essential while planning a short-term development project.

The design and management of training institutions and the approach to the development and motivation of faculty trainers will have a strong influence on training effectiveness.

When high priority is given to government and adequate resources are allocated to strengthen the institutions, training effectiveness is likely to improve.

In private sector, corporations are known to attach high priority to their training activities. A recent ILO study shows that large multinational corporations (MNCs) such as Nestle, Siemens, and Unilevers, spent 2.6 per cent, 4.8 per cent and 5 per cent respectively of their total payroll on employee training.

In contrast, it will be difficult to find systematic data on training. For example, data on the number of the employees trained, numbers of mandays spent on training and total expenditure on public service training are seldom included in assessment and evaluation studies.

The effectiveness of training tends to improve when career planning and development and other personnel policies are closely inter-related with training.

In the absence of the condition, negative consequences result for training. Some observers have also stressed the need for political and bureaucratic commitment in facilitating the integration between training and personnel policies. Business enterprises, for instance, are known for paying systematic attention to this sensitive linkage. The military's tradition of linking career development with training could also be explained in terms of the profession's strong performance orientation. The failure of civilian bureaucracy in showing a similar concern for performance orientation is at the heart of the problem with most governments.

1

HUMAN RESOURCE DEVELOPMENT: INTERNATIONAL SCENARIO

ILO Standards on Human Resources Development: Implications for Industry

An Overview of HRD Convention

According to the HRD Convention 1975, each member country of ILO should adopt and develop comprehensive and coordinated policies and programmes of vocational guidance and training. These should take into consideration employment needs, opportunities and problems; stages and level of economic, social and cultural development; and mutual relationship between HRD and other macro-level objectives of the country concerned. The vocational guidance to children, youths, adults and handicapped and disabled persons. The vocational training system should aim at meeting the training needs throughout life in all sectors and branches of economic activity, and at all levels of skill and responsibility. All these policies and programmes should be formulated and implemented in cooperation with Employers and Workers Organizations, in accordance with national law and practice, and in conjunction with other interested bodies.

An Overview of HRD Recommendation

The HRD Recommendation provides more detailed statements of the expectations from member countries from their vocational guidance and training systems. It essentially builds upon the minimum and generic provisions contained in the HRD Convention, and has the following main sections:

(a) Policies and programmes
(b) Vocational guidance
(c) Vocational training
(d) Vocational training standards
(e) Training for managers and self-employed persons
(f) Programmes for particular areas or branches of economic activity
(g) Particular groups of population
(h) Promotion of equality of opportunity for women and men in training and employment.
(i) Migrant workers
(j) Training of staff for vocational guidance and training activity.
(k) Research
(l) Administrative aspects and representative bodies
(m) Periodical reviews
(n) International cooperation.

Focus on the Individual

A considerable attention has been paid in these standards to the development needs of individuals, whether employed or not. For instance, it is stipulated that "the policies and programmes for vocational guidance and training should be designed to improve the ability of the individual to understand and, individually or collectively, influence the working and social environment." Further, they should "encourage all persons... to develop and use their own aspirations, account being taken of the needs of society."

The Standards recognize that the vocational guidance related information needs of an individual are quite comprehensive, and include aspects such as choice of an occupation, the employment situation and prospects, promotional prospects, conditions of work, safety and hygiene at work, and other aspects of working life. This needs to become rights and obligations for all concerned under labour law.

The Standards emphasize that the policies and programme for vocational guidance and training should "ensure entry into productive employment..., which corresponds to personal aptitudes and aspirations". They should "facilitate occupational mobility" and should "promote and develop creativity, dynamism and initiative with a view to maintaining or increasing work effectiveness". They "should assist persons in their quest for satisfaction at work, for individual achievement and self-expression, and for the betterment of their lot in life."

According to the Standards, the vocational guidance system of a country should inform employed persons of opportunities for improving their occupational development potential, their level of performance, their earnings and their positions. Besides, it should promote general awareness, regarding the contributions made by various sectors of economy, to enable individuals make informed decisions of the career options available to them. The Standards stipulate the use of both group and individual counselling, and also envisage the use of "appropriate tests of capacity and aptitude of individuals, including both physiological and psychological characteristics".

Occupational Value System promoted by the Standards

The Standards appear to be promoting certain occupational value systems, the key ingredients of which are occupational mobility and equal access. The mobility sought to be encouraged by the Standards includes mobility within and between various occupations and sectors of economic activity and between different levels of responsibility. Re-entry of the workers into the educational system, at a level which takes account of their work experience, is a cherished objective. Trade union education to the workers is also considered desirable. Besides, it is sought to protect persons against excessive physical or mental strain in employment, against occupational hazards and against loss of income or earning capacity, the right to freedom of choice in selecting an occupation, to fair promotion opportunities and to education, have also been emphasized. An important provision of the Standards is the need for prospective employees to gain an appreciation of the value and importance of work and an understanding of the world of work. The Standards also envisage that promotion opportunities (in industry) should be open to persons with desire and ability to reach higher levels of skill and responsibility.

Responsibility of the Industry

The Standards envisage that the industry should accept responsibility for training workers in their employment. The training programmes should be so conceived as to promote full employment and the development of capabilities of each person.

According to the Standards, the industrial undertakings should arrange vocational training programmes in progressive stages, providing adequate opportunities for initial training, further training, retraining, such further education as is necessary to complement the training, training in safety and health at the place of work, and information on rights and obligations in employment, including social security schemes.

Training for Managers

According to the Standards, the programmes for training of management and supervisory personnel should be designed with a view to:

(a) develop an adequate knowledge and understanding of the economic and social aspects of decision making.

(b) foster attitudes and abilities for leading and motivating their persons, while respecting human dignity, and for developing sound industrial relations.

(c) develop initiative and a positive attitude towards change and a capacity to appreciate the effect of change on other people.

(d) develop the capacity of assuming new responsibilities on the job.

(e) develop awareness of the importance of education, vocational guidance and training for the personnel of the undertaking.

(f) develop awareness of the conditions of workers in their occupational life, concern for their welfare and knowledge of labour law and of social security schemes.

(g) develop understanding of the value of efforts towards self-improvement.

(h) provide the basis for further training in accordance with changing requirements.

Training of Faculty

The Standards envisage training of all persons responsible for planning, organizing, administering, developing, supervising or giving vocational guidance and training. It is stipulated that these persons must be given frequent opportunities for refreshing and updating their knowledge of social, economic, technical and psychological elements relevant to their line of work and of learning about new methods and techniques applicable to their work. The training of such persons should include study of various characteristics and attitudes of different groups of trainees and of specialized training methods.

Implications for Industry

A perusal of the provisions of the Standards, stated above indicates that the industry has an important role to play in creating a more effective vocational guidance and training system for the development of human resources. The Standards symbolize the best practices towards that end, while a major initiative can be taken by the industry to emulate these practices. No doubt, the industry is not the only stakeholder responsible for compliance with the Standards: the Government and the workers Organizations too have to make significant contributions in this regards. Nor can the compliance with these provisions expected to be a smooth affair, given the challenges and complexities of the existing labour market and constraints of resources. However, an awareness and appreciation of these Standards and a conscious attempt to comply with their provisions can be helpful in focusing the HRD policies of the industry towards systematic manpower development.

Institutional Arrangement for Human Resource Planning and Development

What is Involved?

The process of human resources management has three interrelated issues. First, the development of skills, knowledge and work attitude. Secondly, the management of the human resource. Thirdly, to coordinate the three interrelated functions of planning, development and utilization of human resources. The last aspect which is of primary concern in this chapter requires planning within the context of set policies and national development objectives. It also requires pursuing strategies to implement programmes in such a way so as to ultimately satisfy labour and production market conditions. This implies among other things, that the entire process of human resources management principles, practices and techniques at specific levels fall within the areas of interest such as a district/region/state/nation, sector of economy and manpower groups.

A useful starting point in addressing this problem is to undertake the functional inter-relationship which exists between the various levels and link it to overall national development objectives with a focus on the human stock as both generators and recipients of development.

The Machinery and What is Expected of it?

To adequately perform this task in relation to the three aspects of the process, three inter-related human resources management subsystems within the framework and context of the national development process and system have been identified. These are as follows:

1. The human resources planning subsystem (a) provides the basis for establishing operational linkages between human resources mobilization, human development, and utilization with the view to bring equilibrium to labour market conditions; and (b) set broad policy and operational guideline for ensuring efficient planning, development and utilization of present and future human resource for national development.

2. The human resources development subsystem (a) develops programmes, strategies and institutions that would ensure the production of human resource base, and (b) undertake actual activities in human resources development and quality enhancement programmes such as education, training, health, nutrition, environment, etc. to implement planned programmes.

3. The human resources utilization subsystem (a) develops programmes, strategies and institutions that would actually identify and place workers; and (b) develop, execute and monitor activities to enhance productivity.

Each of these three subsystems will have to be developed taking the need for productivity and different types of linkages into account.

Major Issues to Consider While Designing the Machinery

For effective human resources planning the organizational structure, responsibilities and the functions of the required institutional machinery need to be appropriately defined and designed to:

* initiate, formulate, administer and/or delegate the execution of comprehensive human resources mobilization, development and utilization policies and plans;
* identify, analyse and specify manpower development and utilization programmes, strategies and priorities;
* co-ordinate, monitor and evaluate the execution of measures as adopted, and
* develop guidelines and strategies for the synchronization of inputs and outputs of the entire human resource planning, development and utilization system.

What are the Linkages and how are they vital to the process?

(i) Intersectoral Linkages

The implications of these are twofold. On the one hand, all human resources planning activities should be inter-linked with activities undertaken in all sectors of the economy. On the other hand, each sector should develop its own human resources management capacities which would make the linkages more meaningful and operational.

A point of departure towards the establishment of such linkages is to view human resources, within the development equation, as a vital sector interacting with and re-inforcing other vital development sectors. In other words, human resources management ought to be seen and treated as a priority sectoral management issue in the same way as policy makers see and treat financial management or energy resources management.

These organizational sector plans should assess and prescribe needs, programmes and policies that would enhance their respective delivery capabilities and the quality of their outputs. Needless to state that organizational or sectoral, or even national plans should in effect be an aggregation of individual's articulated needs and programmes, within the organizational, sectoral/ministerial, and national human resources policies.

(ii) Internal Linkages Within the Subsystem

There are various components within the human resources planning. These components need to be solidified and linked to each other for greater effectiveness.

How do We Ensure Productivity and Efficiency of the Process?

The inter-connection of the entire network constitutes the human resource management system. However, the strength or effectiveness of the system depends on the level of planning. First, planning activities should be geared towards planning for the development and utilization of requisite skills, knowledge, fitness and work attitudes for national development. Secondly, there should be harmony and consistency within and among the various planning activities particularly under the given limited resources.

Efforts, programmes, and strategies and the necessary institutional arrangements need to be made if they have to be solidified and operationalized within the macro-framework of development. Again appropriate administrative divisions and units will need to be instituted and interlinking functions clearly defined, allocated and executed. In addition, the intersectoral decision making and co-ordinating body would need to play a leading role not only for ensuring these internal linkages, but also for ensuring the required intersectoral linkages.

Elements of Human Resource Planning and Development Plan

The plans, while varying from situation to situation in the extent and nature of their contents, should contain at least six different items:

1. Planned programme activities, and their anticipated products and problems;
2. Organization and management of programmes;
3. Implementation schedule for the major activities;
4. Development and operating budgets for the programme;
5. Outline the roles and responsibilities of the participating agencies, institutions, and interest groups and of the arrangements for coordination and communications; and,
6. Procedures and indices to be used for plan evaluation and monitoring.

How should the Plan Preparation Process be Organized?

The objectives specified should refer to the most important goals of the programmes.

At the stage of plan formulation, there is need of continuous communication within the group and regular meetings with institutions and organizations, to ensure that the detailed plan is realistic. It is important to agree in advance on the outline of the planned document and to see that the outline is followed strictly.

The HMP working group itself may continue to formulate the detailed programme. The agency may usefully be enlarged to include representatives of those groups that will carry out the programmes, as well as of other important units. The agency may either consider various constituent programmes in sequence, or split them into sub-groups so that the work proceeds simultaneously on different programmes. The latter is the better alternative, if several programmes have to be formulated in a short time and if they demand different kinds of expertise or agency participation.

What are Programme Activities?

Having clarified and re-defined the objectives of the programmes, the agency must begin to plan the programmes in detail.

Programme activities can be divided into two broad groups, (i) Developmental, and (ii) Continuing activities: Developmental activities are aimed at improving the effectiveness and efficiency. They are usually intensive and time bound and take the form of projects. For instance, all the activities needed to expand a training institution can be grouped as a time-bound project e.g., constructing facilities, procurring supplies and equipment, recruiting and training teachers, and increasing the intake of students.

Once the developmental phase is finished, the training institutions continue to operate at their level of training and it becomes a continuing operation. These continuing activities include payment of salaries, admission, monitoring and improvement of curriculam and appointments. A distinction cannot always be made between developmental and continuing activities, since some activities belong to both categories. However, one can make distinction between the two as developmental activities have a definite life time and cease when the project ends while the continuing activities continue indefinitely.

The following are examples of the types of activities that might be included within a programme plan:

1. Policy, communication and coordination: activities to bring about changes in policy, legislation, methods of interagency coordination and communication, and levels and forms of participation.

2. Job design and task analysis: studies of job tasks and functions, and to determine among others the job descriptions and staffing patterns.
3. Training: revision of curricula, design and execution of continuing-educational programmes, in-service training, upgrading of training facilities, recruitment of teachers.
4. Administrative and support: activities directed towards strengthening programme administration, support activities such as the recruitment of staff or consultants, purchase of equipment.
5. Plan for the design and construction of new or expanded facilities.
6. Evaluation : Specific indicators and measures of progress towards achievement of targets or objectives.

All these types of activities may not take place in all programmes. Whichever activities are included should be quantified if possible, i.e., what will be done, by whom, how and when, and to what extent. Thus, targets should be set for programme operations, such as the number of students to be trained, the number of service staff to be re-trained, arranging these activities into an orderly array for the purposes of coordination between activities may pose difficult problems. To overcome these difficulties, different activities should be arranged in an "activity matrix". In this matrix the types of activities are on one axis and the types of changes that are being attempted through these activities are on the other. This matrix (Health Manpower) provides a visual aid to ensuring that all aspects of the programme are considered systematically.

Once the activities are defined, these must be converted into resource requirements.

Resources for developmental activities have to be considered in total, while for continuing activities only the programme components will undergo change.

Human Resources Policy Formulation and Policy Administration

What should A Human Resources Policy Package Provide?

(i) Is policy formulation interrelated with policy administration?

It is one thing to have a clear focus on what direction human resources policies should take and quite another when it comes to their actual formulation and administration. In the first instance, the provisions within the policy package will have to be understood fully and secondly, the policy must be accepted.

With regard to the first set of issues, the package ought to provide: (a) the necessary guidance for making administrative decisions regarding human resources planning, development and utilization; (b) a nation or organization's viewpoint and vision towards the development and utilization of human resource; (c) a framework for establishing a way for directing specific actions to specific areas of concern on which different human resources development and utilization programmes are to be integrated, executed, coordinated, monitored, evaluated and adjusted for maximum results; and (d) the legal authority and institutions for executing those actions. The second set of issues relate to the implementation of the policy. This would involve policy approval acceptability and monitoring, on one hand, and establishing the legal and institutional basis for implementing the policy on the other. It would also involve the determination of goals, objectives and strategies which ought to be consistent with and lend support to other national/organizational policy objectives, goals and strategies.

(ii) What Role has the human resource planner?

The development of people and their professional competence is intimately inter-related with the growth process of organizations. The knowledge which people imbibe and the motivation and development which organization provides can significantly contribute to the achievement of the objectives of the enterprise. In view of these imperatives, organizations are now becoming more and more concerned with the inter-linkages which organizational growth demands in terms of manpower and professional requirements. The efforts made so far by the organizations have proved that an integrated approach to Human Resource Development has vast potentialities of growth and development.

HRD is the process of providing relevant learning experiences to people, as to facilitate their personal and professional growth. A successful implemented HRD Programme influences both the individual and the organization. At the individual level, it contributes to improvement in satisfaction and performance; at the organizational level, it leads to efficiency and growth. The process of initiating learning for individual growth involves a number of organizational functions.

To achieve the above-mentioned condition, the human resource should be concerned with the undertaking of two main tasks which unfortunately are not being adequately performed in many organizations. These are:

(a) The determination and analysis of critical factors and policy areas that influence supply and demand in order to effectively initiate and formulate objectives and policies that are integrated and consistent with other organizational objectives and policies;

(b) The design, adoption and execution of concrete techniques and measures that would ensure acceptability, implementation, and re-appraisal of the formulated policies.

References

1. Bhatia, B.S. Verma H.L. and Garg M.C., *Studies in Human Resources Development,* Vol. 1, 2 and 3, Deep and Deep Publications, New Delhi, 1996.
2. Ginzberg, E., *Manpower for Development,* Praeger Publishers, New York, 1971.
3. Harbison, F.H., *Human Resources as the Wealth of Nations,* Oxford University Press, London, 1973.
4. Levitan, S.A. et. al., *Human Resources and Labour Markets,* Harper & Row Pub., New York, 1972.

5. Rashid Amjad, *Human Resource Planning the Asian Experience ARTEP,* New Delhi, 1989.
6. Srivastava, M.P., *Human Resource: A study of Approaches Needs and Priorities,* Manak Publications, New Delhi, 1997.
7. Flesch, R., *The Art of Plain Talk,* P.F. Collier & Son Corporation; New York, 1967.
8. Rowe, M.P. and M. Baka, "Are you Hearing Enough Employee Concerns?" *Harvard Business Review,* Vol. 62, No. 3 (May-June 1984), pp. 127-35.
9. Schein, E.H., "Improving face-to-face Relationships, *"Sloan Management Review,* Vol. 23 (winter 1981), pp. 43-52
10. Srivastava, M.P., *Human Resource Training Paradigms Need for change,* Manak Publications, New Delhi, 1999.

2

STRUCTURAL AND TECHNOLOGICAL CHANGES: ITS IMPACT ON ECONOMIC SECTORS

Economic process, can be divided into three sectors of the economy, i.e. primary (agriculture and allied activities), secondary (manufacturing) and tertiary (services). Fully recognizing the value of the division of the economy into three distinct sectors based on the activities performed in each sector, an attempt has been made in this book to study in detail the shift of the human resource from one sector of the economy to the other.

The workforce can be divided into three major activities. Agriculture marks the first activity, it includes all activities related to growth and development of agriculture, fishing, forestry and mining. The common feature is that they all depend on direct and immediate utilization of natural resources.

The second activity is manufacturing. Manufacturing can precisely be defined as the continuous transformation of raw material into transportable products. The operative word 'continous' excludes such processes as hand tailoring, shoe repairing and the like. Similarly, the word 'transportable' excludes all processes of building, construction and installation, which are more conveniently classified under service industries.

The remaining group of economic activities come under services sector of economy. The term tertiary had so far been used for these activities, but is now replaced by the term 'service'. The Service Sector, among others, relate to building and construction, transport and communication, commerce and finance, professional services, public administration, defence and personnel services both domestic and commercial.

In the context of the division of the economy, there is an important issue to understand, i.e., the distinction between "industry" and "occupation". This distinction is explained in modern Census tabulations. It was first introduced in Britain in 1921, and later in some of the other industrialized countries. A man's "occupation" is the nature of the work he actually performs, his "industry" is defined as for whom he does the work. For purposes of our present analysis, the objective among others, is to examine the activities of human resource rather than to examine their occupational distribution.

The National Industrial Classification (NIC)[1] 1970 groups together economic activities which are akin in terms of process, type, raw material used and finished goods produced. The classification does not make any distinction according to the type of ownership or economic organization, however, in some cases the classification does not distinguish between large scale and small scale industries.

The basis of classification, being the nature of economic activity carried out in an establishment, it follows that the unit of classification is taken as the establishment. The term, establishment is defined as an economic unit, which is engaged in an economic activity at a defined physical location under single ownership of a firm or enterprise, which may have more establishments engaged in different activities at the same location or the same activities in different locations. The major activities of the establishment should be measured with regard to the value added to the total production by different products and services, or net revenue derived from various activities. Where such assessment is not possible, classification may be determined in terms of gross revenue attributed to the products, or services of the establishment and the number of persons employed for various activities.

The National Industrial Classification (NIC) 1987, which is presently being followed is based on international system devised by U.N. in its International Standard Industrial Classification 1968, Rev. 2. The NIC 1987 is being revised by Central Statistical Organization (CSO) Government of India.[2] CSO for revising NIC 1987 is following International Standard Industrial Classfication (ISIC) 1990 Rev. 3 which is also harmonized with the International Harmonized Commodity Description and Coding System (HS) 1996 prepared under the auspices of the United Nations Statistical Division. It has been recommended to be adopted by the member countries of the U.N.

CSO has divided all the economic activities (primary, secondary and tertiary) into ninteen categories so as to conform to statistical measurement for a systematic classification of economic process and development. The division of economic activities would facilitate international comparison of macro economic aggregates.

Primary Sector: Agriculture, hunting and forestry, fishing and mining

The departure in the present attempt is that it has also included the service activities in agriculture, hunting, forestry, logging, fishing, operation of fish hatcheries and fish farms, mining of coal and lignite, extraction of crude petroleum and natural gas excluding, surveying mining of uranimum and thorium ores, and other mining and quarrying activities.

The three activities identified above—Agriculture, hunting and forestry, fising and mining and quarrying are the Primary Sector of the economy.

Secondary Sector: Manufacturing, electricity, gas, water supply and construction

The activities under manufacturing cover food products and beverages, tobacco products, textiles, wearing apparel, tanning and dressing of leather, wood and products of wood, cork, except furniture and articles of straw and planting materials, paper and paper products, publishing, printing and reproduction of recorded media, coke, refined petroleum products and nuclear fuel, chemicals and chemical products, mineral products, basic materials, fabricated metal products except machinery and equipments, accounting and computing machinery, electrical machinery and apparatus not elsewhere classified (NEC), radio, television and communication equipment and apparatus, medical, precision and optical instruments, watches and clocks, motor vehicles, trailors and semi-trailors and other transport equipment, furniture manufacturing (NEC), recycling of waste.

The activities under electricity, gas and water supply cover their collection, purification and distribution.

The construction covers among others the activities relating to site preparation, building construction, general construction and construction and maintenance of roads, rail-roads, bridges, tunnels, pipelines, rope-ways, harbours and run-ways.

Tertiary (Services) Sector

We have so far reviewed the productivity of agriculture and manufacturing. There remains an important residue which can be described for convenience as Service Sector. The sector covers, of course, a great variety of activities. Many of them are performed with the help of much less capital, equipment and labour which is required for primary and secondary sector activities but others like wholesale and retail trade, repair of motor vehicles, motorcycles, restaurants, transport, storage and communications, financial intermediation, real estate, renting and business activities, computer and related activities, research and development, public administration and defence, compulsory social security, education, health and social work, social and personal service activities, private households and extra territorial organizations and bodies require more capital and equipments.

It is noticeable that 'Services Sector' by no means implies that these are necessarily services rendered to the final consumer. A substantial part of the output of services such as goods transport, maintenance, communication, etc. are services rendered at early or intermediate stage. Even services such as passenger transport and hotel which appear at first sight to be services to the final consumer may in effect be services rendered to business.

Economic Development and Structural Change

Industry is at the heart of contemporary social and economic development. It is generally admitted that one of the crucial problems of industrialization—perhaps even the most crucial—is the development of human resource or sector specific human resource, i.e. primary, secondary and tertiary sector. This development occurs within the framework of the change in the workforce.

An early contributor to the modern discussion of economic development was A.G.B. Fisher, who introduced the concept of primary, secondary, and tertiary activities.[3] Fisher observed that countries could be classified with respect to the proportion of the total labour force engaged in these sectors.

Fisher's insight was supported by a host of statistics assembled by Colin Clark in his book 'The Conditions of Economic Progress',[4] Clark argued that there was a close relationship between development of an economy on one hand, and activity status on the other as the economic progress is generally associated with certain distinct, necessary and predictable changes in activity status. He further writes, that: "A high average level of real income per head is always associated with a high proportion of the working population engaged in tertiary industries.... low real income per head is always associated with a low proportion of working population engaged in tertiary production and a high percentage in primary production.[5] A.G.B. Fisher had also reached the same conclusion: "We may say that in every progressive economy, there has been a steady shift of employment and investment from the essential 'primary' activities.... to secondary activities of all kinds and to a still greater extent into tertiary production."

This is also supported by the fact that the proportion of work force engaged in primary sector generally declined from 70 to 80 per cent to 45-60 per cent of the total population in under-developed countries and to the level of 12 or even 6 per cent in the most highly developed countries such as the United States and Britain.

Economic development and its impact on the labour force has three main features:

(i) The productivity of agriculture increases faster than the production.

(ii) Large scale manufacturing establishments based on the use of machinery and equipment sprang up and promoted the economic activities.

(iii) Industrial development caused a structural change, and this led to a shift from primary sector to manufacturing and services.

(iv) The educational level of the labour force has risen substantially.

It should be mentioned that Fisher's generalization puts a variety of services under tertiary production and that the demand for these is by no means uniform from service to service. This of course is not surprising as demand for various items differ widely. Similarly, it differs with secondary production system, which includes both necessities of low income-elasticity, such as clothing and luxury products. But tertiary production system seems even more disparate in its productive process behaviour. Most services— education, entertainment, transport, communication and commerce, have high income-elasticities at early stages of economic development, and grow faster than total output. But others, particularly domestic service, follow mixed trends, depending upon the level of income, its distribution, and social attitude towards the occupation.

This and other examples suggest that demand patterns, at least in the field of service sector, are by no means identical from country to country, and that, even if all countries experience the same growth in income per capita, their requirements as to transformation may significantly differ.

An increase in the number of white collar workers, in particular the highly qualified technical specialists, is a well known phenomenon accompanying economic and technical development. What is less known is how the share of this highly qualified resource in the total labour force is distributed among the main sectors of the economy and among the individual sectors of agriculture, manufacturing and services in developing and industrialized economies (Table 1).

TABLE 1

Changes in Occupation and Production Structure between 1960 and 1990

(Per cent)

Sector	*Agriculture*		*Industry*		*Services*	
Countries	***1960***	***1993***	***1960***	***1993***	***1960***	***1993***
Distribution of Labour Force						
Asian Developing						
India	74.0	63.0	11.0	14.0	15.0	23.0
Pakistan	61.0	47.0	18.0	20.0	21.0	33.0
Indonesia	75.0	50.0	8.0	16.0	17.0	34.0
Thailand	84.0	66.0	4.0	12.0	12.0	22.0
Philippines	61.0	45.0	15.0	16.0	24.0	39.0
Republic of Korea	66.0	17.0	9.0	35.0	25.0	48.0
Malaysia	63.0	31.0	12.0	22.0	25.0	47.0
Latin America						
Brazil	52.0	24.0	15.0	23.0	33.0	53.0
Mexico	55.0	23.0	20.0	28.0	25.0	49.0
Industrialized Economics						
Italy	31.0	8.0	40.0	32.0	30.0	60.0
UK	4.0	2.0	48.0	29.0	48.0	69.0
Japan	33.0	7.0	30.0	34.0	37.0	59.0
France	22.0	6.0	39.0	29.0	39.0	65.0
USA	7.0	3.0	36.0	26.0	57.0	71.0
Distribution of GDP						
Developing Countries						
Asia						
India	50.0	31.0	20.0	27.0	30.0	41.0
Pakistan	46.0	25.0	16.0	25.0	38.0	50.0
Indonesia	50.0	19.0	25.0	39.0	25.0	42.0
Thailand	40.0	10.0	19.0	39.0	41.0	51.0
Philippines	26.0	22.0	28.0	33.0	46.0	45.0
Republic of Korea	37.0	7.0	20.0	43.0	43.0	50.0
Malaysia	36.0	0.0	00.0	-	46.0	-
Latin America						
Brazil	16.0	11.0	35.0	37.0	49.0	52.0
Mexico	16.0	8.0	29.0	28.0	55.0	63.0

Industrialized Countries						
Italy	13.0	3.0	41.0	32.0	46.0	65.0
UK	3.0	2.0	43.0	33.0	54.0	65.0
Japan	13.0	2.0	45.0	41.0	42.0	57.0
France	10.0	3.0	39.0	29.0	51.0	69.0
USA	4.0	0.0	38.0		58.0	0.0

Source : Extract from the Indian Journal of Labour Economics: Conference Issue Volume 38, Number 4, October-December, 1995. World Development Report, Various Issues.

Table 1 shows that labour force participation in services sector has increased in all the countries as compared to agriculture and industry which shows a decrease in the number of people engaged in these sectors.

The 1990's liberalization initiatives are ushering in a greater change. They provide four major features for 2011. The first relates to retail patterns. Another feature is the rapid rise of employment in unorganized sector. In 1951, there were 125 million unorganized sector workers and 15 million organized sector workers, making a workforce of 140 million. In 2011, there will be 430 million workers in unorganized sector while only 30 million will be in the organized sector.

In other words, while organized sector employment will double in 60 years, in unorganized sector it will be more than three-fold. It is also interesting to note that even within the organized sector, employment in services is growing faster than manufacturing, e.g., increasing employment in trade, banking, insurance and public administration.

Nobel laureate and economic historian Simon Kuznets first proposed that economic development involved the transformation of agrarian economies into industrial ones and thereafter into service-orientation.

It appears that India would also follow the same path and may move directly into the service economy as can be seen from the figures that services were 25 per cent of GDP in 1951, and now they are 45 per cent of GDP. And by 2011, it is expected to be around 55 per cent of the economy, as downsizing in the organized manufacturing and service sector consequent to liberalization is an ongoing process.

In 1971, there were one million vehicles on the road. Today there are 30 million and in 2011 there will be 90 million. These numbers will require more drivers, cleaners, petrol pumps. These are some examples of the growth of employment in the service sector.

The 430 million strong unorganized labour and the increasing importance of services sector employment, therefore, has some implications.

Nature and Role of the Service Sector

The service sector has a crucial role to play in the economy of any society. Services create value by providing a bridge between the producers of goods and the beneficiaries, or between the production and consumption segments of society. Thus, the growth of the services sector in modern society is linked with the increased productivity in the manufacturing sector.

Services, especially 'producer' services or 'knowledge-based' services, have a key role to play in enabling a country to adopt and apply advanced technologies in the production process, to innovate, to produce more efficiently and to adjust to competitive forces, where the development of human capital and supportive infrastructures is being seen as more central to the HRD process than traditional resource allocation. The need to develop such services in the service sector as a means of furthering this process rather than simply as a means of resource allocation is being widely recognized.

Service Sector and Economic Development[6]

The relation between service sector and economic development raises important sets of concern. Some of them are briefly dealt here. First, it is misleading to use the term economic development and economic growth synonymously. While economic growth is usually quantified in terms of the increase in aggregate national income or per capita income, economic development also implies a reduction in poverty, inequality and unemployment and in the improvement in living conditions for the majority of the population.

Economic development as such, is not merely a matter of resource allocation based on efficiency, it concerns, perhaps even more fundamentally, the terms and conditions of resource creation, resource mobilization and resource utilization.

Secondly, it is concerned with the interrelationship between services and development. The literature on the subject has largely conceived this in rather unidirectional terms, confining itself to the role of services in development.

The service sector satisfies the basic needs of the society through education, health care, income generation and employment creation, etc. It also provides inputs for material production in other sectors, creates in infrastructure to meet national development needs and facilitates the development of markets. It contributes to resource mobilization through financial services, to resource utilization through infrastructural services and to resource creation through technological services. It continuously defines and redefines the boundaries of production and consumption.

On the other hand, the stage of development of an economy has a clear impact on the nature and evolution of the service sector. For example, at early stages of development, the share of services in employment was low despite the importance of the informal sector.

This reflects a basic failure of the development process in many developing countries, where labour absorption in the manufacturing and non-agricultural rural employment is not enough to cope with the increments in the workforce. Such situations also represent a failure in the mobilization and utilization of human resources. Thus, the evolution of the service sector is partly determined by the nature of economic development and influenced by factors such as capital accumulation, technological change, land use and distribution pattern, education and the nature and degree of state intervention.

It is true that the domestic service sector contributes substantially to both output and employment. However, this sector usually fails to satisfy the demand for specialized knowledge that arises from the other sectors. This has led to a reliance on HRD in services.

Service Sector and Its Linkages

Traditional economic models that classified services as a tertiary sector have sometimes postulated a linear theory of the evolution of the economies, usually denoted by the term "three-stage theory".

Firstly, the "three-stage-theory", developed mainly on the basis of employment-shifts in Western Europe, does not generalise even to other major developed countries, let alone to developing countries. In Canada and the United States, labour moved to manufacturing and service sectors concurrently rather than consecutively. In Japan, labour movement in the service sector occurred before the movement in manufacturing sector. In Singapore, over 60 per cent of the population was employed in the service sector as early as in 1920, and over 70 per cent of the GDP (in constant prices) has originated in services since 1960. In the case of West Africa too, the shift of labour has been from the extractive sector to the service sector.[9]

Secondly, an assumption behind the "three-stage theory" is that the growth and vitality of the service sector depends on the dynamism of the manufacturing sector. However, even before the eighteenth century, service industries played an important role in the countries of Western Europe. This is evidenced by the centrality of shipping and retail trade in the economies of pre-eighteenth century England, Netherlands and Portugal.

Thus, the development of the service sector in the domestic economy is of central importance for a variety of development objectives. Services are needed to create improved employment opportunities, to increase productivity in other sectors and for a number of national and social objectives such as health care, education and administration. This makes it necessary to formulate appropriate policies concerning the development of HRD in service sector in particular, so that they can be adequately integrated into the larger context of the development process.

Policies for the Development of Service Sector[10]

An important policy objective in this context is the adequate development and utilization of human resource. This can be realized through improved education and specialized vocational training and through the creation of an increased number of higher quality, knowledge-intensive job opportunities. The growth of the manufacturing sector, which provides substantial employment opportunities and absorption depends crucially on the development of those services which can form the largest source of knowledge and intensive job opportunities.

In relation to the national and social policy objectives, it has been argued that sectors such as banking, shipping, transport and telecommunications constitute the infrastructural core of the development process.

The Role of Service Sector in Economic Development: Problems of Definition and Measurement

A case of Indian Economy India made the transition from an agricultural economy to a service economy around 1979. In this respect, it has followed a development pattern similar to that of Japan and the United States. Both of these countries switched from primary to service economies without losing sight of the period in which the manufacturing sector was dominant. India is often referred to as an "industrializing" country and manufacturing has retained a consistent 15-16 per cent of the Gross Domestic Product (GDP) for the past two or three decades.

In 1985, the service sector accounted for 47[11] per cent of GDP, having expanded at an average annual growth rate of 7 per cent between 1980 and 1985. Of total service sector activities, social and community services represented 31 per cent and retail/wholesale growth, which is most highly correlated with overall economic growth, represented only 16 per cent. However, it has been growing at an averge annual rate of almost 7 per cent.

Turning to sectoral employment, official statistics indicate that 65 per cent of India's active labour force was employed in the service sector in 1985.[12] Of total service sector employment, 59 per cent was in social and community services, with transportation/communication employing 18 per cent. The service subsector that generated the largest number of jobs during the period 1980-85 was financial and business services, where the number of employed increased at an average annual rate of 6 per cent.

Definition and Measurement

The question of definition of services is crucial for the clarity and effectiveness of human resource planning. However, in the absence of a universally accepted definition of services as well as the recent changes in the nature of services complicate this matter.

The basic problem with regard to understanding the role played by services is that yet there is no commonly-accepted definition of services.

Traditional attributes of the service sector such as nonstorability, intangibility, high elasticity of demand, low productivity, etc. seem inadequate in that they do not cover the entire range of service activities. Many of these attributes have been invalidated by the increasing use of information technology in the delivery of services.

The definition raises complex problems. These can be grouped into two sets. The first is related to the distinction between goods and services. For example, while goods can be shipped or transported many services need to be delivered 'on the spot'. Therefore, movements of capital and labour, are complementary or essential to measure services. The second set concerns the lack of homogeneity of characteristics in the service sector itself.

Many resist the concept of "services" as a coherent category altogether, arguing that various service industries are too diverse to be treated together. However, agricultural products (ranging from wheat to animal husbandry) and manufactured goods (ranging from clothing to computers) are equally diverse, yet we have no problem in conceptualizing them as analytical categories.

In approaching the definitional issues, it is useful to distinguish the unique functions of the three sectors:[13]

- *Extractive Industries:* Make raw materials available for other economic activities.
- *Manufacturing Industries:* Convert raw materials into equipment and supplies for use in other economic activities.
- *Service Industries:* Facilitate other economic activities by providing time, place, and/or form utility.

Such distinctions place mining/quarrying in the extractive sector and construction and utilities in the service sector. The World Bank, however, in its annual World Development Report, uses a different grouping that maximises focus on "Industrial Sector", Mining, Manufacturing, Construction and Utilities.

The common perceptions regarding the three economic sectors can be summarized as follows:

- *Primary Sector:* decreasing returns, low productivity, slow technological development, low income-elasticity;
- *Secondary Sector:* increasing returns, high productivity, fast technological progress, income-elasticity smaller than unity; and
- *Tertiary Sector:* Proportional or, at the most weak increasing returns, low productivity, very slow technological progress, high income-elasticity.

Impact of Economic Reform on Service Sector Employment

It is possible that the economic reform programme under the World Bank direction would bring about a change in the share of service sector employment. The change in fact, is more negative than positive. Because of liberalization programmes the role of the Government has reduced and some globalized standardized set have entered into local economic system. There are massive cuts in Government expenditure, including that on activities which give a fillip to services. In India, in 1992, of the total service sector employment of 158 lakhs, 137 lakhs was in the public sector (86 per cent).

In the wake of liberalization the public sector share is likely to come down. It is an acknowledged fact that the macroeconomic stabilization, liberalization of trade and internal markets and institutional reform will have an impact on labour. Demand for labour would, therefore, suffer during the initial period of adjustment (World Development Report, 1995).

In the Indian context it is too early to study the impact of the economic reforms on service sector employment. An attempt has been made to examine the impact by looking at the data relating to fifteen countries, where economic reforms have been pushed through.

The data in Table 2 relates to the service sector's share in total employment and the share of the individual components in service sector employment. This data has to be read with caution, for the reform policies have different starting points in different countries. Further it is not proper to compare the average share of the countries in reforms with the average share in large countries.

TABLE 2

Share of Employment in Services as a Function of Per Capita GDP Log-Linear Regression Co-efficients: Based on Time Series Data

Country	*Period*	*Reg. Constant*	*Reg. Coef. (with Sta. Error)*	*R*	*F*
1. Australia	1972-92	-0.5169	0.6184* (0.0492)	0.9191	217.6170*
2. UK	"	-1.4869	0.6241* (0.0643)	0.8473	94.3128
3. France	"	-4.4043	0.3812* (0.0396)	0.9649	494.2580*
4. Canada	"	1.6170	0.3385* (0.0313)	0.8600	116.7520*
5. USA	"	0.9871	0.4253* (0.0404)	0.8537	110.9070*

6. Japan	"	1.8826	0.2696* (0.0183)	0.9155	205.7210*
7. West Germany	1972-91	-1.3824	0.6575* (0.0369)	0.9464	317.5830
8. Pakistan	1974-92	-0.2743	0.4108* (0.0615)	0.7243	44.6563
9. India	1975-91	2.8324	0.1407* (0.0208)	0.7781	45.5773*
10. Italy	1977-91	2.6276	0.3697* (0.0776)	0.9061	125.4600*
11. Phillippines	1980-92	8.0427	-0.5959* (0.1813)	0.4954	10.7998*
12. Greece	1981-91	-9.6902	1.4646* (0.2277)	0.8278	43.2467*
13. Brazil	1981-90	0.2049	0.6876** (0.3124)	0.3772	4.8453**
14. Columbia	1985-92	2.3595	-0.0027* (0.0083)	0.6345	10.4161*
15. Malaysia	1983-90	2.8969	0.1072 (0.1152)	0.1259	0.8649

Notes : * Significant at 1 per cent level

** Significant at 5 per cent level

b1 is the co-efficient of per capita GDP at 1990 prices.

Source: 1. The shares of services sector's employment are calculated using the data available in ILO, Year Book of Labour Statistics, 1982, 1986 and 1993;

2. Time Series data on GDP at 1990 prices and population figures are taken from International Financial Statistics, IMF, 1994.

3. Extract from the Indian Journal of Labour Economics: Volume 38, Number 4, Page 673 October-December 1995.

Three conclusions follow from the above analysis: Firstly, patterns of development exist in the service sector, secondly, economic reforms have had a favourable influence on the share of service sector, and thirdly, the relative significance of the share of the sector's components does not undergo any great change in the face of reforms. Based on these conclusions we may speculate that the share of service sector will expand in India in the due course as the reform programme gathers momentum. In the immediate context this increase in the share may occur both because of positive and negative factors. As things are left to the sway of market forces, employment in the sector may increase, mainly in the private sector, under exploitative conditions. Also, the productivity of the labourers in the sector is unlikely to be high because the increase in employment in the sector is associated with disguised unemployment in certain spheres of economic life.

The examination of long-term changes in the industrial structure of industrialized countries leads to two broad generalizations. First, agricultural employment is steadily declining and second, all countries have experienced an increase of employment in service industries. In some countries, the proportion of agricultural employment has become so small that the rate of decline is levelling off, but yet this is not the case with the rate of increase of services. Today the growth of services is at the cutting edge of many economic and sociological issues.

Given such a knowledge of the emergence of the service sector and its changing structure in industrialized countries, it will be feasible to show that countries might follow quite distinct patterns of sectoral transformation of the labour force, depending on the time at which they started the process of industrialization, their internal economic and demographic conditions, and their position within the system of international trade. In many developing countries today, the service sector is much larger than in the developed countries at comparable levels of development. This growth of services is often viewed in negative terms due to the implicit assumption that major growth of services should come after the expansion of the other economic sectors.

In past, various attempts have been made to classify industries into a manageable number of broad groups in order to detect changes in the distribution of the labour force over time. Most of these divisions form a three-sector model, e.g., Wolfe, 1955: Fourasties, 1966 and the idea of a tripartite division of industries in effect can be traced back to the Swiss Census of 1888 (Menz, 1965). But it was the scheme advanced by A.G.B. Fisher (1935) and Colin Clark (1940) which became most popular in the literature (see Fuchs, 1968), perhaps due

—in part—to the simplicity of their sectoral allocation and the way they suggested that it becomes transformed. The Fisher Clark model consists of the following three sectors:

(1) Primary industries (agriculture, fishing, forestry, mining)

(2) Secondary industries (manufacturing, construction, utilities)

(3) Tertiary industries (commerce, transport, communication, services).

Any classification, of course, must be evaluated in its substantive context. Depending on the specificity of the problem, one or another classification is useful, and no sector allocation scheme can claim to be equally effective in all situations. It was the intent of both Fisher and Clark to analyze the relationship between economic development and changes in the industrial structure of the labour force, and their classification, therefore, need to be examined in those terms.

A.G.B. Fisher (1935:) stated the following relationship:

> We may say that in every progressive economy there has been a steady shift of employment and investment from the essential "primary" activities, without whose products' life even in its most primitive forms would be impossible, to secondary activities of all kinds, and to a still greater extent into tertiary production.....
>
> The shift of employment towards secondary and tertiary production revealed by the census are the inescapable reflection of economic progress.
>
> And in a similar vein, Colin Clark (1940) wrote:
>
> While studying economic progress in relation to the economic structure of different countries, we find a firmly established generalization that a high average level of real income per head is always associated with a high proportion of the working population engaged in tertiary industries.

Since 1971, however, a renewed interest in this topic has emerged and more attention has been given to empirical documentation of sectoral employment changes, especially the shift towards services. Probably, the two most interesting recent attempts to distinguish between different kinds of services and to allocate them to economic sectors have been generated by Katouzian (1971) and Singer (1971).

Following Bauer and Yamey's (1951) notion of the heterogeneous character of the tertiary sector, whereby some services industries may grow in the course of economic development while others decline, Katouzian suggests a division of the tertiary sector into three categories: (1) complementary services, (2) new services and (3) old services.

Complementary Services: This category includes banking, finance, transportation, wholesale and retail trade. This category is most closely linked to the transformative industries, and its services "expand in response to a rise in demand in a new productive situation" (Katouzian, 1971: 366).

> These services have been complementary to the growth of manufacturing production in two ways: as complementary factors to urbanization, and as necessary links to the process of round-about or capitalistic production. The growing demand for labour in industrial centres attracted migrants to urban areas, and factory production necessiated a high degree of urbanization. The growth of round-about production increased the range and complexity of intermediate goods and with the underlying specialization process that was taking place it helped the conversion of local markets into a unified national market and expanded foreign trade all demanding services included in this category. Therefore, as the rate of growth of industrial production increased, so did the rate of growth of these services, and vice versa (Katouzian, 1971).

New Services: This category "includes education, consumption of modern clinical and medical services, entertainments in general including holiday resorts, hotels, restaurants, cinemas, concerts, nightclubs, and the like and such other services that may be appropriately included in this category" (Katouzian, 1971). These services are labelled new because of the recent features of mass consumption in advanced industrialized countries, whereas in earlier phases of industrialization the demand for these services was mainly restricted to the aristocracy.

> The demand for these services is highly sensitive to the growth of per capita incomes, and it is also an increasing function of the amount of per capita leisure-time especially if the community curve of the distribution of leisure-time is not lopsided (Katouzian, 1971).

Old Services: The services in this category consist of those activities which flourished before industrialization and whose importance and contribution has almost continuously declined since" (Katouzian, 1971). One of the largest industries in this category is domestic service, and its share of the labour force has steadily declined. Although, Katouzian is not very explicit about the services to be included in this category, he seems to refer mainly to personal service.

In terms of the function of social services, however, a distinction between two different types must be made: (1) activities serving the reproduction of labour power basically health, hospitals, education, and welfare and, (2) activities that primarily function to maintain the existing social relations among classes—police, public administration. In some ways, education serves two functions: besides providing people with necessary skills, it also acts as a socializing agent and keeps surplus labour from entering the labour force.

Some Dimensions of Service Sector

It is evident that there has been an important restructuring of the tertiary sector from distributive and personal services to producer and social services. It is the latter two types of services that have been expanding most rapidly and continuously. The universal growth of these services is particularly remarkable in view of the persisting differences in the industrial structure and their different patterns of the sectoral transformation.

The advanced industrial countries have either already developed a service economy or are rapidly moving towards one. If the future employment opportunities are to be provided mostly by the various service industries and many signs point to that direction we must come to a better understanding of the environment in which this development takes place, and of the economic and sociological consequences of this shift in the industrial structure of employment.

The growth of services can also influence the relationship of labour and capital. While economic theory "traditionally assumed that capital is a fixed factor and that labour is variable" (Funds, 1968), this is not true for many service industries.

Much capital equipment can be leased today such as office, machinery and computers whereas employment in the government sector, for example, often cannot be discharged at will. Moreover given the greater labour intensity in services than in goods-producing industries, the former must rely more on labour-embodied technology which can usually be upgraded only through a replacement of older workers by new one. (Training and Re-training)

Despite the large amount of capital investments in services such as hospitals and communication, most service industries remain less conducive to the introduction of technological innovations. This will have an important effect of slowing down the rate of growth of a country's economy, and it is no coincidence that the contemporary discussion of the future of growth in economic or demographic terms, parallels the emergence of a service economy.

While there are other important economic consequences of the growth of services that could be noted here, they have received more attention than have the sociological implications of the sectoral transformation. Therefore, the remainder of this chapter will point out some of the most essential features.

Up to this point, the discussion has centered exclusively on the industrial structure of employment and its changes during last few decades. However, there exists a close relationship between the industrial structure and the occupational distribution of the workforce. In an agriculture oriented economy, most workers will be in farm-related occupations. As agriculture declines in terms of employment, the occupations of farmers and farm labourers will also become less prominent. In contrast, social and producer services require a large proportion of professional and clerical skills.

While the growth of these occupations is fairly well documented, a closer inspection of the industrial occupational relationship yields some very interesting results. It can be argued that changes in the occupational structure come about as a result of two types of shifts:[14] (1) the sectoral transformation of employment and (2) shifts in material technology, organization of work, and demands for different quality of work within industries. Studies have shown that the industry shifts are the primary source of occupational changes..

The expansion of the social service sector has led to a substantial shift of economic activities from a market to a non-market context. It has also very important repercussions for the expansion of the public sector, because the three of the largest social service activities are: hospitals, education, and public administration (including postal service) which are overwhelmingly government run. The growth of social services, therefore, has increased the role of the state as employer.

Policy Implications for Sectors of the Economy

Two kinds of quantitative exercises have been undertaken to evaluate the role of services and particularly producer's services, in the development process through their interlinkages with the productive sectors of the economy. These two exercises are input-output analysis and regression analysis. These exercises are complementary in the sense that the former uses data relating to services at an aggregate level while the latter uses data relating to services at a disaggregate level. Both exercises have confirmed that the service sector has been growing. Services have been using inputs from the productive sectors and also creating intermediate demand for themselves in other sectors of the economy.

Services sector is contributing significantly to GDP and Employment (Table 3 and 4) in Developing Countries. Tables clearly show that in all the economies employment in services has increased considerably from 1980 to 1994. The growth of output in developing countries also shows an increase in services from 1980-90 to 1990-96. However, the same does not hold true for industrialized economies where average annual (per cent) growth in services shows a decline.

On account of the increasing contribution of services in GDP and employment and of the recent transformations in communication technology, some leading economists have emphasized the service-led growth strategy for developing economies on lines similar to that of the 'industry-led growth in the past. In economically advanced countries such as the United States, services have been contributing significantly towards GDP and employment. In United States, the service sector has experienced considerable technological transformation. It is on account of this that a country like the United States can think in terms of 'service-led growth' strategy. Whether the 'service-led growth' strategy is viable and appropriate for developing countries such as India, is an important question that deserves attention.

On the basis of the quantitative exercise in the form of input-output analysis and regression analysis, one can definitely say that services cannot be termed as the 'unproductive sector' of the economy. This is simply because production in the productive sectors require services as input and at the same time the production of services require inputs from 'productive' sectors of the economy. In the last 10-15 years, services[15] have displayed faster growth compared to manufacturing and agriculture. Through forward linkages, services generate intermediate demand for them in other sectors of the economy. Hence, during a period when the industrial sector is stagnant, a boost in the investment and production of services can help to revive the economy. However, if one tries to extend this logic to make a case for 'service-led growth' for a country like India, one may perhaps be reading too much into the issues relating to the inter-linkages. Services providing a boost to the economy is different from services being perceived as a growth strategy because it should not be forgotten that the growth of services is linked to that of the productive sectors.

GROWTH OF OUTPUT

	GDP		Agriculture		Industry		Manufacture		Services	
	Average annual per cent growth 1980-90	1990-96	Average annual per cent growth 1980-90	1990-96	Average annual per cent growth 1980-90	1990-96	Average annual per cent growth 1980-90	1990-96	Average annual per cent growth 1980-90	1990-96
Developing Countries										
India	5.8	5.8	3.1	3.1	7.1	6.8	7.4	7.5	6.7	7.0
Pakistan	6.3	4.6	4.3	3.8	7.3	5.5	7.7	5.5	6.8	5.0
Indonesia	6.1	7.7	3.4	2.8	6.9	10.2	12.6	11.1	7.0	7.4
Thailand	7.6	8.3	4.0	3.6	9.9	10.3	9.5	10.7	7.3	7.9
Phillippines	1.0	2.9	1.0	1.7	-0.9	3.1	0.2	2.6	2.8	3.3
Rep. of Korea	9.4	7.3	2.8	1.8	13.1	7.5	13.2	7.9	8.2	8.0
Malaysia	5.2	8.7	3.8	1.9	7.2	11.2	8.9	13.2	4.2	8.5
Latin America										
Brazil	2.7	2.9	2.8	3.7	2.0	2.1	1.6	2.2	3.5	3.7
Mexico	1.1	1.8	0.8	1.2	1.1	1.8	1.5	2.0	1.2	1.9
Industrialized Countries										
Italy	2.4	1.0	0.1	1.4	-	-	2.9	1.0	-	-
UK	3.2	1.6	-	-	-	-	-	-	-	-
Japan	4.0	1.4	1.3	-2.0	4.2	0.2	4.8	0.0	3.9	2.0
France	2.4	1.1	2.0	0.1	1.1	-0.3	0.8	0.0	3.0	1.6
USA	2.9	2.4	4.0	3.6	2.8	1.2	3.1	1.6	2.9	1.6

Source : World Development Indicators, The World Bank, 1998, pp. 176-78

EMPLOYMENT BY ECONOMIC ACTIVITY

	Agriculture				Industry				Service			
	Per cent of Economically Active Male Population		*Per cent of Economically Active Female Population*		*Per cent of Economically Active Male Population*		*Per cent of Economically Active Female Population*		*Per cent of Economically Active Male Population*		*Per cent of Economically Active Female Population*	
	1980	*1994*	*1980*	*1994*	*1980*	*1994*	*1980*	*1994*	*1980*	*1994*	*1980*	*1994*
Developing Countries												
India	63	59	83	74	15	17	9	15	22	24	8	11
Pakistan	56	45	73	72	15	20	12	13	29	34	15	15
Indonesia	59	54	56	56	12	14	12	13	29	31	32	31
Thailand	-	42	-	38	-	26	-	19	-	26	-	31
Phillippines	61	54	37	31	15	16	16	14	25	29	47	56
Rep. of Korea	29	13	38	17	30	37	23	25	35	47	36	56
Malaysia	36	28	49	26	19	23	18	23	44	48	33	52
Latin America												
Brazil	41	28	26	14	28	28	14	13	31	43	60	74
Mexico	43	35	19	12	30	25	28	20	28	40	53	69
Industrialized Countries												
Italy	11	7	14	7	40	35	24	18	40	49	48	59
UK	3	3	1	1	44	32	21	13	44	51	72	80
Japan	8	5	13	6	39	39	28	25	50	53	57	65
France	9	6	7	4	43	38	22	17	48	56	71	78
USA	5	4	2	2	39	34	19	13	52	62	78	84

Source : World Development Indicators, The World Bank, 1998, pp. 58-60

A country like India which has followed the path of industrialization, needs to follow it along with an appropriate stimulus to service sector being provided side by side. India is a country where balance of payments figures have shown deficits of a structural nature. Its exports are not growing fast, and its import capacity is reduced. Invisibles have been positive in India's balance of payments for most of the years and the positive invisibles have mitigated the current account deficits in India's balance of payments to some extent. Yet, India's service sector is not very highly developed compared to that of the developed countries. Some services are in their infancy and cannot compete with the international market. While a country like the United States can earn enough through services and can import goods from other countries, a country like India cannot afford this. It is in this respect that the 'service-led-growth' strategy is neither viable nor appropriate for India, keeping in view the long-term development considerations. However, this is not to deny the need for a boost to the service sector which may help to provide a stimulus to the productive sectors of the economy.

The services sector in other words has truly come of age and the time is probably ripe for the Government to "look up" increasingly to it for augmenting its tax base, rather than focussing on the already over-taxed manufacturing sector.

Within the services the sub-sectors financing insurance, real estate and business services and community social and personal services have notched up impressive growth rates of 8.6 per cent and 5.2 per cent respectively during July-September 99 (as quoted in The Hindu Business supplement January 1, 2000).

The real impetus to higher services sector growth, however, has come from trade, hotels, transport and communications, among others.

Human Resource Development cannot be promoted by a single minded pursuit of economic growth. The quantity as well as quality of growth is important but without sufficient human resource very little achievement can be made. The reduced importance and even neglect of the qualitative aspect of all developmental (definitional) paradigm is now being considered as one of the main bottleneck for sluggish holistic development all over the globe.

However, Human Resource Development has not received its due importance. Therefore, one finds distortions in development strategy of India in the initial stages of development. But now the human resource has gained importance both at micro and macro-levels. Human resources are viewed as a form of capital, wherever production is required whether it is in the primary, secondary or tertiary sector of the economy.

Human Resource whether educated, skilled and experienced can play a very vital role in the all round development of the different sectors of the economy. A developed human being can very easily and efficiently adopt a new technology in agriculture which is growing very fast in our economy. New agriculture technology that consists of new farm equipments, new varieties of high yielding seeds, new inputs such as chemical fertilizers, pesticides and insecticides and proper management of water resources calls for new brand of human resources who are educated, fully developed and free from evils like superstitions, ignorance and conservatism.

Like primary sector the role of human resource for the planning process in the secondary sector also requires a certain specialized type of value orientation. Besides value orientation, usable specialization for professionals should be encouraged, in secondary sector.

Human Resource Development in financial and technical institutions should go in a major way for skill formation in the entrepreneurship sector. This would involve greater funds being made available for training of people for the medium and small sector industrial undertakings. Productive management of such units should be ensured. Innovative entrepreneurship should be encouraged in the industrial sector to make proper use of available science and technology base. Science and technology entrepreneurship bank was seen as a fit instrument to tap not only this segment of skilled manpower but also for drawing a reasonable proportion of the best scientific talents to the field of entrepreneurship development.

The greater cooperation amongst the large institutions is required for effective utilization of human resource, was felt not only in agricultural and industrial sector, but in the tertiary sector as well. The proper evaluation method of human resource development in tertiary sector is needed. There need to be rigorous and imaginative performance audit before any further HRD activities are undertaken. All in all, rationalization of human activities and developing standards in tertiary sector is the need of the hour. A national wage policy and national labour policy can help in developing such standards. Above all, the tertiary sector will have to become more productivity oriented if it is to survive. With these perceptions of Human Resource Development problems in various sectors of economy, holistic approach to human resources development acquires greater significance and acceptability.

Confederation of Indian Industry (CII) President Rajesh V. Shah said that the growth areas of the future will be in the services sector and India should recognize this as an engine of growth.[16] He further said that in the services industry, whether, growth in software, hardware or the internet, India has the ability to provide world class services at lower cost than other countries.

Colin Sherman,[17] World Wide Chairman of KPMG International also expressed this view that India should accelerate its move from basic industries to services. He further suggested that India has a long way to go as also the country's expertise is proven and the leadership skills are there, still the country is not doing enough to exploit its intellectual capital.

He gave an example of United Kingdom and said that in UK basic industry has gradually given way to a bias towards services and India has the potential to move in the same direction.

Similarly, Industry Ministry[18] officials pointed that the services sector had been the fastest growing sector in the post-liberalization phase. Thus, while agriculture and allied activities have been growing at negative rates of growth in the past few years, industry has been averaging around 5-6 per cent growth per annum. In contrast the services sector has been showing an average growth of around 8-9 per cent per annum.

Human resource development has certainly moved to the centre stage of development priorities, but in actual practice sufficient importance is still not attached to study the shift of human resource from one sector of economy to the other. This is specially true in economic sectors in terms of adoption of policies which have a direct bearing on the development of activities in services sector of the economy.

Second, there is considerable need to integrate human resource planning and to increasingly view Human Resource Development from sectoral perspective.

Third and last, the rather slow realization that human resource planning is not a question of just projecting requirements of demand and supply. The severe limitations of projection approach must be realized and the need for sector specific analysis and an understanding of the labour markets must be increasingly recognized.

These factors have brought to the forefront the need for effective programmes and policies for human resource development.[19] There is a need for an inter-disciplinary and holistic approach to human resource planning in order to ensure efficiency in human resource allocation. In view of the linkages between human capital and economic development, approaches to Human Resource Development need to be broad-based and comprehensive. Thus, human resource planning has to be fully integrated with the overall development planning process rather than treated as a one dimensional by-product of planning.

Human resource development determines and gets determined by the pace and pattern of growth. It is dialectically related to the given perception of growth. Per capita income is a functional outcome of human capital and physical capital. While per capita income, literacy levels and life expectancy rate together influence the rate of savings, a rising investment rate would make large social sector investments and hence higher levels of human resource development status. The magnitudinal aspects of human capital formation are determined by population growth and changes in labour participation rates both of which are influenced by the growth rate while investment and production pattern have a relation to the demand for goods and services flowing out of population—the derived demand for labour and skill confronts the supply of labour. How these interact is determined by the extent of competitiveness of the labour market which is also a function of growth. The human resource development—economic growth linkages operate through the labour market.

In view of this, what is needed is an integrated approach to Human Resource Development encompassing population planning, planning for a better educational and health status of the labour force, planning for higher productive and efficient absorption of the labour force, planning for a more competitive functioning of the labour market, and planning for better training and delivery systems. An integrated approach to Human Resource Development basically implies due recognition to the interactive processes between demographic and socio-economic systems in terms of suitable programmes and policies and developing an employment strategy and human resource planning in the framework of the development plan.

Human resource development calls for an inter-disciplinary approach insofar as it emanates from environments to productivity and has a bearing on social consumption, labour time disposition and industrial/occupational distribution of work-force. The arithmetical entities need to be replaced by measures for removing labour market distortions and wage disparities and for improving social mobility, so that there is efficiency in human resource allocation and optimisation of production levels.

In the context of the above issues the study of the organizational pattern of services sector as well as Human Resource (power, transport, railways, health, education, insurance, communication, etc.) will be found useful amongst others for the policy planners.

While considering the strategy for Human Resource Development, an important question to be considered is, at whom the human resource development effort is aimed? Are we talking of only the elites? In fact, what we find today is that most of the training programmes are aimed at senior and middle management, or at the most supervisors in the organized sectors, but even these programmes are not really adequate. What about the workers and the vast number of people who are self-employed, employed in the agriculture and unorganized sector? Should we not cover the unemployed and under-employed persons so as to develop them and enable them to make the desired contribution to the economy and society? What about the disadvantaged people, the tribal people, the backward classes, the physically handicapped, etc.? In fact, considering the total labour force in the country, one can see that human resources development effort generally leaves many of these categories uncovered, and thus, a large proportion of the labour force which can contribute to the country's growth, both economically and socially, is left out.

About eighty per cent of our population lives in the rural areas, but 80 per cent of our human resources development effort seems to be concentrated in the urban areas, and most of that too for the elite class. This imbalance requires quick change if the process of growth has to be accelerated.

Human Resource Development for rural sector is one of the most important and possibly the most difficult area. Here we have the problem of vast numbers, large physical distances in rural areas, deep rooted value-systems, differences in culture and work practices, and the non-availability of what we can call as the "barefoot" trainers. Much of the effort in the past has been of extension type rather than on human resources development. While we have embarked upon massive rural development and poverty alleviation programmes, it appears that the associated human resources development effort, which is essential for the successful and effective implementation of these programmes, has not yet been effectively undertaken. The emphasis on decentralization during the Seventh Plan coupled with the focus on agriculture and rural industrialization and development, makes it imperative that adequate training and development effort is undertaken in rural areas, at the district, block and village levels.

The second important area relates to the infrastructure and industry. While the Human Resource Development in the organized industry, particularly the large organizations, is perhaps better undertaken, it is greatly lacking in infrastructure sectors such as irrigation, power, transport and communication. Performance in these sectors has considerable potential of improvement. A large-scale increase in productivity is essential which calls for a massive training and development efffort. The numbers to be covered are large and the existing training in these sectors is still in its infancy. Training and retraining of these sectors will need to receive considerable attention.

The third important theme for service sector is 'Human Resource Development' in the social sector. We have the social services like health and education, where some training is going on in the conventional manner. New approaches and ideas are yet to be tried. Then, there are large public services including police. A lot has been said about their training but the study of actual work done by them and its impact is still pernicious for scholars. A plan scheme on "Training for Development Administration" was initiated in a modest way during the Fifth Plan. It was successful in making a small dent during the Sixth Plan. It expanded during the Seventh Plan and the Working Group has recommended many new thrust areas in keeping with the overall Plan strategy. The fact remains that if 'Plan' goals are to be achieved then the public servants at all levels have to be geared up and trained effectively to produce the results. Their training methodologies need to be geared to meet the needs of modern times. The professional services, consultants and institutions also require training inputs.

To what extent, we are able to achieve the objectives of the economic development, will largely depend on improving the productivity of our human resource. Now let us have a look at the human resource development role, scope and priorities both at macro level as well as at the enterprise level in the organized sector.

HRD at Macro Level

There is a lot of ambiguity about the meaning of the term human resource. One school of thought says that all the human beings are the resources. Human beings can be resource only when they have productive uses. In a broad sense human resource denotes; energy, skill, talent, knowledge and attitudes of the human beings which can be used for productive purposes. At the macro level Human Resource Development has a much broader meaning. It not only includes training and education, it includes other developmental inputs like, health, nutrition, family welfare, housing etc. While considering HRD at macro level another point to be clearly understood is whether it is the population in the working age-group, i.e., 15-59 years that is to be formally included under HRD programmes or the entire population. Some may argue that even children below 5 years in age or between 5 and 14 years in age also need developmental inputs and their development is vital for the future of the country.

The present decade is really the decade of challenge to HRD as a profession and as an independent scholastic domain in the hierarchy of sciences. Looking at all these developments during the last four decades, today, a HRD professional can hardly say that industry and other service organizations do not have faith in HRD or do not encourage HRD.

Primarily, HRD is a management function and has to be tackled within the paradigmatic scheme, orientation and perceptual foundation of the dialectics between human resource and future development of the organization. Again, each organization has its own ethos and ideas of work culture and development. In the corporate world, HRD is basically associated with the managers and workers in an organization. But essentially HRD functions are organizational and each management has to address itself to this task.

Human Resource Development in the Service Sector

The end of all economic activity is consumption and welfare. This is predominantly achieved through the provision of services to the population.

The term "Services" is interpreted in many different ways and can cause ambiguity. In common usage it could mean the defence services—Army, Navy and Air Force, or it is used to refer to the administrative or judicial services. But, in fact, it is a much broader concept, with a wide scope, as we shall see in the following paragraphs.

Services have a crucial economic role. It is the process of creating value by building a bridge between the provider and the beneficiary. The value may be of private benefit, which is paid for, or a social benefit, which is free, or a blend of both, which is subsidised. The benefits may be food, clothing, shelter, health, education, entertainment, culture, etc.

Services have other (unique and varied) role in a developing economy. Investment in education and health is a necessary input for skill and productivity. Village level extension services are necessary for raising food output and curbing population growth—the two most crucial objectives of early stages of economic development in reducing inequalities of all kinds—regional, religious, caste, class, sex, etc. This is especially true of social services. They enable the individual particularly from weaker sections to have access to the benefits of modernization. These groups develop and, in turn, become a catalyst for the overall development. Further, people from different strata have to encounter each other in gaining access to the common services, and thus, contribute in reducing the social distances.

Professional services also have a similar effect. Those in government service such as administrative or the judicial have to provide the service to any legitimate claimant, without discrimination. Those from disadvantaged groups who enter such services can make further dents in stratification. Those in private professional services like medicine, law or architecture would respond to any one who is ready to pay the prescribed fees, independent of social origins.

Thus, there is an essential element of HRD in services. They do affect in at least, two ways—firstly by developing the individual and deprived groups, and secondly, by gradually changing the social-culture values in a more democratic and rational direction.

Rapid rationalization and innovations are taking place in the service sector and are an indispensable feature of service sector. The few examples relate to:

(i) Financial services. These services have gone far beyond deposit banking and life insurance. They have introduced hire, purchase and leasing systems. Banks are entering into project lending, merchant banking, foreign exchange, etc. Various personal and business risks can also be insured.

(ii) There are several categories of hotels, motels, restaurants, cafes and fast food outlets, etc.

(iii) Within the health services, it ranges between government hospitals, community hospitals, public sector township hospitals, primary health centres, private clinics, among others.

(iv) Professional services include legal and private clinics.

(v) Besides central and state education, there is a growing market for educational and training services.

The US Trade and Tariffs Act of 1984 has defined services as those economic activities whose output is other than tangible goods. Commonly accepted definition of services sector includes labour services, travel, transportation, port and shipping and other related services, insurance, banking and other financial services, construction and engineering design services, education, tourism, health care, and other private services.

The service sector contributes about half of the world's GDP (Table 3). The advanced economies are predominantly service economies in the sense that services produce, on an average, is over 60 per cent of the GDP and generate about 60 per cent of the total employment.

Services assume special importance for developing countries. Services like banking, communication, transportation, and others provide infrastructure services to the entire economy. The share of the services in India's GDP increased from 34 per cent in 1965 to 41 per cent in 1991. The distribution of GDP between agricultural, industrial and services sector is roughly spread between 29 per cent, 19 per cent and 41 per cent respectively.

TABLE 3

Distribution of Gross Domestic Product (GDP)

(Per cent - Value - added)

	1980	*1995*
Agriculture	38	29
Industry	26	29
Manufacturing	18	19
Services	36	41

Source : World Development Report, 1997.

TABLE 4

Occupational Pattern of Main Workers : 1991

(Figure in Lakh)

	Organized	*Unorganized*	*Total*
Agriculture and allied	14	1,848	1,862
Cultivators	-	1,071	1,071
Agriculture Workers	-	732	738
Others	14	39	53
Mining and Manufacturing	96	259	355
Mining	11	6	17
Manufacturing	73	211	284
Construction	12	42	54
Services	157	415	572
Transport and Communication	31	48	79
Trade and Commerce	5	203	208
Other Services	121	164	285
Total (Excl. Jammu & Kashmir)	267	2,522	2,789

Source : Centre for Monitoring Indian Economy, India's Social Sectors, February 1996.

In 1991, about 69 per cent of the population was engaged in agriculture and allied activities as can be seen fromTable 4. A shift in the sectoral shares of employment is noticeable with the workforce moving away from agriculture during the eighties. India appears to be shifting directly from an agricultural economy to one dominated by services.

According to Centre for Monitoring Indian Economy (CMIE) only about 10 per cent of the working population is employed in the organized sector. About 55 per cent of the total employment in the organized sector is in the services sector and less than 30 per cent is in the manufacturing sector. Needless to repeat that services sector is playing an important role in providing employment in organized sector.

In India,[20] services are looked at sceptically and it is claimed that they are no more than adjuncts to manufacturing. This conventional attitude will have to be changed. In the USA the share of manufacturing in GDP is around 23 per cent, of services more than 70 per cent, and this is reflected in employment patterns too. This is a lesson for India.

Indian[21] industrialists need not focus on manufacturing alone. Similarly, the government needs to shift its thinking to create institutional structures that encourage private investment in services and remove road blocks and delays. That will create far more jobs than public sector investment. (Table 5)

Action Issues

Fruitful actions for HRD in the service sector can be taken up by many agencies including:

- Government
- Public/Private Sector Organizations.
- Organizations in Service Sector (Professional Services)

We began this chapter by noting that service sector is the fastest growing sector and has important economic and social roles. Therefore, HRD in this sector can bring the most valuable contribution and would make a difference to developing economies, organizations and employees, if practised and managed effectively.

TABLE 5
Employment in Public and Private Sectors in Major Industries and Services

(Per cent)

End of March	*Construction*	*Wholesale and Retail Trade*	*Transport, Storage and Communication*	*Financial Insurance, Real Estate, etc.*	*Community, Social and Personnel Services*
(1)	(2)	(3)	(4)	(5)	(6)
Public Sector					
1981	7.03	0.76	17.49	4.83	47.50
1986	6.68	0.74	16.56	5.82	47.06
1991@	6.03	0.79	15.88	6.27	48.42
1993@	5.97	0.76	15.81	6.48	48.52
1994@	6.00	0.83	15.86	6.55	48.74
1995@	5.99	0.83	15.97	6.60	48.87
1996@	5.96	0.83	15.91	6.59	49.00
Private Sector					
1981	0.97	3.75	0.81	2.65	16.52
1986	0.94	3.76	0.73	3.00	18.07
1991@	0.95	3.91	0.69	3.31	19.35
1993@	0.93	3.83	0.70	3.53	19.74
1994@	0.63	3.80	0.71	3.56	19.99
1995@	0.66	3.82	0.72	3.64	19.89
1996@	0.62	3.72	0.70	3.59	19.47

* Including agriculture, hunting etc., mining and quarrying, manufacturing, electricity, gas and water.

@ Data based on Quarterly Employment, Review.

References

1. National Industrial Classification-1970 Government of India Cabinet Secretariat, Central Statistical Organisation.
2. Draft National Industrial Classification of all Economic Activities; 1998.
3. Fisher, A.G.B., "Economic Implications of Material Progress," *International Labour Review,* July 1935, pp. 5-18; and "Primary, Secondary and Tertiary Production," *Economic Record,* June, 1939, pp. 24-38
4. Clark, C., *The Conditions of Economic Progress,* Ist ed., Macmillan & Co., Ltd., London, 1940, Chap. V; 2nd ed. (Completely rewritten), Macmillan & Co., Ltd., London, 1951, Chap. IX.
5. Colin Clark, T*he Conditions of Economic Progress* (Third Edition) Macmillan & Co. Ltd., New York, 1960.
6. M.B. Athreys, "HRD in the Service Sector," *Indian Journal of Training and Development,* XV(1) Jan-Mar 1985, pp. 46-48.
7. UNCTAD, "Services: Issues raised in the context of grade in Services" (TD/B/1197).
8. Daniel Bell, "The Coming of the Post-Industrial Society: A Venture in Social Forecasting", (New York, Basic Books, 1973) as quoted in *Services and Development Potential: The Indian Context,* United Nations, 1989.
9. Dorothy Riddle, *Service-led Growth: The Role of the Service Sector in World Development,* Praeger, New York, 1986, pp. 5-6.
10. *Ibid.,* p. 6.
11. ESCAP, *Statistical Year Book for Asia and the Pacific 1986-87,* Bangkok, 1988.
12. Ibid., p. 38
13. *Services and Development Potential: The Indian Context:* United Nations Conference on Trade and Development, 1989.
14. Singleman, Joachem, *From Agriculture to Services: The Transformation of Industrial Employment,* Sage Library of Social Research 69.
15. D. Riddle, *Service-led Growth,* Preager, New York, 1986.
16. *The Economic Times,* New Delhi, 15th October, 1998.
17. India to take a Shine to Services, *The Economic Times,* 19th October, 1998.
18. "Services Sector may be left out in WPI revamp," *The Hindu: Business Line,* October 28, 1998.

19. R. Thamarajakshi, "Human Resource Development in Asian Countries: An Integrated Approach", *HRD Working Paper,* New Delhi, 1987.
20. Vijaya Kath, "Service Sector and Employment", Yojana, August, 1998.
21. *Ibid.*

3

MANAGEMENT AND DEVELOPMENT OF HUMAN RESOURCES: INDIAN SCENARIO

The 1980's saw the emergence of a major paradigm shift in the activities of different sectors of the economy. This trend is not only a part of the global situation but is also reflective of a favourable economic environment for the growth and development of the economy and nation as a whole. The advantage of this paradigm shift is that it has broken away from the past economic structure and identifies with the current scenario. This development has provided the sector specific shift a greater credibility. The recent economic changes suggest that the shift from primary and secondary sector activities to services sector activities requires a powerful workforce, which needs careful examination and analysis.

On the face of it, as skill requirements will continue to increase in response to rapid technological change, the trends under reference seem to have a global validity and, therefore, with few modifications could be plausibly extended to Indian conditions as well.

The techonology-skill gap is going to grow steadily everywhere and more so in India. We have an appallingly low level of literacy in an evergrowing population along with a poor infrastructure for technical education. This scenario projects a future trend where finding men with the right skills for right jobs in right time would be both a necessity and a daunting challenge for HRD. At macro-level it could be seen into the following issues:

1. Industry-Education interfacing for improving technical education in the country facilitating the development of tomorrow's workforce.

2. Recruiting the right skills would emerge as a specialized function and would call for greater professionalism. At the industry level, different sectors would witness technological change but perhaps the pace of change would not be as rapid as, say, in infotech industry. However, since the delicensing of the certain economic sectors, there has been a mushroom growth of new players causing a serious threat of skill migration.

What role can HRD play here? The challenge is enormous and calls for a multipronged approach. Some points worth considering are:

(i) If there are any possibilities of skill retention, they can be created only by way of generating more 'employability' amongst the existing workforce by imparting them skills in a much more effective way.

(ii) Considering the prospect of skill migration, HRD will have to continuously identify pockets where skills are depleting and are likely to deplete and ensure quick replacement. This must work out as a system.

(iii) Considering the business and technological changes, HRD must enable the organization to predict its skill requirements at various levels say for next 10 or 20 years.

(iv) Workforce of tomorrow will be significantly different and diverse. This problem though unlikely to be encountered in the near future, could start showing up way after 15-20 years when cross-border movement would become the order of the day. Notwithstanding the low potential for diversity, the new age workforce is certainly going to be a different entity in many other ways. This will pose a typical problem for the HRD professional.

(v) The greatest challenge for HRD in future is, therefore, finding ways of meeting the work expectations of the new worker.

What is required is a battery of HRD initiatives including work re-design, more innovative ways of empowerment, career planning and above all a strong induction system combined with other socio-economic interventions that can help restore dignity of labour while offering prospect of career advancement. HRD Planners as yet have not squarely faced this problem but in future it will be a burning and inevitable issue for HRD. In addition, with emergence of multi-nationals in a big way, workforce would become multi-cultural, HRD will therefore also have to face with the challenge of preparing global professionals of tomorrow who will be required to be equipped with cross-cultural management skills.

HRD practitioners should start gearing up for meeting this scenario, or proactively they should start creating one. This would call for a clear vision and conviction. It would also call for systematic long-term planning, exit systems and a high level of integrity to implement things over a long stretch of time.

A paradigm shift, is well underway in which training professionals have redirected their focus from traditional development inputs (classes, hours and so forth) to outputs such as performance at individual level and development of human resource information system at organizational levels.

For this to happen effectively, it will be critical for HRD and training department to bridge the gap between the recognized goals of a alignment and the perceptions of the organization needed for short-term interventions. Further, more holistic human resource management for performance improvements will replace temporal concerns for training. In order to meet the needs of the organization and the individual, HRD will have to contribute to the creation of such a systems. Secondly, it will have to impart training to make people a part of such learning systems. Thirdly, it will have to make the system a team-based and reward based system. Lastly, in the process of organizational reengineering, it is felt that HRD may lose its present identity as a stand-alone department and continue only as a performance improvement and evaluation process.

Since all future changes strongly indicate the centrality of the people processes, training and HRD are likely to assume greater significance. The size, shape, composition and approach of HRD will, however, undergo major changes. But for all this to happen tomorrow, the preparation and groundwork must begin in right earnest, today.

The 'first wave' of Human Resource Development which changed man's life-style significantly came around 7000 B.C.

The 'second wave' came when the economy started becoming self-sufficient. (Alvin Tofler)

The 'third wave' came, among others, along with information system.

However, HRD gained its present status during 1980's and was considered as 'training' activity of human resource management but was limited to executives only. In addition, performance appraisal system, job rotation and career and succession planning was developed.

The workers were out of the ambit of HRD. HRD was seen and believed to be an isolated cell—unconnected with the main stream activities concerning planning, development and utilization of workforce.

Now there is a paradigm shift in the activities pertaining to Human Resource Development and the purpose and objective of the activities have also undergone a subtle and significant change. HRD[1] has started inculcating among the employees (a) attitudinal changes (b) willingness to learn new skills, and (c) willingness to be redeployed in one of the sectors of the economy.

Human Resource Development is the process of facilitating and ensuring the acquisition of competencies required by employees and supervisors to perform certain activities or tasks intended to achieve desired outcomes. These outcomes are defined by the organization in an organizational setting.

Objectives of a programme or an organization can be achieved only when employees work to achieve them. What they do or are expected to do may be called "activities" or "task". These activities or tasks are grouped into categories and are sometimes called "functions". If the task or activities have to be performed well, certain conditions have to be met. The following are some of the important conditions that need to be fulfilled:

1. The goals or objectives should be clearly started and preferably in observable and measurable terms.
2. The activities or tasks required to be performed for achieving the goals should be exhaustively identified and listed.
3. Each employee should have a complete list of the activities he is expected to perform and should be motivated to perform the activities.
4. Each employee should have the capabilities or competencies required to perform these activities. If he/she does not have them, he/she should be helped to acquire those competencies.
5. Periodically the list of activities should be reviewed and competency gaps need to be identified.
6. Competencies should be developed in employees on a continuous basis.

HRD is nothing but a planned way of ensuring that the organizational goals are met. In order to ensure this there are a number of instruments or mechanisms. These instruments, among others, include activity analysis/task analysis/role analysis exercises, critical attribute identification exercises, performance analysis, feedback and review discussions, potential development exercises, training among others.

For quite some time HRD was equated to training, however, gradually, it was recognized that there was much more to HRD than training. Training is only a sub-system of HRD. The evolution of a total model of HRD came about in the following ways:

1. How to decide who should get what kind of training?

   Some training is required for present role, and some for future roles.
2. For the current role of training, one way to identify the training need is to see in which areas the employees performance is relatively weak. This requires a review of evaluation system.

3. Similarly, for identifying future role-related to training needs, the organization has to design a qualitative evaluation system.
4. How much future role-related training would be required will depend upon the number of vacancies on account of superannuation, expansion, acquisition, diversification, personnel turnover, and others.
5. Not all training can be formal, much of it has to be, on the job.
6. As one progresses on HRD, individual expectations also rise. Such expectations cannot be met unless each individual also prepares himself fully. This requires Self-Development.
7. Successful HRD leads to frustration unless it is simultaneously linked to planning and development. So, the Human Resource Planning needs to be linked to the organizational planning.

Mechanism of Human Resource Development

Job Redesign	Training (Education and Development)
Rewards	Performance Appraisal
System Development and Research	Potential Appraisal
	Performance Feedback and Councelling
Human Resource Information System	Career Planning and Development
Small Group Activities	Organization
(Quality Circles etc.)	Development

The Emerging HRD Canvas

We are at the threshold of new millennium. It gives us a vintage point, wherefrom we can reflect and assess the 20th century and foresee the 21st, can learn from the past and prepare for the future.

The human resource strategies need to be addressed to the achievements and failures of the past and vision for the future. It has to acquire a mature professionalism that organizations and employees of tomorrow will demand.

The fragmented concept of HRD that it is training and is only concerned with the management development, has no connection with personnel or industrial relation, requires immediate attention. It is a holistic concept interfacing all the human segments and activities in the organization right from pre-selection processes and even post retirement case. It concerns both individuals and groups in the organization.[2]

"Two roads diverged in a wood and I took the one least travelled by and that has made all the difference". HRD professional should be something like the traveller in Robert Frost's "The Road Not Taken".

Scope of HRD

The scope of HRD activities should not be, therefore, confined to the training activities alone. Though, the acquisition of capabilities required to perform various tasks relating to present and future roles—is the basic thrust of HRD, it also strives to develop an organizational culture that emphasizes among others, team work and collaboration for enabling the organization to cope with the future changes.

Needless to mention, HRD activities should be linked with the strategic planning to be precised Human Resource Planning activities. The system of human resource planning proposed in this chapter is described below:[3]

Training and Development

Training including education and development will continue to remain the main focus of the HRD activities. The following systems are suggested to be developed for achieving the objectives of training and development:

Training needs identification system.

Training planning system

Training control system

- Training information system
- Training evaluation system.

Future Role of HRD

HRD professionals need to assume the role of a change agent, a torch-bearer and be a beacon light by perceiving the need for change, by committing the organization to change, by evolving appropriate strategies for change. This requires a total support and co-operation of the organization which is missing in most of the organizations today, both public and private.

Training appears to be the main thrust of HRD profession. Perhaps, no other area requires more clarification than this. Training is an organizational requirement, which is to be imparted to each one, on a regular basis according to his needs. An integrated approach to impart training-skill development, attitudinal change, professional development, refresher and orientation package, etc. needs to be developed. Creating a learning organization, which ensures action learning and action research is a welcome proposition. But most of the organizations today pay lip-service to training. Training department, in fact, is an asylum for incapacitated incapable employees. Training is to the organization what physical exercises are to human beings, therefore, training need to be taken as a long-term investment in building human capital.

HRD is at crossroads, caught between the *vortex* of deep rooted traditions and ever emerging organizational compulsions. It has to evolve a new set of paradigms and core values and a new mindset to meet the challenges, as it is passing through an evolutionary stage and is in the state of transition. It is busy acquiring required capabilities and evolving appropriate strategies to match the situation.

Human Resource Management

A further evolution about HRD is that it has to be placed in a broader context of Human Resource Management. A higher level model[4] of HRM could be as follows:

Utilization. A decade ago, a question was frequently raised about the degree of effectiveness of training. The same question is today relevant about HRD, which involves much more effort, because it encompasses several subsystems already discussed in previous pages. The utility of HRD depends on the organizational commitment to utilize the talent developed by HRD.

Planning. At any given time, an organization has a backlog of strengths and weaknesses of its employees. Even with efforts in the three areas, namely human resource planning, development and utilization, the strengths may not have been fully exploited, and the weaknesses eliminated. There will be some improvement, but much will remain as it is. Thus, there is need for long-term human resource planning.

Human Resource Management; Strategic Interventions

The challenges before the human resource management is complex and multifold. This necessitates evolving HRM strategies both at the macro and micro level not only to cope with the fast changing environment but also to create an atmosphere conducive to growth and development of the economy.

Macro strategies, in this context signify strategies, which have to be implemented on a national scale. Hence, governmental action becomes vital for success. The crucial macro strategies are given below:

In an information era, the foundation of any organization is its data-base and human resources. Developing a human resource database at the national level, therefore, becomes the basic strategy. The data has to be comprehensive, accurate and updated, with regard to all aspects of human resources planning, development and utilization.

Coming to the HRM strategies at the organizational level, the foremost need is to understand the environment and the area within which it operates, and the needs, aspirations and drives of its employees.

Several specific issues have contributed to the strategic role of HRM. One is the productivity concern of the organizations that emerged in the early 1980s.

A second issue has been the need for a sound human resources strategy to effectively manage the highly diverse work force of the future. Projections suggest that the future work force will be more diverse in gender, race, ethnicity and age, as well as in attitudes, beliefs, and values.

Broadly defined, human resources planning is the process of analysing an organization's human resources needs under changing conditions and developing the activities necessary to satisfy these needs (Walker, 1980).

The scope and focus of such planning varies according to the issues addressed, competitive practices, the organizational context and culture, the rigour of planning, and other factors. For some organizations, human resources planning is essentially development planning, for others, it is the staffing process, including forecasting and planning for recruitment, deployment, and attrition of talent in relation to changing needs. (Walker, 1992, Ulrich and Lake, 1990, Schuler and Walker, 1990).

A Look into the Future

It would perhaps be meaningful to picturize the shape of things to come, i.e., the HRM facets of tomorrow.

First of all, government's intervention will enter the HRM activities of the individual organization in a substantive way. This is anticipated because of the fact that the competitive advantage of human resources will be at the leading edge against the background of a growing economy, where productivity issues are going to attain much more criticality than what exists today.

Continuous training to cope with changing technological infrastructure will continue to have a vital significance. Programmes to educate the worker in sensitive areas like quality and cost consciousness will also gather material importance in the near future. Retraining will be essential at all levels of management to successfully cope with the changing demands of the internal and external environment. Management of personnel in the future will reflect changes in human resource practices, systems and activities.

The following paragraphs, will deal with the development and management of human resources in the organizations. However, before going into details let us deal with the theoretical framework of organizational management.

The Theoretical Framework

Broadly conceived, organizational management is concerned with policies, procedures and practices which enable an organization to meet its requirements of external capital, internal capital and human resource for different services or occupations. It includes among others the assessment of manpower needs of different categories, evolution of suitable criteria, policies and procedures of recruitment, appropriate career patterns, training and placement in a manner best suited to their development and utilization. The broad objective in view is to enable the organization[5] to meet its current and projected needs of human resource. However, in its narrow context, organizations deal primarily with ways and means for achieving optimum development and utilization of skills and potential of human resource in meeting the organizational needs. As organizations are equally concerned with the qualitative and quantitative aspects of human resource planning and development.

Organizational programmes involve long-range, manpower projections for the growth and development of the organization and their employees. Another important goal of management is career development which relates to experience, such as training, work assignments, education and allied activities. Such activities prepare employees for anticipated needs as well as for the work which is being currently performed.

Development implies a planned system of development and career progression of employees, which may not be within a single functional group but may stretch across functional and organizational lines when it is felt that an employee can be developed or utilized more effectively.

Long-range programmes for the human resource development and utilization have several aspects, the following are of particular interest:

1. To determine the requirements of human resource at different level, such as professionals, middle and junior management and associate professionals.
2. To study personnel policies and practices of the organization with a view to ensure the proper utilization and by putting the right man in the right job; and
3. To ensure intake of talented personnel, and train them to study the given situation in the organization, and ensuring that steps are taken in a phased manner to prepare the persons with the requisite skills.

To carry out this process, organizational pattern need to be studied with respect to duties, responsibilities and functions. The positions in the organization, therefore, can be classified through the study of duties, responsibilities and functions. Jobs must first be classified according to major functions, then divided into groups, and further subdivided into fields of specialization. The broad classification plan mentioned above will serve the following objectives:

(a) To establish and maintain an orderly functional structure which will both reflect and accommodate a wide variety of functions and positions,

(b) To identify and describe the key characteristics of functions that are significant for distinguishing one job from another,

(c) To set out the knowledge, skills and abilities required for the performance of work at different levels in each functional group or specified field,

(d) To provide insight into those elements of education and training, which are significant in identifying individuals capacity to perform the functions and the duties.

(e) To facilitate the judgemental processes involved in carrying out placement, training, promotion and other personnel functions.

Preparation of Human Resource Information System : (HRIS)

Compilation of various types of statistics will be of considerable assistance in preparing an HRIS but it cannot be regarded as the sole basis of quantitative and qualitative analysis of jobs, functions and activities. At the most, such compilation may give a quantitative and qualitative break-up of personnel working in an organization.

It may be emphasized that although the human resource requirements can rarely be predicted on a precise basis, they are nevertheless essential for effective human resource planning to meet the long-range manpower needs.

In the preparation of human resource information system the following information will be required:

(a) Personal data,

(b) Data on Education,

(c) Data on Training,

(d) Position data: Functional group, level and organization,

(e) Chronology of experience, and

(f) Performance Appraisals.

The inventory of projected human resource should be based on potential for growth.

Utilization of HRIS

The inventories of current and projected human resource will be useful in the following ways:

(a) To provide a means for identifying weaknesses in personnel and thus helping to establish a management development programme,

(b) A basis for planned career progression,

(c) To provide a scientific basis for selection from eligible candidates for career advancement and promotion. The system will help in the identification of those employees who are within the 'eligibility zone'.

Thereafter the candidates can be evaluated by promotion panels and by other means,

(d) To locate qualified employees for filling up positions in a systematic manner,

(e) To locate professionals or consultants and experts in specific areas,

(f) To identify human resources based on a criterion which will enable them to meet the immediate and future needs for development, and

(g) For projecting human resources.

The field of human resource management (HRM) has emerged, developed, and evolved during the last few decades and represents one of the most important and interesting areas of organizational management. The field of HRM has not developed in isolation, rather it has developed in the context of sectoral change and economic development. As such, HRM represents a response to the changes, that development, particularly after industrialization has had on society and the world of work (Miller and Coghill, 1964).

Organizational Pattern

The organizational pattern of India can be discussed under the following sub-heads:

1. Salient features of the Constitution of India
2. Central government
   (a) Secretariat and other agencies
   (b) Public undertakings
3. Local governments.

Salient Features of the Constitution of India

The Constitution[6] provides for a federation in which each level of government has a parliamentary form of democracy based on the Westminster model. The Constitution[7] enumerates the powers and functions of both the levels of government in a detailed way—union list has 97 items, state list 66, and the concurrent list 47 items and most substantive functions like agriculture, animal husbandry, education, cooperation, public health as well as law and order are the direct responsibility of the constituent states, the central government's major direct responsibilities being defence, external affairs and communications among others.

Machinery of Government

The Constitution of India[8] does not refer to the machinery of public administration nor does it use a term like the secretariat. What the Constitution says is that the executive action of the central government shall be expressed to be taken in the name of the President and the President shall make rules for the transaction of business of the Government of India and for the allocation among ministers of the said business. The secretariat consists of a number of ministries and departments, the exact number varying from time to time, depending on the volume and variety of work, work priorities, valuational orientation, political expediency, to name a few.

The Secretariat The secretariat is primarily a policy making organ of the government, leaving execution of policies and programmes to another set of organization, called attached and subordinate offices, which emerged in Indian administration as a result of a belief in policy administration dichotomy.

The machinery of government at the centre[9] and also in the states is designed on the basis of two important administrative principles. An over-riding belief in the desirability of structural separation of policy-making and administration which led to the creation of an organization exclusively concerned with policy-making and another one charged with implementational responsibilities. As a result, the machinery of the Government of India is a three-tiered one.

Creation and steady expansion of public undertakings constitutes perhaps the single most conspicuous development in the field of public administration in India since Independence.

Starting with First Five Year Plan in the year 1951, their number had increased to over 200 in the mid-eighties. Key and strategic areas of national economy are under public ownership but public undertakings also cover fields like manufacturing, mining, petroleum, chemicals, pharmaceuticals, financial and insurance services.

Public undertakings in India are organized in several forms but the important forms are: The departmental form of organization is the oldest one and is associated with the regular departments of the government. This form has been adopted in the case of railways, posts and telecommunications, broadcasting and ordinance factories. The other is the company form of organization which represents the Fertilizer Corporation of India, the Heavy Engineering Corporation, and others are among the one-hundred and odd public undertakings under Company Act, 1956.

The holding company form of organization for public undertakings is the newest one, first tried in 1978 when the Steel Authority of India Limited (SAIL) was set up. The SAIL is the apex organization and the public sector steel plants like the Hindustan Steel and the Bokaro Steel were made its subsidiaries.

Public undertakings have remained in existence for over fifty years which surely is a long enough period to create its broad image in the society. Both its large size and its long existence have not, however, imparted a distinctive professionalism to its management and executive cadre. A lack of professionalism should evoke a measure of surprise as undertakings are engaged in production of items which constitute the infrastructure for the society and their performance ultimately affects the efficiency of the entire national economic system.

Civil Service

The civil service consists of a number of unequal services with little inter-service communication, much less mobility. Administration being an integrated process, the resultant inter-service disharmony poses a problem in the way of synchronized action. This is recognized by many but with no serious determination to curb it. The Administrative Reforms Commission 1966-70 had sought to open the road to the top to all possessing merit and recommended a unified grading structure but the recommendation was rejected.

Local Government

In India, local government, in the modern sense of the term, is an old institution dating back to the year 1687 when a municipal corporation was set up in Madras through Lord Ripon's Resolution of 1882. One need not go into its history but should focus on the issues in its existing organization, functions and problems. Local Government in India is organized on rural-urban dimension or, to be more correct, on rural-urban dichotomy. Rural government, called Panchayati Raj, is a hierarchically integrated one, consisting of Panchayat, Panchayat Samiti and the Zila Parishad at the village, block (a cluster of villages) and district levels. These are elective bodies enjoying defined civic and developmental powers and are vertically integrated.

The urban local government is organized on the following medium-sized cities, cantonment boards for military stations, notified area committees and town area committees for nascent small towns and other urban areas, and townships for a newly established industrial complex. The corporation form of urban local government has traditionally enjoyed more powers and autonomy than others, and being a prestige symbol this status is cherished by an increasingly large number of cities, not yet incorporated.

In view of the challenges faced and tasks lying ahead, a substantial transformation of the administrative capabilities in all sectors and levels of activity seem urgent, which is also realized by the national political leadership. As many as twenty-one committees on administrative reform have been set up by the central government since 1947 to revamp the administrative system of the country. These committees among others have, for instance, examined issues like the following:

1. How should the machinery of government be reorganised?
2. How should procedures of work be improved?
3. How should financial administration be conducted in the context of planning?
4. How should planning be organized at different levels of government?
5. How could better co-ordination be secured between various agencies?
6. How should the various processes of personnel administration such as recruitment, training, placement, performance appraisal, promotion, salary-fixing, etc. be improved?
7. What should be the staffing policies in the Government, particularly at senior levels?
8. How should the grievances of public personnel be redressed?
9. How should corruption be controlled in public administration?
10. How should citizens' grievances be redressed?
11. How should waste and extravagance in public administration be controlled?
12. How should public undertakings be organized?
13. How should project planning be organized and control mechanisms designed?
14. How should plan progress be monitored and programme evaluation carried out?

The important among them, for the purpose of this book relate to. organization of government machinery, how it should be organized at different levels.

One must also note that public administration is the accredited instrument of development in India, which imparts special significance to it in the society. It has to its credit many achievements the most impressive ones being the unabridged practice of democracy, and sustained promotion of developmental activities.

Human Resource Development in Government System

HRD in administration is an important part of macro-level resource planning. Government that does not plan for its human resources will often find that it is not meeting its developmental goals. There are four basic steps in human resource planning:

(1) Planning for future needs,

(2) Planning for future balance,

(3) Planning for recruitment and selection, and

(4) Planning for development.

With the introduction of the Five Year Plans after independence, the Government of India took upon itself a developmental role in addition to the conventional regulatory role. The assumption underlying the new role was that along with looking after law and order, the Government is required to pay attention to resource mobilization and utilization.

Some important HRD developments in Government[10] are given below:

1. Initial attempts were made to improve organizational effectiveness in Government. Paul Appleby from the US Public Administration came and studied the Indian Administrative set up. One of his recommendations was the need to transform the administration from a 'colonial' to a development oriented one.
2. The Administrative Reforms Commission of 1967, emphasized the importance of better system of training and development. This led to the setting up of an Administrative Reforms Cell, within the Home Ministry. This later became a Personnel Department. The three activities which were specifically strengthened included, among others, nominations of more officers for training within and outside the country, computerization of human resource data and a more systematic postings for specialized assignments.
3. The Indian Institute of Management, Calcutta and

Ahmedabad were started in 1962. By the early seventies, Indian Administrative Service recruits were given training in management concepts and these were also brought into the training institutions of Income Tax, Postal and Police, among others.

Phases of Growth in Public Sector[11]

Productivity was never the issue in the post-independence socialistic thinking of Pt. Nehru which established large public sector corporations, but public sector today is riddled with ills and with few exceptions, consists of ill-managed corporations despite strong management systems.

Economists believe that the failure of the public sector was inbuilt in the foundation, with five crucial phases. The first phase was concerned with building core industries from fertilisers to telephone, trading to ship-building, watches to steel plants. The goal was a self-reliant India.

In the second phase Indian industry and financial institutions came under government control. Banks, insurance, coal and oil were nationalized, sick units were taken over, and interests safeguarded. The government entered transportation, consultancy, contracting, and consumer goods.

In the third phase the consumer goods industry was consolidated and the public sector took on services from hospitals to textiles, pharmaceuticals and bakeries.

The fourth phase, which saw tremendous growth, strengthened manufacturing to counterbalance large independent business houses. It also covered roads, power and potable water and new townships and facilities were initiated.

The fifth phase, after liberalization, served up some rude surprises as the government withdrew budgetary supports and called for rationalization without giving the time to readjust to changing realities. Reforms in the government and in the bureaucracy in particular, are essential in an age of globalization and fierce competition. Partnerships with the private sector, as in case of Maruti, have proved that such relationships can work.

"In 1947, infrastructure was needed for development. This was true for areas like transport and heavy industry. The financial resources required to manage them, made it unthinkable for the private sector to participate. In the 50s and 60s, the growth and development of private sector enterprises began decreasing and a number of them closed down completely displacing thousands of workers. To protect workers' interests, the public sector took over.

HRD for Public Sector Enterprises

Different countries have chosen different strategies, and management styles to face the challenge of globalization and privatization. Japan has emerged as the leading nation with the unique style of management—thanks to its overwhelming reliance on the use of major asset, viz., the human resource. The key issue for the public sector enterprises in India[12] is also to develop its human resources in such a way that organizations become effective. Thus, in order to meet the challenges of change there is a need to institutionalize the system of Human Resource Development (HRD) in all public enterprises. According to Y.S. Mahajan, "human resource being the most vital factor of production and labour productivity, a positive, forward looking, human resource development policy is sine-qua-non for the efficiency and effectiveness of public sector employees".

The HRD programme, however, has to be designed after careful assessment of employees' profiles and organizational needs. In other words, the first primary challenge for the successful implementation of HRD policy is to develop the 'HRD climate' in an organization which is also termed as the 'development climate'. Rao and Abraham have mentioned that an operational level of development climate is essential for facilitating HRD. To Finkel also, the management of an organization must create specific surroundings that will meet the need of the participation and the requirement of HRD. The HRD climate is, thus, fundamental to an organization as it facilitates HRD programmes.

The first "Annual Report" for Public Sector Enterprises in India was prepared in 1960-61 giving a composite picture of the working of these undertakings.

The number of public enterprises as on 31.3.1991 was 246 excluding 7 enterprises with Central Government investment but without direct responsibility for management, 6 insurance companies and 2 financial institutions as against 244 enterprises on 31.3.1990.

For the purpose of planning and national accounting, public sector in India includes all activities funded out of Government's budget. In this sense, the size of public sector is, indeed, very large. It includes not only government departments but also government companies, whether in the Central or the State Sector. The details are as under:

(a) Enterprises Under Construction	10
(b) Enterprises under Manufacturing/Producing goods	163
(c) Enterprises Rendering Services	73
Total	246

The cognate groups under which these enterprises have been classified are as given below:

Cognate Group	*Total Enterprises*
I. Enterprises under Construction	**10**
II. Enterprises Manufacturing/Producing Goods	
(i) Steel	9
(ii) Minerals and Metals	12
(iii) Coal and Lignite	8
(iv) Power	4
(v) Petroleum	14
(vi) Fertilizers	8
(vii) Chemicals and Pharmaceuticals	19
(viii) Heavy Engineering	16
(ix) Medium and Light Engineering	23
(x) Transportation Equipment	13

(xi)	Consumer Goods	19
(xii)	Agro Based Industries	4
(xiii)	Textiles	14
	Total II	163
III. Enterprises Rendering Services		
(i)	Trading and Marketing	20
(ii)	Transportation Services	12
(iii)	Contract and Construction Services	8
(iv)	Industrial Development and Technical Consultancy Services	12
(v)	Tourist Services	8
(vi)	Financial Services	7
(vii)	Telecommunication Services	2
(viii)	Section - 25 Companies	4
	Total III	73
Grand Total (I+II+III)		246

Source : Public Enterprises Survery, 1990-91, Annual Report.

To bring about development of human resources, public sector has been one of the important instruments. These enterprises have been able to build up a corps of personnel at all levels from skilled workers to executives so that they are considered to be fairly self-reliant.

Government has also recognized the culture of participative management to bring about further improvement in the functioning of enterprises in the country. In this context, a comprehensive scheme for workers' participation in management was devised in 1983 which is in vogue in all public enterprises at various levels of management. The scheme has been successful both at shop-floor and plant levels.

Personnel Policies and Human Resource Development in Public Sector Enterprises

The human resource development programmes assume a special importance in the management of public sector enterprises. The PSEs now employ a large workforce in different disciplines. The success of PSE's would depend largely on skills and capabilities of their workforce. The personnel policies of an enterprise are therefore required to be developed carefully to meet its human resource requirements at all levels. The development strategies developed for each group of employees will have to be different keeping in view their job requirements and skills needs to handle specific work areas.

Department of Public Enterprises is a nodal agency for coordinating training and development of managers in the central public sector undertakings. It is concerned with the formulation of training policies and programmes for these enterprises at the national level.

DPE organizes special programmes for the top/senior executives, arrange for deputation of managers on a selective basis for training abroad and play a catalytic role in the development of in-house training facilities in the public sector enterprises. While the public enterprises are responsible for identifying the training needs and providing the training facilities to their managers, DPE supplement their efforts in this regard by organizing programmes in collaboration with the premier/ management institutions in areas where special efforts are needed to meet the training and development requirements not available with the public enterprises.

The training strategy of DPE can be broadly categorised in the following three groups:

(a) Advanced Management Programme

(b) Executive Development Programmes

(c) Overseas Training Programme.

The Department of Public Enterprises, besides other things, is concerned with formulation of policies relating to employment and recruitment, CDA Rules, vigilance matters, deputation, etc. for the Public Sector enterprises. It also advises the concerned administrative ministries/departments on matters relating to labour relations, sports, environment, etc.

Evolution of Human Resource Management in Public/ Private Sector

The evolution of the HR function in India many be divided into four phases.

The first phase was Personnel Administration, during which employees were treated just as another input in the production process.

Personnel Management was the second phase in which systematic efforts were made to identity the requisite skills for a job, recruit suitable employees and get the necessary output from them. Even then, people were not perceived as a resource that could appreciate and stretch.

This awareness was conducive to the emergence of the third phase-Human Resource Development. It emphasized the distinctiveness of human resource, their capabilities, competencies and attitudes. This phase laid emphasis on the conception that while other resources depreciate over time, human resources appreciate. Therefore, organizations should develop employees through different mechanisms such as job training, career planning, job rotation, management development, among others. This was an important phase in the evolution of HRM in India, as it changed the orientation of human resource planners.

This thinking brought in the fourth phase; Strategic Human Resource Management. This phase is still in an incipient stage. The nature of Strategic Human Resource Management elaborated in the following paragraphs.

The HR function becomes strategic when it is actively involved in strategy formulation. This means that HR issues get sufficient consideration in the organizational goal setting process as well as its implementation, i.e. mobilization of the right employees with the right competencies and commitments towards the strategic goals. The Indian Oil Corporation, for example, accomplished this successfully in the early 1980s (Box 3.1).

Box 3.1

Strategic Focus on Human Resources (Indian Oil Corporation)

The Indian Oil Corporation (IOC), a Fortune 500 company, adopted Human Resource Development as a strategic focus and a means for strategy implementation in the early 1983. The top management, in spite of changing chief executives, was committed to the development of human resources.

The interventions that were adopted by HR managers at IOC included improving and strengthening of certain HRM systems, like transfer, training, recruitment, and performance appraisal. In addition, they introduced new HRM systems like manpower planning, career planning, succession planning, role analysis, counselling and human resources data bank. Further, these systems were aligned with the corporate goals. Systematic efforts were thus made by the senior HR managers to creat the climate and systems that were conducive to the development and utilization of employees.

Athreya, M. "HRD Evolution and Practices-A Consultant's Perspective", *MDD Management Journal,* 5 (1) : 15-28, 1992.

Once the environment-industry-organization interface has been analysed, the next step would be to set strategic goals for different functions. The questions at this stage are—What are the requisite knowledge, skills and attitudes needed for the organization today?; What mix of knowledge, skills and attitudes would be required in the near future?; Do employees in various activities and at different levels posses them?; If not, where are the gaps?; What can be done to bridge these gaps? and, What is the cost of human resources?

In order to plug the above it would be necessary to develop an inventory of the employees' competencies and capabilities in different activities and at different levels. This would entail the development of a comprehensive human resource information system.

Human resource planning is affected by the strategic goals and the environment of the organization. The strategic goals determine the requisite level of skills in different activities and the values and beliefs they share. If human resource planning is not matched with the strategic goals, the organization suffers from a human resource imbalance, which may lead to organizational ineffectiveness. In addition, the HR environment refers to factors like the availability of the required human resource in the labour market, managerial resources, labour laws, trade unions, etc.

The next step in the HRM is job training. Whether it is selection or redeployment, employees must first be trained to develop the relevant job skills so that they can perform their task effectively.

Finally, the performance of an employee not only contributes to the achievement of an organization's goals but also helps in the development of the individual. An individual does not work just for earning his livelihood but also for utilizing and unfolding his potential.

Box 3.2

Crompton Greaves developed a system of performance assessment of managers which was open, transparent and fair.

The company was designed along product and regional lines. The marketing regions rank-ordered the product divisions in terms of their effectiveness in customer satisfaction. On the other hand, the product divisions rated the marketing regions in terms of their efforts in promoting and selling their products. These ratings were shared openly at quarterly review meetings. The incentive system was linked with performance. In addition, management development was used as a tool to improve performance.

Crompton Greaves Ltd. (9-491-074).

Box 3.3

The participative process was the hallmark of human resource management in Tata Steel. A three-tier system of joint councils with equal representation from the management and employees was set up in 1957. There was a Joint Consultative Council of Management at the apex, a Joint Works Council in the plants and 40 Joint Departmental Councils. The Joint Departmental Councils considered issues related to manufacturing, productivity, cost improvement, safety, cost reduction, elimination of wastage, welfare, etc. They met once a year and discussed their active subjects related to works organization as a whole. Finally, the Joint Consultative Council of Management discussed matters concerning the company and the industry.

Besides the above mentioned committees there were many other Joint Committees, like Permanent Joint Rates Committee (for grievances related to wage compensation), Trade Test Specification Committee for laying down skill requirements of skilled workers, Joint House Allotment Committee for allotting houses, etc. The participative culture led to a sense of belongingness and internalization of belief in the inter-dependence of personal and organizational goals.

[Based on: Extract from Pandey, S.N. "Productivity and Excellence-Concepts and practices: A case study of Tata Steel" Personnel Today, January-March, 3-12, 1992]

References

1. Singh, I.N., Future Scenario for Training and HRD", *Growth,* Volume 25, No. 1, April-June, 1997.
2. B.D. Singh, "Human Resource Development in Transition" *Growth,* Volume 24, No. 1, April-June, 1996.
3. "Manual on Manpower Planning", Bharat Heavy Electrical Limited, *Corporate Personnel,* New Delhi.
4. A.V.L.N. Rao, "Managing Future Through Learning", *Growth,* Volume 24, No. 1, April-June, 1996.

5. "Managing Human Resources: Some Macro Issues", *Growth,* Volume 19, No. 2, April, 1991.
6. "Article 74" of the *Constitution of India.*
7. "Article 77" (1) of the *Constitution of India.*
8. "Article 77 (3)" of the *Constitution of India.*
9. Committee on Public Undertakings (Seventh Lok Sabha): "Forty Ninth Report on Public Undertakings-Management and Control Systems", Lok Sabha Secretariat, New Delhi, 1982, p.42.
10. "Human Resource Development Comparative HRD Experiences" M.S. 22, IGNOU, School of Management Studies, 1996.
11. Sekhawat, K.S., "Profile Public Sector", *Business Standards: A Special Supplement,* October, 1998.
12. Uddesh Kohli, "On the Role of the Public Sector", A Special Commercial Supplement, October, 1998.

4

HUMAN RESOURCES DEVELOPMENT: AN ORGANIZATIONAL VIEW

The human beings are responsible for making use of physical and natural resources of the economy and for bringing change from the traditional economies to modern and industrial ones. In essence, "the difference in the level of economic development of an economy is largely a reflection of the differences in quality of their human beings. The key element in this proposition is that the values, attitudes, general orientation and quality of the people of an economy determines its economic development".[1]

The shift from manufacturing to services and the increasing pace of technological change has made human resources the key ingredient in the growth and development of the economy. In service-oriented sectors of economy, like railways, telecommunication, health, banking and insurance, among others the planning, development and utilization of human resources becomes all the more important.[2]

The human resources system receives inputs from the organization in the form of goals and objectives, and it results in individual and organizational performance, that may be viewed as individual and organizational input of the human resources system and the entire organization operates under the same cultural, economic, social, legal, political constraints.

In essence, the survival, development and performance of an organization, although not solely but heavily, depends on the quality of human resources.[3]

Before analysing the issue, one must look back at developments in the last 20 years, i.e., the growing concern about employees despite some aberrations and periodic ups and down.

Need for HRD in Organizations

The need for and importance of HRD can be better appreciated when we understand the nature of human development and the nature of the organizational development.

Further, the changing structure of the workforce has led to the introduction of new values of workforce in organization. These are (a) quality of life over quantity, (b) equity and justice over economic efficiency, (c) pluralism and diversity over uniformity and centralism, (d) participation over authority, (e) personal convictions over dogma and (f) the individual over the organization. (See Box 4.1).

Box 4.1

Companies must manage the knowledge of their workers. Says Amin Rajan, Chief Executive of the Centre for Research in Employment and Technology in Europe (CREATE), which has published a study on the subject based on interviews with more than 150 employers in Europe and America, many of them in the finance sector.

Rajan divides knowledge into two categories—explicit, which we are conscious of having learnt, and tacit, which is subconscious and more difficult to communicate. Knowledge management is about converting tacit knowledge into explicit knowledge, so that it can be passed on. Recently, managers in insurance companies and banks have turned tacit knowledge into hard data. Although the phrase "knowledge management" has not been used, this approach underlies the recruitment and career development of fund managers and other staff. Organizational climate is viewed as an important tool of motivating and developing employees in any organization. The concept has gained greater significance in recent times. HRD climate creates interest and motivation among the employees to stay long in an organization. It creates growth opportunities and recognition. The dynamic HRD climate can create the right path for development of both the individual as well as the organization. It is possible through humane treatment of employees by the employers, which would inter-alia help in developing right attitude among the employees. The HRD climate appears in informal and social relations. Therefore, it carries a descriptive role rather than an evaluative role.

Role of HRD

The role of HRD among others is:

- To bring to the surface, those implicit behavioural patterns that are helping and hindering the process of development.

An organization can be compared to an iceberg in which the visible part comprises formal aspects including policies, structures etc., while the invisible part comprises informal aspects including values, feelings, perceptions, assumptions, habits, attitudes, norms, etc. HRD is mainly to reveal and uncover the organization's habits, values, perceptions, and deep-rooted assumptions.

- To deal with the problems of growth and identity.

Any organization is like a living being and hence a growing entity. In the process of consolidation, growth and maturity, it becomes imperative to have formalized systems and procedures to deal with the emergent problems. It also becomes necessary to know its strengths and weaknesses and become aware of the external opportunities and threats.

- To know its human resource base and build them to a strong motivating force who could deliver the desired outcome.

An organization can be said to be functional only if its human resource base is strengthened so that it can cope with the rapidly changing environment. Organizations, right from its inception, need to put considerable imphasis on this aspect of management. Development of human resources speaks of integration of individual needs with that of the organizational goals. It further emphasizes the involvement of its employees in the decision making process that directly affect them and their working conditions. However, of late, a conscious and deliberate HRD intervention was initiated to develop its employees as individuals and as instruments of change.

- To deal with problems of renewal and revitalization
- To sustain an organization, it requires continuous nourishment by the forces of renewal and revitalization.

Principles of HRD Intervention

The following principles serve as the foundation in shaping the HRD practices:

(a) HRD is an ongoing interactive process

(b) HRD is a database approach to plan change

(c) HRD activities focus on team work

(d) HRD emphasizes democratic thinking.

Organizational development helps organizations to improve their problem-solving potentials and innovative capabilities through their efforts, to become more flexible and more effective, to become learning organizations, and to integrate into their self-development, a forward-looking process of adjustment to the constantly changing external environment.

Organizational development aims to strengthen the autonomy of organizations, i.e., ability to develop problem and conflict-solving potentials, and to define and design their own processes of change. The organizational development approach also focuses on the potentials of an organization. As the organization is involved in the problem-solving process, change takes place both at the level of action and attitude of individuals, and also at the structural level—corporate organization structure and structuring of operations, technology, mechanisms of decision-making, etc.

Organizational development is a process-oriented approach of organizational change. The task of the HRD is to support the process of change. (Box 4.2).

Box 4.2

What's this change management thing that everyone's into?

Arthur D. Little. Maira is an authority on the subject and has tackled the subject in his book, "Accelerating Organization". "Take any organization at a point of time, and then at a later point of time, and if the organization as a whole has learnt and improved in a positive way, that's transformation." The success formula is to combine change with improvement since learning is the other side of the changed coin.

Changing structures does not mean that you will produce the results of others. It creates confusion, a lot of turmoil, and it's avoidable on a regular basis," says Maira.

In India, one of the biggest challenges according to Maira is to operate a learning organization—an organization where everyone thrives on change. As Maira puts it, "People in the organization should be hungry for change. People as such don't like being changed. But they do want to make changes if they feel they have a control over the process."

In fact, a complete picture and description of the changed organization has to be first blue-printed. "Only then can you identify, if the employees are behaving in consonance with this vision, or they have to learn something different," says Maira. This vision has to be then shared and communicated across the organization.

Maira separates the formalization of the learning organization into four definite steps—know-what, know-how, know-why and then know-want. The first stage, know-what, is knowledge about processes, "like a cooking recipe," explains Maira. Then is know-how—

the ability to use the processes effortlessly; "like when my wife cooks and not me," says Maira.

The next two are critical. Know-why is the stage when know-how has to be dissected to determine exactly what experiential skills and knowledge goes into creating know-how.

And finally the last stage is the knowledge of how to craft know-what—transforming ordinary recipes to a gourmet dish each time requires know-want; the shared aspiration for a stretch-goal.

So what can be done to enable grass-root organizations, as well as governmental organizations and private enterprises to obtain the professional support they need for the process of change?

The purpose of this chapter is to set forth a comprehensive framework for the identification of needs and its analysis, describe some of the most useful technique for analyzing education and training needs, examine the most important strength and weaknesses of the various methods of instruction and programme of development, and review the concepts and techniques of evaluation and training needs, examine the most important strength and weaknesses of the various methods of instruction and programme of development, and review the concepts and techniques of evaluation, the latter being the knottiest problems in social science, management and education.

The approach is to explain the possible methods for determining who needs which type of development opportunities for a particular stipulated purpose in the organization. It is felt that the basis for effective human resource development is on-going research on needs and results.

Megehee and Thayer have devised a threefold approach which helps resolving complex problems connected with human resource planning and development in an organization / division/ unit of any organization.

It consists essentially of the following :

- *Organizational Analysis :* To determine whether within the organization, the education and training emphasis should be placed.
- *Operations Analysis :* To determine what should be the contents of programmes in terms of what employees must do to perform a task, job or assignment in an effective way.
- *Man Analysis :* To determine what types of behavioural change are required on the part of an employee if he is to perform the tasks which constitute his job in the organization.

The three types of analysis are closely related and are not performed in isolation of each other but the tools for making these analysis are not fully developed. Although the literature of the social sciences and management has been replete with references to organizations, organizational theory, organizational planning and organizational analysis in the last few decades, but there has been actually only a small part of the literature that has tied together organizational analysis and the development of human resources. In order to be organizationally effective, a human resource development programme must develop a linkage on the following functions :

- Define objectives, identifying the scope and the emphasis of the programme.
- Guide about the proper utilization of human resources by identifying broad policies, advising the human development staff, and evaluating present human resources.
- Study long range resource needs.
- Evaluate available resources periodically and follow up on the status of individual and organizational development plans.[4]

A wide range of information is needed about the employees in the organization, especially those having technical and managerial responsibilities. As a rule, improved job performance appraisal information is needed based upon how well the individual is doing things that he is supposed to do in his present job. (Box 4.3)

Box 4.3

The critical attributes of the employees today among other are mindset, vision, flexibility and agility, multiple skills, and communication ability, says Jaydev Raja, Managing Director of Iridium India. The employees need to be technology proficient, analytical with a quick grasp of issues, and address tasks hand-on.

ABC Search calls for three-dimensional vision. Subject depth on one axis, and future perspective on the other and at the same time keeping track of wider perspectives while making judgements. The need for vision, obviously is a function of the fact that areas like business portfolio and competitive strategy, managing productivity, delivering shareholder value and customer orientation has become essential for survival, says G C Burman. One has to sacrifice short-term gains for long-term goals.

Versatility is the other significant difference. Says Shitin Desai, Vice-Chairman DSP Merrill Lynch. "Multiple skills is the challenge. This does mean he is a generalist, but has basic knowledge across the board." Cross-functional expertise is an imperative in a CEO resume. Finance, marketing, operations, HR, strategic planning, technology-working knowledge and experience in all areas is required, as compared to the earlier trend of rising to the top from a single function, usually finance or marketing.

There is an increasing evidence today that bureaucratic models are changing and are undergoing modifications. The characteristic trend is towards loosening of structure through the creation of more fluid and informal organizational arrangements. Among the devices leading to such results are project management. techniques, the use of task forces, management team concepts, and the management-by-results school of thought in administration.

The changes that are taking place describe implications of manpower and organizational planning. The education, training, and development of professional, managerial, technical and skilled workers cannot remain the same as in the past. The challenges before the organizations today is to wrestle with the new problems of organizational change and human resource developement, even if this means discarding the ways of the past. For competent professionals and executives these changes will seem like opportunities for development rather than threat to their growth and development.

Changes currently under way in thinking about human resource development and organizational development are typical of the times and indicate that in these fields turmoil is apparent as it appears to be in the developed economies.

HRD Climate: Conceptual Concerns

An organization nurtures and establishes its own climate over a span of period. The climate signifies commonly shared beliefs, values, expectations, working styles, leadership and commitment and goes a long way towards influencing performance and ensuring job satisfaction.[5] However, the HRD climate is much more comprehensive and is essential for executing HRD mechanism. Rao and Abraham[6] have mentioned that the HRD climate is characterized as consisting of the following tendencies on the part of an organization.

- A tendency at all levels starting from top management to the lowest level to treat the people as the most important resources.
- A perception that developing the competencies in the employees is the job of every supervisor.
- Faith in the capability of employees to accept change and acquire new competencies at any stage of life.
- A tendency to be open in communications and discussions rather than being secretive.

- Encouraging risk-taking and experimentation.
- Making efforts to help employees recognize their strength and weaknesses through feedback.
- A general climate of trust.
- A tendency on the part of employees to be generally helpful to each other and collaborate with each other.
- Team spirit.
- Tendency to discourage stereotypes and favouritism.
- Supportive personnel policies.
- Supportive HRD practices including performance appraisal, training, reward management, potential development, job rotation and career planning.

The HRD climate is, thus, essentially an integral part of an organizational climate and is additionally characterized by the presence of values of openness, confrontation, trust, authenticity, proactivity, autonomy and collaboration. Besides, a general supportive environment which includes commitment of the top management, positive attitudes and good personnel policies are necessary aspects of the HRD climate.

In short, one might say that all of what has been set forth amounts to a dynamic concept of what used to be called "staffing" a rather passive appearing organizational function in traditional personnel work. Human resource planning, when followed up by the systematic development of human resources, will bring us closer to the development of individual and the organization. If done, then we shall have accomplished more than the staffing of our organizations: we shall have enhanced and enlarged the quality of our human resource through the system developed within the organization.

Human Resource Development Policies and Programmes in Services Sector

From the stand-point of development linked with a common concern for human resource, it is relevant to consider the results in terms of human resource development under different service sector activities. It can be said at the outset, however, that there have been no independent consideration of results of employees evaluation under the scheme of human resource development organized by different segments of economy such as government, public and private sector but there have been a number of studies on training needs, training evaluation, performance appraisal, among others. Most of these studies have concluded that human resource development programmes improve the labour market position and help in the betterment of employees in a large number of cases and also suggest that training programmes help in securing better growth and development. Human resource development programmes organized by different organizations have become a lever for changing traditional manpower, educational and training institutions.

Every training effort adds to the total supply of skills available in the labour force of the nation. The contribution to human resources of this general upgrading process depends upon the degree to which the skills provided are relevant and transferable to other uses, but under these programmes the individual is still the focus and not the organization.

For the future, the solution to the development of human resource, if at all there is such a solution, will depend upon a number of factors:

The first is that the organization should become aware of the fact that human resource is an indispensable economic asset so that out of this awareness appropriate human resource planning can begin to be implemented.

The manpower planning, development, and utilization in the decade 1960's marked the beginning of widespread interest in planning at the area—district, state, nation, sector and manpower group levels.

The economic opportunity, through the globalization in 80's and 90's, among others, marked the beginning of human resource development programme for individual and organization in which professional, technical, managerial and other manpower groups were able to develop in time.

Our concern here is to examine opportunities, which have come through proper programmes of human resource development for the individual and the organization in services sector of the economy such as Communication, Banking and Railways.

Here, the human resource development planner must have a new outlook and a new sophistication in respect of the development of the individual in the organization vis-a-vis education, training and evaluation. These values centre upon human resources.

In the last 30 years and specially in the last five years, the character of organizations whether government, public or private are in the process of transformation reflecting the enhanced position of the individual specially in the organizations of services sector of economy which has come on account of paradigm shift from primary and secondary to services sector.

Our approach is to set in this context such apparently diverse human resource development opportunities as: the future of skill development, new views on the inter-relationships of government, public and private sector in respect of human resource development planning. There is little doubt that we have much to learn about manpower planning and Human Resource Development. Practice will probably run ahead of theory and research because the latter two tend to lag behind with the fast moving world of everyday life.

Need for Strategic HRD Perspective

The experiences gained from the functioning of the HRD during the last three decades indicate the need for a fresh perspective in all HRD related tasks. Traditional assumptions and approaches are now passe. Both public and private sector will need to do fresh strategic thinking about their organizational HRD policies and procedures. They will also have to consider the positioning which is set against the backdrop of underlying characteristics of the organizations and also the slow but distinct developments that are taking place in line with the changes elsewhere in the world. Runaway successes achieved in the past through segmentation of personnel policies and evaluation may need to be revisited. They will have to be based on meaningful research, in the light of some of the new understanding and experiences.

In this new scenario, the organization's management must function with a strategic development perspective. Strategic HRD differs from the generally understood concept of HRD in the sense that the former concerns itself with the issue of deciding the broad parameters of organizations and employees including specific segments to be served within the organization and defining the scope of the development mix in the context of long-term development the organization is aiming at. A strategic HRD perspective enables an organization to continuously assess the changing behaviour of employees in the segments being targeted and also monitor actions in response to the same. It also helps in tracking fundamental shifts that may be taking place silently in organizations value expectations, the process through which values are created and delivered, approaches and practices used in communicating to employees or methods adopted to make innovative changes and services available physically and to reflect the new insights suitably, through altering the development mix well in time. As against this, the organizations management function is oriented towards maintaining the existing directions and associated development mix at a more efficient level. (Box 4.4)

Box 4.4

In a study, conducted by BHEL to examine the organizational climate, the opinions of different cadres of employees working in different units was sought and the line managers employees' perceptions regarding organizational climate was that (weighted average + 1.5) favoured the view that opportunity for promotion exists in BHEL. They also favoured the views like limited resistance to change in BHEL, clarity in priorities of BHEL, cooperative attitude is conducive among the existing departments and freedom to change the things in employees own job. However, they were against the views like job offers one to grow as a person, equal pay scales, logical division of work and friendly relations with the members of department. They totally rejected the view that there was no evidence of unresolved conflicts in BHEL.

In the category of Junior Managers, the respondents had positive perception towards, 'opportunity to grow as person', 'logical division of work tasks', 'friendly relations', 'clarity in goals', 'harmonious relations with superiors', 'clarity regarding the job' and the ability of the organization for changes'. However, they have negative views for statements like 'BHEL not introducing enough new policies and procedures', unresolved conflict incidents', and 'equal treatment in case of pay scales'.

In cross analysis, it was observed that all the categories of employees seem to have more or less similar perceptions towards the views highlighted.

Middle and Senior Managers had expressed that HRD climate in BHEL encouraged them to experiment with new methods, creative ideas and they do not feel and difficulty in expressing their ideas with subordinates and superiors. They also felt that the company ensures employee welfare to such an extent that the employees can save a lot of their mental energy for work purposes. They respond averagely to the views 'in understanding the mistakes done by the subordinates and make them to learn not to commit mistakes in future'. 'Team spirit was not of a high order in this company' as per the responses of middle and senior level managers.

They poorly responded to 'the development of subordinate as an important part of their job' and to 'take active interest in helping the juniors and also in development of competence among the subordinates'. There was also no climate to take initiative in the decisions without waiting for instructions of superiors. Delegation of authority to encourage juniors to develop and handle higher responsibilities is not quite common in the company. The juniors do not view delegation of authority as an opportunity for their development. The discussion on problem solving is also not encouraged in the organization. No employee responded that job rotation is useful for his development.

Importance of Research on Strategic HRD Issues

In order to respond adequately to strategic shifts that are already experienced in the economy, organization and their HRD agencies will need to alter their approach to meet the requirements of employees. This is because strategic issues concern themselves with long-term or fundamental shifts and employees requirements help the decision makers to gain insight on such critical issues, and also to develop a foresight for the future. As Hamel and Prahalad have observed in their book, Competing for the Future, the new strategy paradigm will require organizations to foresee the future five to ten years down the line and get answers to such questions as to how the organization will succeed, what changes are expected in the behaviour of their employees and what new services will be needed to be offered to sustain organization. Needless to say, answers to these and many other futuristic issues are not easy to find, not only because these are difficult to deal with but also due to the fact that they do not figure in the agenda of HRD of the organization.

HRD today is mostly focussed on the mechanics of getting answers to a whole lot of questions concerning training and personnel management and performance evaluation. No attempt is made to bring out underlying forces or shifts that are taking place in all aspects of HRD. The emphasis is on using time on tested, validated research models that are often not useful to unearth the underlying long-term trends.

Researching on the strategic HRD issues will require extensive debates within the organization and also with its HRD agency regarding specific aspects that are to be explored including identifying the cause and effect factors and not just finding out or describing what is happening at a particular point of time. HRD agencies will need to develop capabilities (can be in-house or networked with outside organizations) and possess familiarity with the employees on a long-term basis in order to effectively participate in such strategic debates. They should be able to help the employees to where the future state lies and what strategic issues need to be studied through formal research.

However, the above questions are only indicative. Obviously, strategic HRD issues will differ from one organization to another and within a category of employee. It is important to note the type of questions raised and to understand how these differ from traditional HRD issues such as demand estimation, personnel policies, recruitment, selection, promotion, profile of employees, etc. In research on strategic HRD, the thrust will have to be on interpreting human resource information data that are collected from primary and secondary sources rather than on debating about the intricacies or sophistication of research models to be used.

In understanding strategic HRD issues, research methodology and framework must support the strategic debates and dialogue within the organization and HRD specialists around the key issues being explored. Several scenarios and multiple perspective, using robust data which may not be always statistically valid for want of large size sample, have been built through a series of iterative discussions, but there is a need to develop a consensus on the fundamental issues that are driving the organization and arrive at specific action plans, not only in the area of HRD, but also for other functional areas as well, to reflect the new understanding.

While the right research framework and technique is the key to identify and address strategic HRD issues, what comes in the way is the lack of perspective among HRD professionals. In most organizations senior personnel are not even asking the questions of strategic importance. Instead they concern themselves in getting more data for describing the current HRD scenario. The emphasis is more on knowing 'what' is happening, and not getting bogged down with the sophistication of research techniques used. The thrust is on why things are happening, the way they are happening and also on finding the long-term directional change is missing. And, obviously, if organizations do not ask the right questions, the possibility is that they will get wrong answers. Large HRD organizations should gear themselves up for developing capabilities to undertake research in strategic HRD issues and impress on their employees the need to continuously track these issues, through formal research, for dominating the emerging future.

The Human Resources Development process should ideally be both multidisciplinary and intersectoral. The diverse institutions, organizations and interest groups involved in this process, as well as their terms of reference, functions, resources, and constraints, constitute an integrated system—the human resources system. The development process encompasses three broad functions:[7]

1. Human Resources Planning "is the process of estimating the number of persons and the kind of knowledge, skills, and attitudes they need to achieve predetermined targets and ultimately status objectives". Over the years this function has been broadened to include human resources policy, where "policy" refers to statements made by relevant authorities intended to guide the allocation of resources and effort. The policy and planning function is as concerned with the qualitative aspects of human resources such as health as with the quantitative aspects of supply and requirements.

2. Human Resources Education and Training refers to "all aspects related to basic and post-basic education and training of the work force. Although it is one of the central aspects of the manpower (development) process, it is not under the system's sole control".[8] The "production" system includes educational and training institutions. Although the term "production" is still used and presents little confusion, the Study Group prefered the term "production" and training".

3. Human Resource Management, defined as the "mobilization, motivation, development, and fulfillment of human beings in and through work", has recently received attention as an important and challenging concept in human resources development. It "covers all matters related to the employment, motivation of all categories of workers, and largely determines the productivity, and, therefore, the coverage of the system and its capacity to retain staff. Organizations also encompasses programmes for in-service and continuing professional education and evaluation. The critical importance of the organization is now acknowledged, and ways of improving it and its effect on productivity have been studied extensively.

HRD Framework

HRD organizations may not always be precisely defined. This being so, the objective should be to identify patterns to use available data from various sources. What is needed is to conduct exploratory research to understand the variables that are driving the organization structure and also to identify factors that are driving these variables themselves. The definition of organization here includes not only the existing ones that are offering the same or similar products and services, but also potential entrants, substitute products and services, existing and potential users.

One, however, will have to be careful in defining the industry: too narrow or too broad a scope can undermine the quality of HRD. Within the scope of this exploratory qualitative research on strategic issues, one can use structured or unstructured interviews, employ Delphi techniques or conduct focus group interviews. All these need to be backed up by high quality research based on secondary data. If properly conducted, exploratory research can give useful insight on underlying fundamental shifts that are taking place in the segments or industry. Once the broad patterns are identified through exploratory research and specific hypotheses of interest are developed, quantitative research on specific areas can be conducted to validate the identified issues.

In addition to exploratory research, it is also useful to study in-depth the pattern of evolution of organization. For example, answers to many of the questions of relevance to strategic HRD can probably be had if one can look at the evolution of the same industry in countries such as China or countries in Latin America or the Far East. However, care is needed while using the available data from these countries given the significant differences that exist in such areas such as political system, governmental control on trade and commerce, demographic profile of people, nature of distribution network, institutional framework, culture, openness to change and innovation, etc. If the differences in all these areas are identified, the pattern seen elsewhere can be suitably adjusted to foresee what possibly should happen in India.

Another approach is to get an insight on HRD marketing issues and develop foresight on future employees needs and how to meet them. For example, the US computer industry can draw important conclusions from the experiences of US companies, say automobile or consumer electronics: in both these sectors, American companies suffered badly at the hands of Japanese companies. Using such experiences, it is possible for the US computer industry to identify certain trends in such areas as technology developments, need for manufacturing efficiency to produce cost competitive products, and importance of brand building.

Is HRD Researched well?

The fundamental conditions to get success is a deep understanding of employees and an excellent appreciation of their activities. This can come about only if the organization has strong systems and methods, not only to collect and analyze data, but also to disseminate the information thus obtained to relevant decision makers within the organization.

The message, therefore, is that you need to review your internal systems and processes for gathering and utilizing HRD data relating to your employees so that your decisions become more sharper and data based.

One of the weakest links in many organizations is the absence of any systematic approach for identifying HRD opportunities, or introducing new methods of assessment. A glimpse at the mindset of organizations indicate that the major source of new HRD ideas is the top management. These efforts are further supplemented with analysis of activities.

Key Messages

The success probability of new HRD initiative today, suggests that a noticeable proportion of organizations do not exhibit strong and systematic approaches to managing employees and depend on either formal or informal HRD research, and seldom do they have a planned approach to identify opportunities.

If one examines those organizations which have significantly higher success rates than others, then the key differentiating factors are their systematic and scientific approach to managing new HRD issues and their much higher dependence on data for decisions. It is said that the fortune often favours the brave. Which are these brave organizations? They are the ones who assess success probabilities at each step while launching new HRD programmes with the sole purpose of reducing chances of failures. It is this orientation that differentiates the concern of the organizations in the development of their employees.

Despite enough causes for satisfaction, there are reasons for dissatisfaction too. The first relates to appropriate skill development which is the organizations basic responsibility. The second is our inability to generate adequate attitude, knowledge, management and relevant training.

If this is so, what is the role of the organizations of tomorrow? Firstly, it is necessary to refer to the new situation created by the structural reforms and globalization. The system of HRD has a critical role in inducing and effecting a genuine development of employees within the organization. The HRD planners of tomorrow would also have to assess the efficiency of employees so that they could further the interest of the employees.

An awakened HRD is the spin of any organization as the employees are becoming more demanding. Education, media and the socio-politico-economic process have created such an atmosphere. The HRD will have to play the role of an enlightened provider of services in a dispassionate, objective and selfless manner.

The employees must increasingly realize that employing them costs the exchequer substantial money. So, the employees have to be sensitive to costs financial, social and economic. Moreover, the employee will also have to show greater feeling for the development of the organization. The employees needs to be tuned to the ground realities that surround him, and cannot afford to be indifferent. Protecting one's colleagues and subordinates is all right up to a point but is unwarranted, improper and, even counter-productive beyond that.

What we need is a demanding organization. A wide awake employee and the HRD culture more aggressive.

To cope with these, the employee must operate with greater wisdom, competence, and sensitivity towards the development of the organization.

Changing times and values reorient the philosophy of a organization, the system of HRD also has to reorient with it.

Approach to Managing Quality

The approach to managing quality is not as difficult as a number of organizations visualize it. It should not take more than eight months as indicated in the book *Quality is Everybody's Business* by Tom Peter. Tom has further indicated that to define the process, complete the training and start improving, it is not as difficult as it may seem. The role of the leadership and the role of organization, if done systematically, makes the human resource development activities viable and is also ethical and correct to introduce.

There are several components to quality process. Taking one component in isolation is neither going to help the organization nor the employee. The components are; reengineering, management commitment, leadership and communication. There are two aspects to communication—transmission and reception. Training comes next. There is normal technical training and quality specific training. Evaluation is another critical part it is vital to measure, otherwise, the efficacy of human resource development within the organization will not be established, and the last component is recognition.

The general expectation of an employee in an organization is existence of good and congenial environment for better working. Creation of such an environment is the responsibility of both management and the workforce. A better climate emerges following due cognizence of the views of employees on the prevailing organizational policies, practices and conditions. The climate varies due to different conditions and nature of activities within the organization. Hence, it is very interesting and important to study as to how the human resource development needs and evolution to be organized for production organizations and service organizations as well as in achieving the goals of the organization.

Following a discussion on issues, significance and methodology adopted by human resource development planners in developing a climate for human resource planning for employees in different organizations—both within public and private sector, an attempt has been made to study the human resource development improvements in human resource planning policies as well as to ensure more effective organizational and HRD climate, as there is tremendous scope for improving the HRD climate for the development of employees and the organization in the service sector both in the 'production' and 'service' functions.

Evaluation of Employee Performance

Employee appraisal techniques are said to have been used for the first time during the First World War, when, at the instance of Walter Dill Scott, the US army adopted the man-to-man rating system for evaluating military personnel. During the period 1920-30, industrial units adopted relational wage structures for hourly paid workers. Under this system, the policy of giving grade wage increments on the basis of merit was accepted. These early employee plans were called merit rating programmes, which continued upto the mid fifties. By then, most of these plans were of the rating-scale type, where emphasis was given to factors, degrees and points. At that time, however, attention began to be given to performance appraisal for technical, professional and management personnel. Since then, as a result of experiments and a great deal of study, the philosophy of performance appraisal has undergone drastic changes. Consequently, a change has also taken place in the terminology used. Now, merit rating is largely restricted to the rating of hourly paid employee and is used for developing criteria for salary adjustments, promotions, transfers, etc. Personnel appraisal places emphasis on the development of the individual and is used by professional and management personnel.

The appraisal of individuals has been variously described over the years as performance appraisal, merit rating, behavioural assessment, employee evaluation, personnel review, progress report, staff assessment, service rating and fitness report, etc. Some personnel authorities use such concepts interchangeably while others interpret some of these phrases differently. However, the term performance appraisal or evaluation is most widely used.

Performance Appraisal

It is the process of evaluation the relative worth or ability of an individual employee against pre-determined, job-related performance standards usually set by job descriptions. Performance appraisal replaces casual assessment with formal, systematic procedures. Employees know they are being evaluated and are being told the criteria that will be used in the course of the appraisal. Other advantages of performance appraisal include generating useful information about the employees and the true nature of their duties. This data can be incorporated into an organization's human resource plans and thus assist in avoiding compulsory redundancies, in career planning and in identifying needs for training and development, forcing superior and subordinate to investigate problems jointly, which helps subordinates in their motivation and involvement, creating an effective system within the organization's management information structure.

In addition, it also provides, at an aggregated level, a profile of the organization in terms of its human resource strengths and weaknesses, an inventory of employee's skills and experience, and an evaluation of the organization's human resource. In short, the main purpose of performance appraisal particularly in the Government Sector is to provide human resource planning data for improving over the personnel information system. In private/public sector organizations, it is the most important tool that can be used by managers or superiors to motivate, encourage, build, train, reinforce and modify behaviour of their subordinates.

Perhaps the least liked activity by the appraiser and appraisee is doing the annual performance appraisal. The activity is often only a perfunctory, paper exercise. Performance appraisals are like seat belts; everyone agrees that they are important and that they save lives, yet no one uses them. The problem with appraisal system includes poorly designed procedures, a psychological resistance of the supervisors to give negative evaluations and a perceived invalidity. The appraisal system, nonetheless, is central to human resource management. It contributes to three essential processes of, seeking to provide an adequate feedback to each employee on his performance; purporting to serve as a basis for improving or changing behaviour, towards more effective working habits; and aiming at providing data for future job assignments. The various stages, therefore are:

Establish performance standards, communicate performance expectations to employees; Measure actual performance; Compare actual performance with standards; Discuss appraisal with the employee;

If necessary, initiate corrective action.

Criteria	*Employee Development*	*Administrative Purpose*
Definition of Purpose	Performance improvement by advising what is expected of an employee	Information for decisions on salary, promotion, reduction in work force
Basis for comparison	Performance related to objectives of the organization	Performance related to other similar employee
Techniques of appraisal	Result oriented appraisal	Employee, Supervisor
Role of Supervisor	Counsellor	Judge
Distribution of evaluation information	Employee and supervisor	Employee, supervisor personnel folder and related personnel

Components of Appraisal Evaluation

In view of the fact that there are a variety of reasons for performance evaluation viz. counselling, promotion, administration or a combination of these factors, it is necessary to understand clearly the objectives of the evaluation process. Having done this, the performance evaluation system should address the question in respect of the five w's, i.e. who, what, when, where and how of performance appraisal.

Who: It is usually the immediate supervisor who is entrusted with the task of rating the appraisee because he is most familiar with his work and is responsible for recommending or approving action based on performance appraisal and for providing a feedback to the appraisee. Supervisor's ratings are, therefore, regarded as the best possible assessment and often considered as the heart of most of the appraisal systems.

What: This includes appraisal of current performance and future potential. It also includes evaluation on human traits.

Why: It is concerned with creating and maintaining a satisfactory level of performance of employee in his present job; highlighting employee needs and opportunities for personal growth and development; aiding in decision making for promotions, transfers and discharges, etc. promoting understanding between the supervisor and his subordinates; and providing a useful criteria for determining the validity of selection and training methods and techniques.

When: It denotes the frequency of appraisals. It has been suggested that informal counselling should occur continuously. The Supervisor should use good work as an opportunity to provide positive reinforcement and use poor work as a basis for training. In most organizations, employees are evaluated once in a year. However, evaluation should not coincide with the date of increment for obvious reasons.

Where: It indicates the location where an employee may be evaluated and it is usually done at the place of work or office of the Supervisor. Informal appraisals may take place anywhere and everywhere, both on the job in work situations and of the job.

How: The organization must decide what are the methods available and which of these can be used for performance appraisal. On the basis of comparative advantages and disadvantages, it can be decided as to which method would suit the purpose best.

In any performance appraisal, due consideration must be given to the ethics of appraisal, failing which many organizational problems may crop up and the purpose of appraisal may be defeated. In this connection, M.S. Kellog has suggested the following do's and don'ts:

- Do not appraise without knowing why appraisal is needed.
- Appraise on the basis of representative information.
- Appraise on the basis of sufficient information.
- Appraise on the basis of relevant information.

These ethical standards are most likely to be met if appraisals are based on information both qualitative and quantitative as well as for each manpower group e.g. health, education, communication, bank, railways among others.[9]

References

1. Eli Ginzberg, "Man and his Work", in Dale S. Beach (ed.) *Managing People at Work,* Macmillan Publishing Co. Inc., New York, 1980, pp. 3-4.
2. Sar A. Levitan, Garth L. Mangum and Ray Marshall, *Human Resources and Labour Markets,* Harper & Row Publishers, New York, 1972, pp. 1-2.
3. Edwin B. Flippo, *Personnel Management,* Mc Graw-Hill Kogakusha Ltd., Tokyo, 1980, pp. 10-15.
4. Orlo. L. Crissey, "The Industrial Psychologist in Manpower and Organisational Planning" *Manpower Planning and the Development of Human Resources.*
5. N. Raja Reddy, "Motivational Climate: A Case Study of Commercial Banks", *The Journal of Institute of Public Enterprises,* Osmania University, Hyderabad, Vol. 14, June 1991, p.163.
6. T.V. Rao and Abraham, "Human Resource Development Climate in Indian Organizations", in T.V. Rao and D.F. Pereua (eds.), *Recent Experiences in Human Resource Development,* Oxford and IBH, New Delhi, 1986, pp. 70-71.

7. Hall, T.L. & Mejia, A., (ed.) *Health Manpower Planning: Principles, Methods and Issues.* Geneva, World Health Organization, 1978.
8. Report of a WHO Study Group, *Technical Report Series,* WHO, Geneva, 1990.
9. Evaluation of Employee Performance, M.P. Srivastava, *Employment News Weekly,* 12-18 December, 1998.

5

EDUCATION: RETROSPECT AND PROSPECT

The activities in different sectors of economy are all interrelated and the shortest and the most effective way to meet their requirements is to make a simultaneous attack on all the issues relating to the growth and development.

This will have to be attempted through two main programmes:

1. The development of physical resources;
2. The development of human resources.

The development of physical resources is acquired through the modernization of primary, secondary and services sectors of the economy. This modernization requires the adoption of science-based technology, information-based technology, capital formation and investment and the provision of essential infrastructure facilities such as transport, communication, credit, marketing and others.

The development of physical resources is a "means to an end" and that of human resources is an "end in itself" and without human resources adequate development of physical resources is not feasible.

The reason for providing greater emphasis to the planning and development of human resources as compared to physical resources is clear as the country's development is dependent on the development of human resources which inter-alia is reflected in the development and acquisition of education, skills and values. This requirement is basic to each programme of development—physical and human.

The professional, technical and skilled human resource required for the development of different sectors of the economy can only come from development of education, i.e., both from general/professional, scientific and technical education.

Education as Instrument of Change

Education as an instrument of change is difficult, complex, significant and of immediate requirement for the growth and development of the economy. Its effective use requires strength of will, knowledge, motivation and dedication to work and this applies to all kinds of education, particularly professional and technical education. The primary purpose of education is to provide an opportunity to develop the potentials of the human resource, i.e., their knowledge and skill among others. But the path to this achievement lies through the development of physical resource of the economy as well as emphasis on their perspective.

This direct link between education and physical resource development which has been emphasized during the last 50 years and in which the country deeply believes in can be achieved only when the system of education is organized both from the qualitative and quantitative points of view. Quantitatively, education can be organized to promote social justice. The same is equally true of the quality of education. It is only the right type of education, if provided on adequate scale that will lead to the development of physical resources and when these conditions are not met the opposite effect may result.

The role of education in socio-economic development has been recognized since Adam Smith, but it was only during the fifties of the present century that it has been identified as an important instrument of national development. Education since then has not only been recognized as an investment sector but it has also been realized that planning for education should be considered as an integral part of over all planning.[1]

Educational Planning is a process and its development is related to the socio-economic needs of the economy. It aims to provide a balance development of education at all levels and for different types of education. It is not only concerned with the quantitative expansion but also with qualitative improvement and aims at making the educational institutions more effective, efficient and appropriate both for the present and future.

In short, development of education necessarily involves making conscious decisions both for the present and the future. The realization of this need is a worldwide phenomenon.

The evolution of the modern approaches to the development of education are listed below:

1. Prior to World War II educational planning was done under conditions of slow socio-economic growth and development.
2. In the post War era a new role was assigned to education, i.e., to promote socio-economic growth combined with the growing demand for education by different sectors of the economy, organizations and individuals.
3. A new kind of educational planning emerged during the last fifty years which had the following characteristics:
   (a) comprehensive development of the educational system, (professional and technical).
   (b) a time perspective for development.
   (c) integration of socio-economic development, educational opportunities through human resources and physical resources.
   (d) attention to qualitative aspects and innovations in the educational system.

In order to adopt a plan on the basis indicated above a system analysis approach to the development of education was suggested. The main components of such a system analysis has been indicated in a book called *World Educational Crisis* by Philip Coombs.[2] In this approach concepts and techniques are drawn from social sciences and engineering backdrop.

Beeby has drawn attention to the new dimensions in educational planning and their contrast from traditional educational planning.[3] However, a number of changes have taken place in educational planning over the decade as a result of socio-cultural, economic and technological reasons.

The following are the most important elements in the new dimension of educational planning:

1. There is an intense interest on the part of the educational planner in economic growth, in human resource development and in what economists call macro planning—the simultaneous consideration of a country's all interlocking development plans.
2. "The Costing of a Global Scheme in advance with a constant eye on the country's economic plans and potentials and on its manpower needs".

It is believed that quantitative expansion of educational opportunities was to accelerate socio-economic development which inter-alia contributed towards skill formation, increase in productivity and learning of new ideas and techniques and also to enhance the opportunities of social mobility among the previleged and the underprivileged.

Role of Education in Human Resource Development

Despite geographical, historical and cultural diversities, the developing countries in general are characterized by an abundance of unskilled and untrained labour, existence of underemployment and "unemployed intellectuals" on the one hand, and serious shortages of persons with critical skills including highly educated professional manpower, technicians, top level management and administrative personnel, qualified teachers, and the like on the other.

It is realized that one of the most important factors underlying the slow and halting socio-economic development in recent years has been the rapid population growth and inadequate utilization and development of the relatively abundant human resources. It is widely accepted now that social and economic development cannot be ensured by making provision for capital, raw materials, machinery, power, etc. unless sufficient attention is given to the role of human factor in the development process.

Planned development envisages its own quantum and nature of skilled manpower supply. Education is one of the means for developing the skills, knowledge and capacities of persons for participation in the labour force. Here education contributes most obviously to human resource development, or, in economic terms, to human capital formation. In all countries the costs of education tends to raise relative costs in many activities. Of all industries, education is one of the most labour-intensive industry, about 75 per cent of its costs are wages and salaries.

A society develops its human resources by educating and training its members. There is as yet no general model or set of models which describes, explains or predicts how this is done.

At the outset, a word on the distinction between human resource planning and educational planning. The first is not merely a mere pretentious synonym of the second. Educational planning covers the arrangement and ordering of school programmes and the more formally managed in-service training courses. Human resource planning has a wider domain. First, it may cover the establishment of standards of nutrition and sanitation and medical care that reduce morbidity and mortality to levels where the population can use whatever education and training it has to produce. Second, human resource development planning can cover all of the institutional and individual ways in which a population acquires and improves knowledge and skill for social, political and economic development. Much of this goes on privately, in the minds and hearts of men, unamendable, fortunately, to observation, characterization and control. Formal education is a large part of human resource development, but not all, planning one will often involve planning the other, but not in all cases.[4]

Social and national integration is crucial to the creation of a strong, united country, which is an essential pre-condition for all progress. It has a varied content—economic, social, cultural and political and its different facets are closely interconnected.

Social and national integration is a major problem which will have to be tackled on several fronts including education. Report of the Education Commission, 1964-66 has laid stress that education can and should play a very significant role by:

- introducing a common school system of public education;
- making social and national service an integral part of education at all stages;
- developing all modern Indian languages, and taking necessary steps to enrich Hindi as quickly as possible so that it is able to function effectively as the official language of the Union; and
- promoting national consciousness.

It has further observed that, the most powerful tool in the process of modernization is education based on science and technology. The one great lesson of the present age of science is that, with determination and willingness to put in hard work, prosperity is within the reach of any nation which has a stable and progressive government. There is no doubt that in the years to come India's trade and commerce will grow: there will be more food for all; more education, better health and a reasonable standard of living will be available. But, India's contribution can, and should be far more than these material gains. It should learn to harness science but she must also learn not to be dominated by science. In this respect India has a unique advantage with her great tradition of duty without self-involvement, unacquisitive temperament, tolerance, and innate love of peace and reverence for all living things. Too often are these precious assets forgotten and we tend to relapse into moods of pessimism, fears and forebodings, discord and destructive criticism. A new pride and a deeper faith expressed in living for the noble ideals of peace and freedom, truth and compassion are now needed.

The report has further observed that the quality of the existing programmes of teacher education should considerably be improved. The essence of a programme of teacher education is 'quality' and in its absence, teacher education becomes, not only a financial waste but a source of overall deterioration in educational standards. We need to attach the highest importance to this programme of qualitative improvement. Existing programmes of teacher education are largely traditional, rigid and divorced from the realities of schools and existing or proposed programmes of educational reconstruction. Reorganization is needed at all levels and in all courses. These are some broad principles on which this reorganization need to be attempted.

- re-orientation of subject-knowledge;
- vitalization of professional studies;
- improvement in methods of teaching and evaluation;
- improvement of student-teaching;
- development of special courses and programmes; and
- revision and improvement of curricula.

The main concern of this chapter is to identify the major activities which have resulted in the educational revolution during the past five decades and what impact it has brought on the socio-economic development of the Indian economy.

Organization and Structure of Educational System in India

In the modern society, knowledge is increasing everyday and the increase in knowledge is influencing the socio-economic development. This development would inter-alia bring a radical transformation in the education system. Education is no longer an instrument for imparting knowledge or the preparation of finished product, but is an instrument of development, of interest, attitude and value and also for building up of essential skill and capacity to think and judge for oneself.

The transformation of human resource with various levels of skills, knowledge, competencies has to be done on the basis of the human resource profiles which are required to work out an emerging scenario out of a given socio-economic goal. At the initial stage of socio-economic development the man was stated as a factor of production. Later, in the wake of industrial revolution when the man was required to be equipped with various jobs/skills he came to be known as a 'shop-mate' instead of a 'factory-mate'. Still later, when the relationship between the industrial employment and the educational level reached its climax, human beings came to be recognized as human capital wherein the investments have to be made for its fuller development.[5]

The educational structure in India with levels and duration of each level and the normal age of entry at each level is given in Figure 1.

Formal education and training are given in India under two systems. The first system can be characterized as the university system which is distinguished from the other primarily by the fact that education and training under this system generally end with the award of recognized degrees, marking the completion of a course of education. All courses of education under this system do not end with the award of a degree, but their completion necessarily takes individuals towards a degree.

The university system of education provides full-time regular courses in most cases running for periods longer than a year. These courses are always graded, so that each course is preparatory for the next higher level course. At the base of this education system is the secondary educational programme which covers a period of 10 years of formal schooling, followed by another two years of senior secondary schooling programmes at which the school level education ends in India.

After the age of 14 years a child can—instead of joining the secondary school providing general education programmes—join a vocational school or an Industrial Training Institute. A person who completes 10 years of general education has a similar choice either to take up academic courses at the higher secondary level preparatory to collegiate education or to opt for vocational streams within the higher secondary programme or to join specialized institutions such as polytechnics and Industrial Training Institutes. Completion of higher secondary education qualifies the individual for entering first degree programmes in general courses or in professional courses like engineering and medicine.[6]

The control of the secondary school education rests with the secondary school boards. It is usually state based, and each State Board has the jurisdiction over the entire state. The State Boards determine the standards of secondary level education

Figure 1 : STRUCTURE OF EDUCATION IN INDIA

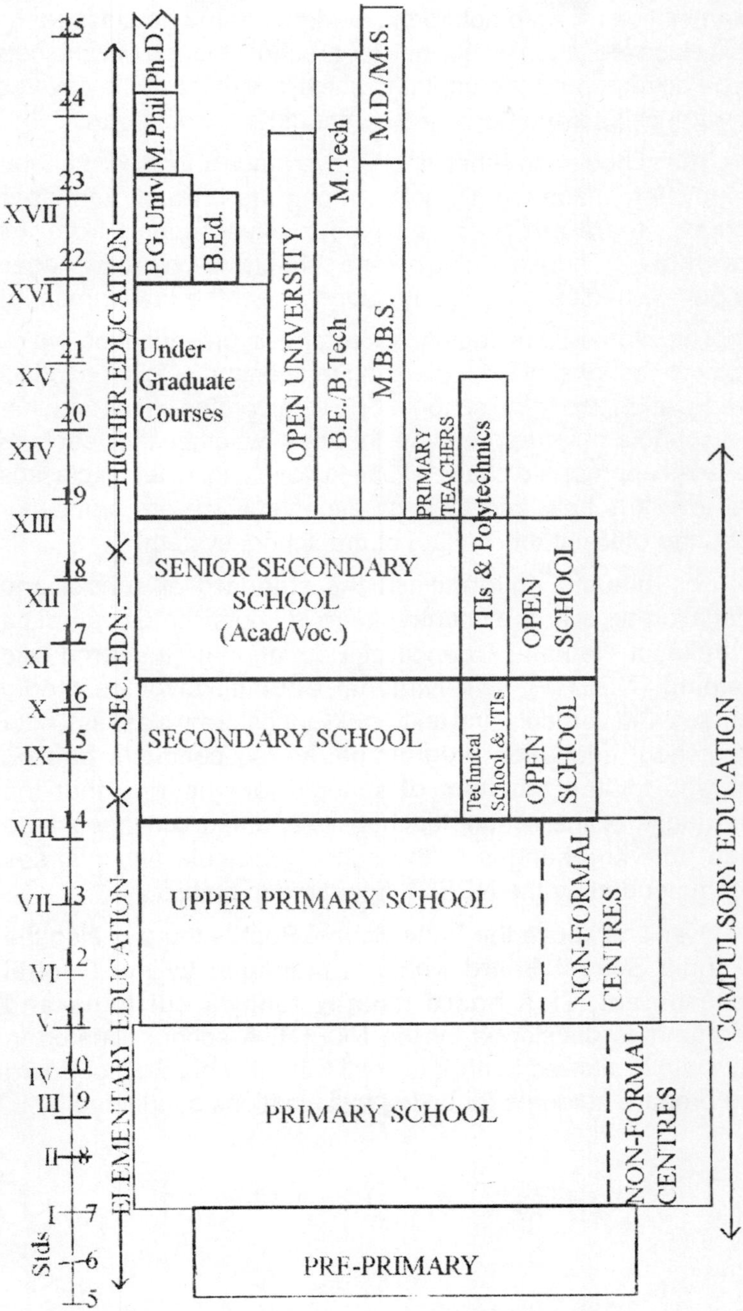

and also hold examinations at the completion of first 10 years of secondary education and again at the completion of the additional two years of senior secondary education. Annual examinations for promoting the students from one class to the next class are taken by the individual school though the subjects to be covered and the depth at which subjects will be covered at each class are determined by the state school boards.

The schools are either wholly government managed schools or privately managed schools. Among the privately managed schools, there are schools which receive support from the government. There are also private schools which are managed by private bodies without any support from the government.

The states have regular Directorates of Education which bear the responsibility for ensuring regular and efficient conduct of education under the schools. The Directorates check whether the schools have appropriate facilities, whether the teachers possess appropriate qualifications for teaching, whether classes are regularly held and all such aspects which are crucial for ensuring efficient functioning of the school system.

For ensuing uniformity in the standard of school and education all over the country, there is under the Government of India, a National Council of Educational Research and Training (NCERT). The National Council develops model courses and curricula and text-books for different classes under the school education programme. It also conducts training courses for the teachers of schools for ensuring that the knowledge of the school teachers is updated continuously to keep up with changes in the school curricula and courses recommended by the NCERT from time to time.

Over and above the State School Boards there is also the All India School Board which is managed by the Central Government. This board usually follows curricula and programmes developed by the NCERT. A school situated in any state is allowed to affiliate itself with All India School Board and prepare students for taking examinations conducted by it.

Education beyond the school level is under the control of the universities. Different colleges offer courses leading to first degree and/or post-graduate degrees and diplomas.

In each state, there are usually more than one universities, which are either unitary or federal or affiliating. The unitary universities are also centres of education both for the first degree and/or post-graduate degree level education. In a federal university, the colleges where education is conducted are constituents of the university. With an affiliating university, the colleges are autonomous teaching organizations affiliated to the university.

Each university develops its own course and curricula and also conducts examinations for the award of degrees to successful candidates. In the case of a unitary university, the university departments also take the responsibility for conduct of the courses and for preparing the students for the examinations. In a federal university the courses are conducted in constituent colleges, where the students are prepared for taking examinations arranged by the university as a whole. In the affiliating universities also, the courses are conducted in different colleges for preparing the students for common examinations arranged by the university. The affiliating university takes on the additional responsibility for ensuring appropriate facilities of education in different autonomous colleges. It also sets the standard requirements for appointments of teachers for different courses.

Each university is managed as an autonomous organization with its own administrative and academic governing councils for determining the standards of education at different levels and courses. Subject to the financial and other constraints which the government imposes through Acts under which the universities are established, the universities are empowered to formulate their own academic programmes like the courses to be offered, curricula for each course, method of examination and evaluation.

For ensuring a certain amount of uniformity in the standards of education and also for ensuring regular improvement in the quâlity of education under the universities, the Government of India has also set up a University Grants Commission. This Commission formed under an Act of Parliament has responsibility for ensuring a minimum standard of education for all levels. The Commission has also funds at its disposal for extending support to universities and colleges towards maintenance and improvement of the standard of education. The courses offered under the university, either in the colleges or in the university departments, are regular full-time ones of duration usually longer than a year. At the post-graduate level, however, there are courses which may run for a year or less.

Formal education and training is also given outside the university system. The characteristic features of the courses under this arrangement are that they are primarily related to a profession or occupation or vocation and the completion of these courses does not lead to award of degrees, nor do they entitle the candidates to get admission in higher level courses provided by the universities in their affiliated colleges. These courses are individual courses and are not preparatory for other courses.

The institutions offering such courses are usually under different government departments. There are also regular full time and time bound courses.

The Ministry of Labour is an important agency involved in this area of education. The Ministry of Labour runs Industrial Training Institutes (ITI) offering both engineering and non-engineering trade courses for supporting industrial manpower developmental programmes in the country.

The ITI courses are available for individuals who complete only middle level education (Class VII or VIII) and also for those who complete secondary level education. The ITIs offer a large number of courses, and depending upon the trade and craft, the courses run for six months to two years. Standards of education in these institutions are maintained through national and state councils for training in vocational trades. These councils have representatives from the government, private agencies and other specialist groups for determining the course, content, curricula and the test and evaluation procedures for different trade courses.

The Ministry of Education also runs a large number of polytechnics for education which may lead to middle level supervisory occupations in various industries. These courses are also regular, full-time and period bound and are open to individuals who acquire general education under the university system upto a certain level. The candidates are offered diplomas at the completion of the courses. These courses are also terminal. However, arrangements have been made for admitting the graduates of these courses to advanced university based courses leading to university degrees.

Vocational, technical and professional educational institutions offering various terminal courses are also run by other ministries. The Ministry of Agriculture has also large number of institutions for conduct of courses for preparing individuals for occupations in the fields of agriculture, forestry, fishing, etc. These courses are also regular, full-time and terminal, preparing individuals for entry into specific occupations.[7]

Education in Indian Planning

Education was exclusively the responsibility of states before 1976. Central Government was only concerned with areas like technical and higher education. Education became a joint responsibility through a constitutional amendment in 1976. Now, the quality and character of education is the responsibility of Union Government. The Ministry of Human Resource Development shares with the states the responsibility for educational planning.

Indian planning has had to balance three competing claims: the constitutional obligation regarding eight years of compulsory education, the manpower needs of a growing economy and the insatiable demand for expansion of educational institutions. The balance has not been static.

The development of education in India since its independence has been guided by national demands as also by the socio-economic and political challenges. The Indian National Commission on Education has also expressed that education should be used as a powerful instrument of socio-economic and political changes.

The national policy on education adopted in 1968 emphasized for considerable expansion of the educational facilities all over the country and at all levels. While these achivements were found impressive, the general formulation incorporated in the 1968 policy did not get translated into a detailed strategy of implementation accompanied by the assignment of specific responsibilities and organizational support and problems of quality, quantity, relevance and financial outlays accumulated over the years.

National Policy on Education (NPE) 1986

It was in response to this that the new National Policy on Education (NPE) was adopted by the Government of India in May, 1986. The policy laid greater stress on the elimination of disparities in the educational system and provision of greater facilities through qualitative interventions.

The policy document also called for appraisals at short intervals to ascertain the development of its various parameters from time to time as also a five yearly review.

Review Committee 1990

A review committe was set up in May, 1990 among others to assess and take cognizance of the developments initiated since the policy 1986 and to monitor the progress of the programmes and accordingly prioritize the goals and strategies of educational programmes. In addition, Central Advisory Board of Education (CABE) was constituted in 1991 to review the implementation of various parameters of NPE, 1986.

The link between education and socio-economic development of different sectors of economy, particularly the services sector of the economy could be forged through the development of the following programmes which need to receive high priority in educational reconstruction of the economy.

These are:

1. Increase Investment
2. Research for Relevance
3. Rapid Multiplication of knowledge and skills, and
4. A change of attitude of Society and Worker.

To make this possible, it was found necessary to bring a socio-economic integration, which need to be tackled on several fronts including general education and professional education.

System of Educational Administration

At the central level, the Department of Education in the Ministry of Human Resource Development is responsible for all matters connected with education, including overall planning of programmes and providing guidance for their implementations. The creation of the Ministry of Human Resource Development in September 1985 is a landmark in the organizational history of the Union Government; it marks the institutionalization of the seminal idea that the people of the country should be looked upon as the most valuable resource, that development should go beyond economic growth with its calculus of Gross National Product (GNP), investment and growth rate, and that, instead, development should aim at integrated development of the citizens, beginning with childhood and going right through life and drawing upon all factors having a bearing on the condition of the masses, including science and technology, culture, education, arts and crafts, sports, humanities and human values.[8]

The state level organizational structure and administrative set-up varies from state to state. Given that the states have to manage an immensely larger number of institutions than the centre, in most states there is more than one Department of Education each looking after a few stages of education. The most prevalent pattern comprises the three departments, i.e., department of school education, higher education and technical education. The organization and functions of each of these departments are similar to the Department of Education at the centre. To each department a few directorates are attached to each looking after a particular stage of education such as elementary education, adult education, collegiate education and so on. In larger states, each of these directorates have field-formations at the regional, district and sub-district levels.[9]

Institutional Support

The implementation of educational programmes, for better planning, development and utilization of human resources requires tremendous support from a wide range of Government institutions. Apart from those ministries with a direct responsibility for human resource planning, development and utilization such as HRD, Labour and Planning, much support is required from other ministries such as Health, State Governments, Industry, among others. The priority for this support institutions would orient their activities which would inter-alia enhance the national effort to develop and utilize human resources.

Human Resources Development: Education Sector

The concern in human resources development is not just on improving work and productivity but all aspects that are vital to the improvement of the welfare of the people and their active participation in the development process. It encompasses a whole array of social, economic and cultural variables. Given this inter-relationship, policy interventions can be in the form of broader educational opportunities, among others.

In India, high unemployment and/or poverty rates have persisted despite the provision of free education up to the university level because the output of the educational system has not fully corresponded to human resource needs. Such mismatch arises from the lack of coordination among human resource, education and planning.

Education can be regarded as constituting the core of the human resources development strategy in India. However, it is not education in the narrow sense of schooling, but a broad concept encompassing health, nutrition, employment, science and technology. Education is an instrument of people's development and their access to opportunities and facilities in these areas. These concerns underlie the New Education Policy and the programme of Action passed in 1986.

The government has implemented the Minimum Needs Programme to ensure the universal satisfaction of such basic needs as elementary education, adult education and rural education. The programme complements the target group approach since it also focuses on the poverty groups.

Many human resources development policies and programmes in India can best be understood in terms of the target groups and programmes designed for them. Some of these programmes include:

(a) Integrated rural development programme

(b) National rural employment programme

(c) Programme for scheduled castes and tribes

(d) Integrated child development services programme

(e) Special nutritional programmes.

Despite all efforts no well-knit system exists at present to ensure coordination and integration of human resources development programmes in India. The responsibility for the implementation of human resources development is shared between the central and state governments, because planning for a country of India's size and diversity is not so easily organized, supervised and controlled by the centre. As the primary implementing agencies in human resources development, the state governments determine their own policies and also draw up their five year and annual plans of development. The Central Government, however, influences state policies, by initiating national level programmes in crucial areas, by developing an ensuring national standards, and providing substantial financial assistance to the states.

Government of India constituted Planning Commission and vested it with responsibility of developing prospective long-term plans as well as mid-term plans and annual plans, and undertake evaluation. The Planning Commission is in a unique position to ensure the development of human resources development and to monitor their implementation.

Government efforts in the area of Human Resource Development include constitution of a separate ministry, the Ministry of Human Resources Development. It comprises the Departments of Education, Culture, Youth Services and Sport and Women and Child Development.

Institute of Applied Manpower Research was established by the Government of India in 1962, as an autonomous organization. The Institute functions under the agies of Planning Commission. The Institute stimulates interest in manpower planning and manpower development issues, among sister institutions with similar objectives, Central and State Government departments, and public sector undertakings through its activities in training, seminars and conferences as also through sponsored research activities.

Taking Stock of Educated Manpower: Role of Institute of Applied Manpower Research

The Institute of Applied Manpower Research (IAMR) for the first time in the country has developed information system, i.e., The National Technical Manpower Information System (NTMIS) for one of the important and crucial categories of manpower viz. engineers. The system provides a comprehensive information on labour market conditions of different categories of engineers both at the national level and at the individual state level.

The other type of information system relates to National Science Manpower Information System. An effort has been made under this system to study scientific activities, i.e., (i) research and development (ii) scientific and technological services (iii) teaching (iv) science administration/management and (v) other scientific activities. The third system relates to Agricultural Manpower Information System. The system when operational will provide information on demand and supply of agricultural manpower and would develop an agricultural manpower Information System and also identify a model for agricultural manpower planning, among others. The details of the first two systems are presented below:

National Technical Manpower Information System[10] (NTMIS) Labour Market Information for Engineers

Development of an information system for a given category of manpower would need a multipronged approach. It has to explore the possibilities of making best use of the data and information available from different sources and also develop methodologies for generating additional information that is required for bridging the gaps in the existing data system. Though, several approaches are available for generating such information in the NTMIS we have adopted the tracer study approach for generating labour market information in respect of engineers. These tracer studies focus on generating information on the characteristics of flow of degree holders and diploma holders in engineering from the engineering educational institutions in the country are covered through the tracer studies two years after their graduation from the respective levels, starting from the batch year 1982. The information on the following aspects is elicited from each and every graduate through the tracer study viz.:

1. Subject of education like Civil, Mechanical, etc.;
2. Level of course viz. (i) P.G. Degree, (ii) P.G. Diploma, (iii) Degree, (iv) Post-diploma and (v) Diploma;
3. Date and month of the results;
4. State of permanent residence;
5. State of education;
6. Current activity status viz. (i) wage employed, (ii) self-employed, (iii) student, (iv) looking for job, (v) not available for job, etc.;
7. State for first employment;
8. Month and year of first employment;
9. Characteristics of the establishment where employed like main activity of the establishment, sector of employment, and size of employment;
10. Nature of employment viz. permanent, regular, ad-hoc;
11. Function performed;

12. Emoluments received;
13. If self-employed details like activity in the employment venture, financial assistance received, etc.;
14. If unemployed details like number of times applied for jobs, number of times appeared for interview, job/location preference, etc.

Structure of Information Generated through the Tracer Studies

1. Flow of graduates into various economic activities, by discipline and level in each state.
2. In and out migrations for education by discipline and level in each state.
3. Migration for employment by discipline and level in each state.
4. International migration by discipline and level in each state.
5. Net availability of a given year's out-turn for job by discipline and level in each state.
6. Annual absorption in percentage term, of a given year's out-turn, by discipline and level in each state.
7. Waiting period for 100 per cent employment of a given year's out-turn, by discipline and level in each state.
8. Size of unemployment of a given category of engineers at the end of a specified year by discipline and level in each state.
9. Average monthly emoluments earned by fresh engineers by discipline and level in each state.
10. Percentage of a given year's out-turn taking up self-employment by discipline and level in each state.
11. Activity type of the self-employment ventures taken up by the fresh engineers.
12. Expectation of the unemployed engineers in terms of emoluments and locational preferences, if any.

In addition to the tracer studies, surveys are also conducted regularly, and on the annual basis, covering all the engineering degree and diploma institutions and also the employing establishments in the socio-economic sectors. The broad parameters on which information is elicited from these two groups of respondents and the structure of information generated are as under:

Parameters on which Information is Elicited from the Engineering Educational Institutions

1. General particulars of the institution;
2. Courses available, discipline-wise and level-wise;
3. Size of intake by discipline and level;
4. Size of enrolment and its characteristics by discipline and level;
5. Facilities available for continuing education in terms of courses available, admission capacity and duration of different courses;
6. Characteristics of the teaching faculty;
7. Sanctioned and actual strength of teachers;
8. Characteristics of the non-teaching faculty;
9. Consultancy projects undertaken and particulars thereof;
10. Financial data;
11. Physical facilities.

Information sought from the employing establishments

1. General particulars of the establishment;
2. Principal activity of the establishment;
3. Size of total employment;
4. Size of technical manpower in employment its structure;
5. Size of formally trained engineers by discipline and level;
6. Total turnover;
7. Total investment;

8. Total capital;
9. Total value of output.

Structure of Information Generated

1. From Engineering Educational Institutions

(i) Courses available at degree and diploma levels in engineering, state-wise;

(ii) Total number of students admitted to the first year of the course, discipline-wise and level-wise, state-wise;

(iii) Net out-turn of the state, taking into account the incidents of in and out migrations for education, discipline-wise and level-wise, state-wise.

(iv) Students per teacher, department-wise in engineering colleges and polytechnics, state-wise;

(v) Shortage of technical teachers, department-wise in engineering colleges and polytechnics, state-wise;

(vi) Courses available for continuing education;

(vii) Details of sponsored projects undertaken by engineering institutions and the particulars of the faculty involved in such projects.

2. From Employing Establishments

Manpower coefficients of the following types are generated

(i) Ratio of technical manpower in employment to total employment;

(ii) Ratio of a particular category of technical manpower in employment to total employment;

(iii) Ratio of a particular category of technical manpower in employment to total technical manpower in employment;

(iv) Ratio of degree holders of a particular category in employment to diploma holders of the same category in employment;

(v) Ratio of practicals to total technical manpower in employment.

Labour Market Information for Scientific Manpower

In order to forecast demand and supply of science post-graduates in a scientific manner, it is essential that the following issues may be resolved. They are:

(i) Identification of Science Subjects

First of all, one should have a clear idea about the type of science subjects which form science education at post-graduate level. In the Indian Universities, there is no uniform system of awarding science post-graduate degrees in science. The prevailing system of awarding science post-graduate degrees is as under:

(i) Most of the universities award M.Sc. degree under faculty of science for science subjects;

(ii) Some universities for some science subjects award M.A. Degree under faculty of Arts/Social Sciences, and

(iii) Some universities award both M.Sc. and M.A. degrees under Faculty of Science and Arts/Social Sciences, for some subjects.

Based on the National Science Manpower Information System conducted by IAMR, the following 15 subjects have been identified where the universities have difference in awarding post-graduate degrees:

1. Anthropology
2. Applied Geography
3. Applied Mathematics
4. Applied Psychology
5. Criminology/Forensic Science
6. Defence Studies
7. Earth Sciences
8. Geography
9. Home Science
10. Mathematics
11. Math-Statistics

12. Military Science
13. Pure Mathematics
14. Psychology and
15. Statistics.

For the above mentioned subjects, some universities award M.Sc. degree under faculty of Science, while some universities award M.A. degree under faculty of Arts/Social Sciences. In addition, there are some universities which award both M.A. and M.Sc. degrees under faculty of Arts/Social Sciences and faculty of Science respectively. Under these circumstances, it is suggested that all the subjects for which M.Sc. degrees are awarded by any university under faculty of Science may be considered as Science subjects at post-graduate level irrespective of whether some universities award M.A. degree for the same subjects.

(ii) Scientific Activities

Another important aspect of manpower forecasting is to assess demand of science post-graduates for scientific activities. The information which is analyzed may help to identify: (i) whether science post-graduates are joining the scientific activities for which they were normally trained; (ii) is there any shortage/surplus in any category of science post-graduates in the labour market vis-a-vis their demand; (iii) what is labour market position of science post-graduates vis-a-vis other post-graduates; (iv) whether the science post-graduates are joining non-scientific occupations due to either non-availability of jobs in scientific occupations or there is a better prospect of science post-graduates in non-scientific occupations, etc.

For conducting manpower planning to provide answers to above queries, it is important to identify scientific activities. It is difficult to define scientific activities precisely and prepare a comprehensive list of such activities. This is due to overlapping of functions and duties of organizations engaged in the area. As such some arbitrariness is bound to creep up in the identification of such activities under this system, an effort has been made to identify scientific activities into five broad categories as under: (i) research and development, (ii) scientific and technological services, (iii) teaching, (iv) science administration/management, (v) other scientific activities.

Planning for an educational system has certain other crucial dimensions also. Institute visualizes that a more comprehensive information system could be built to facilitate policy formulation and implementation of a variety of development programmes in education.

Linkage with other Organizations

In the process of acquiring the status of the focal institution in the field of manpower and employment research, the Institute has established formal linkages through the General Council/ Executive Council and the Standing Committee on Research Programme (SCRP) with Central Ministries, State Governments, public and private sector organizations, professional bodies, and academic and research institutions.

Organizations within the formal frame of linkages participate in formulating the policies and programmes of the Institute. On occasions, they have also collaborated with the Institute and aided its efforts to find solutions to critical problems in manpower and employment planning.

IAMR is a founder member of the Asian Human Resources Development (HRD) Network among the nations in the Asian Region set up under a programme of the Asian Regional Team for Employment Promotion (ARTEP) of the International Labour Organization (ILO). Major activities of the Asian HRD Network are training in HRD and documentation on manpower and employment research. IAMR has been a leading participant in these activities. The institute also has informal linkages with international agencies such as FAO, ILO and WHO; and professional associations in India and abroad such as the Indian Association of Social Science Institutions, Association of Development Research and Training, Institutes of Asia and the Pacific (ADIPA) and Society for International Development (SID) (Figures 2, 3, 4, 5 and 6).[11]

Figure 2 : LINKAGES WITH OTHER ORGANISATIONS

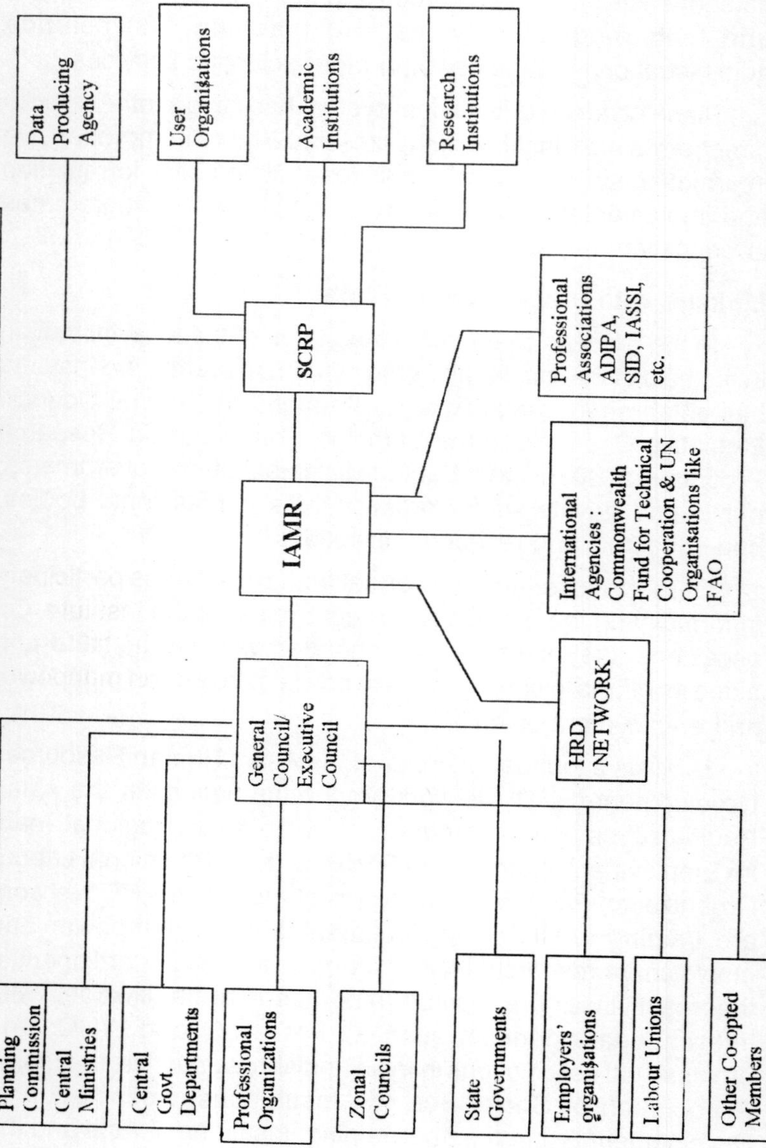

Figure 3 : DIMENSION OF MANPOWER DEVELOPMENT ISSUES : AREA BASED ISSUES INVESTIGATED

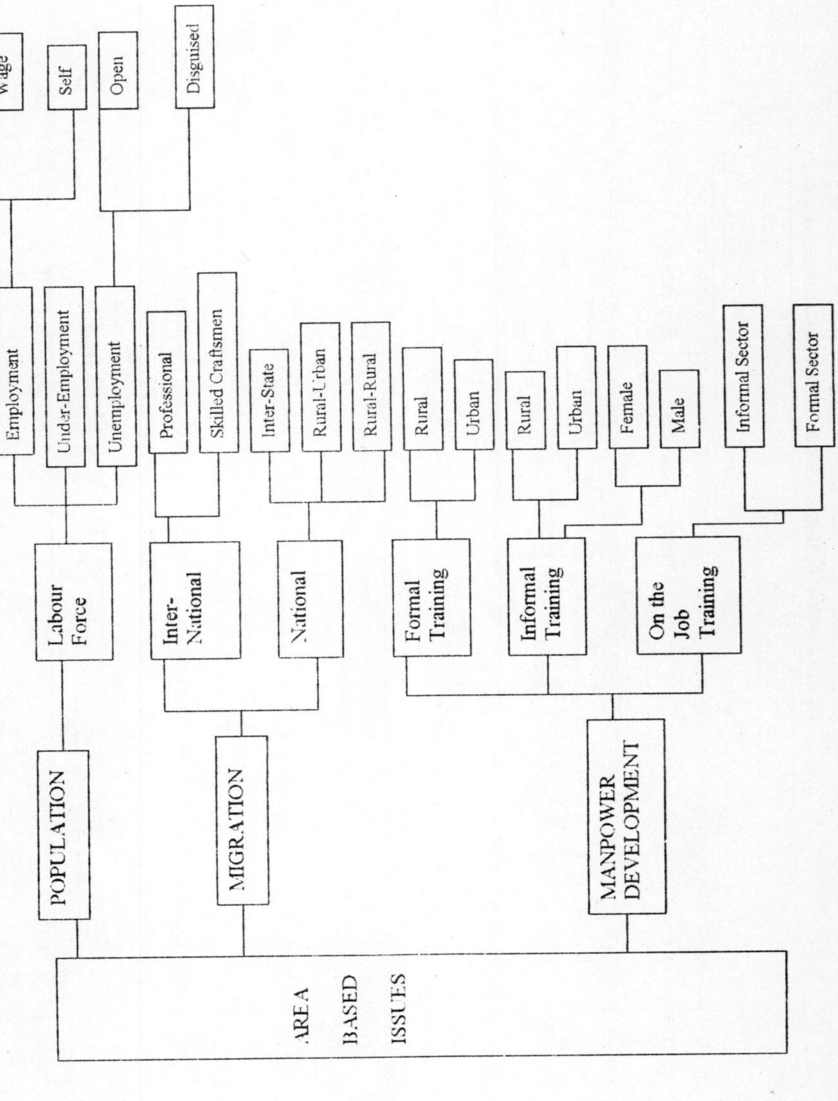

Figure 4 : SECTOR SPECIFIC MANPOWER DEVELOPMENT ISSUES

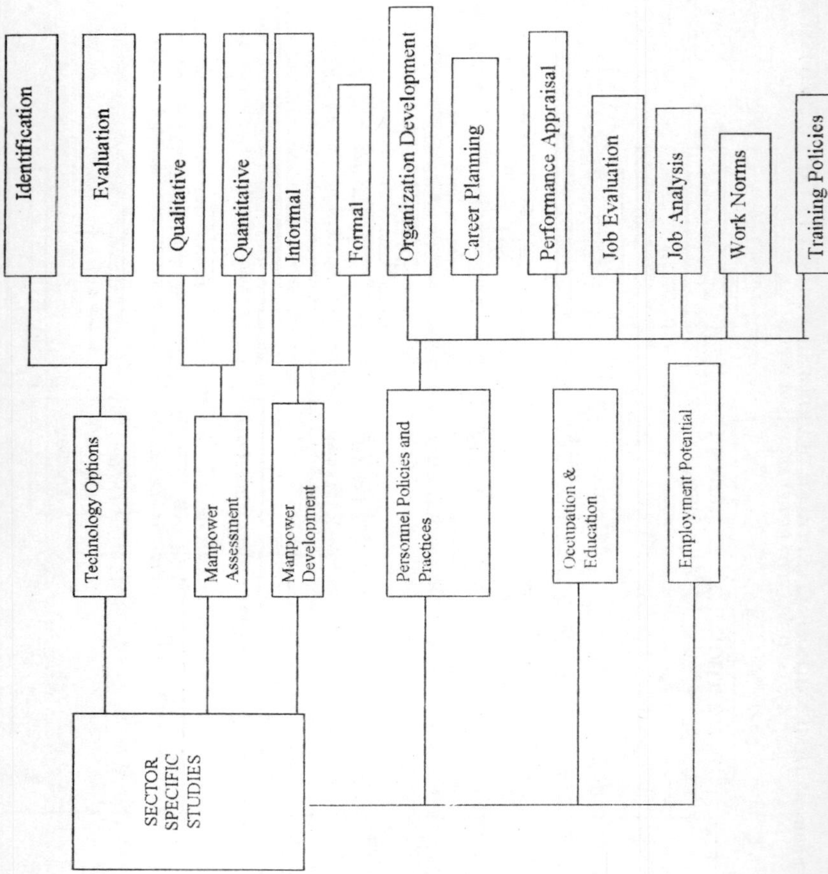

Figure 5 : DIMENSIONS OF MANPOWER DEVELOPMENT ISSUES : MANPOWER GROUP STUDIES INVESTIGATED

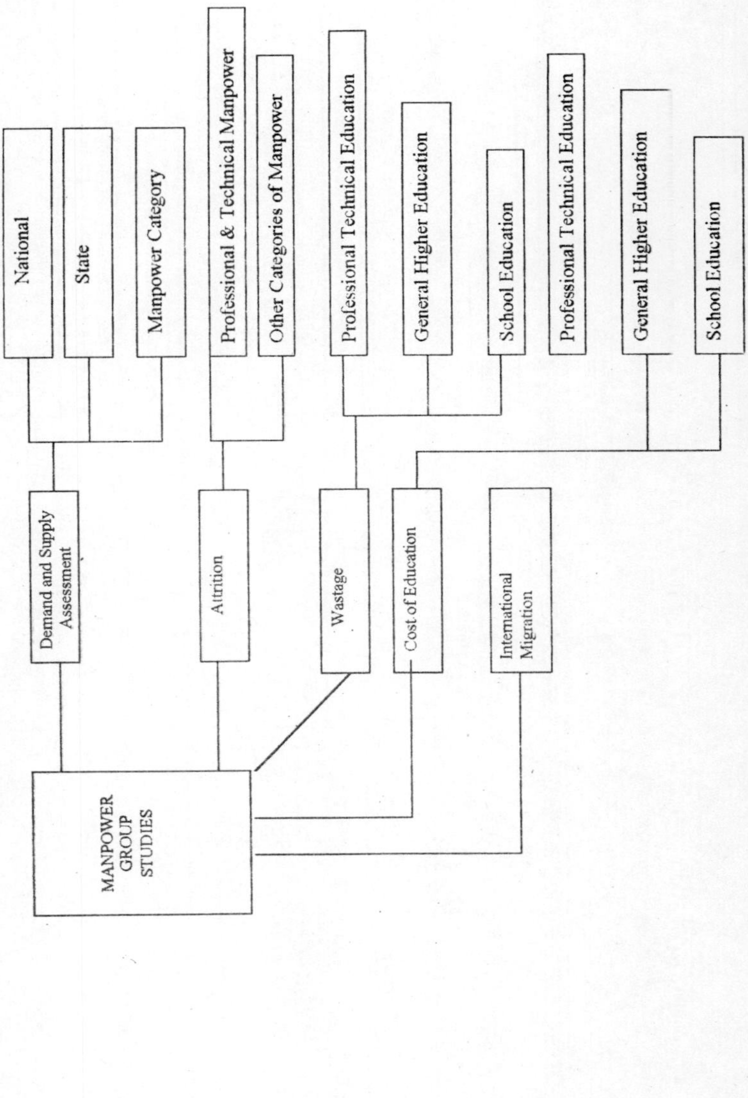

Figure 6 : MANPOWER DEVELOPMENT ISSUES : MANPOWER INFORMATION SYSTEM

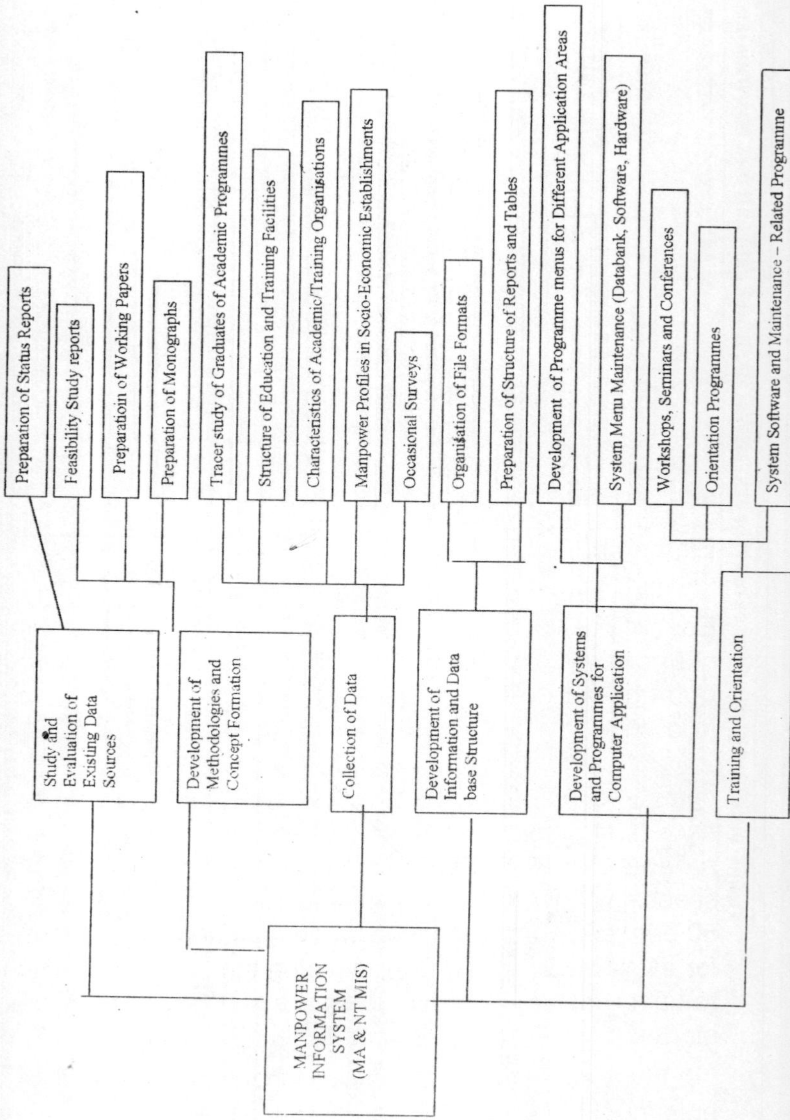

In summary, while it can be observed that there is no single agency responsible for all human resources development coordination, a strong lead has been taken in this regard by the Ministry of Human Resources Development and the Institute of Applied Manpower Research, which have sought to establishes linkage with other departments and agencies concerned with human resources development.

Shifting Focus in Educational System

The purpose of this part is to explain the shifting focus in education and its implications for HRD.

It is evident from the past experience that the principal reason for non-cooperation between the national economy and the national educational system is largely on account of the proportion of the national stock of higher educated manpower which is employed in the organized sector. Therefore, it is of paramount importance to review the changes in occupational structure and education per-se.

Elementary Education

The revised Programme of Action 1992 of the New Education Policy, 1986 has resolved to ensure free and compulsory education enter the 21st century. In order to operationalize the revised policy of the Government, the following three sub-schemes were proposed under Operation Blackboard during the Eighth Plan: (i) continuation of the ongoing scheme to cover all the remaining schools identified as on 30 September 1986: (ii) expanding the scope of the scheme to provide three rooms and three teachers in primary schools with enrolment exceeding 100 with provision for about 50 per cent women teachers in primary schools as mandatory for all states/UTs; and (iii) extending the scope of the scheme to upper primary schools. The expanded schemes have been started since 1993-94.

In elementary education the focus has been shifted from enrolment per-se to retention and achievement. The Minimum Levels to Learning Programme answers the third dimension of Universalization of Elementary Education, namely, universal achievement, laying down competency to be mastered by all children in the country at a particular grade, the programme envisages a package of quality improvement. It incorporates curricular revision, teacher orientation and improved pedagogy to handle multi-grade situations. A committee has also been constituted to lay down Minimum Levels of Learning for subjects taught at upper primary stage.

Secondary Education

Vocational Education

The National Policy on Education, 1986 accorded high priority to vocationalization of eduation at the secondary stage. The NPE as revised in 1992, set the target of achieving diversion of 10 per cent of the students at the +2 level to the vocational stream 1995 and 25 per cent by 2000 A.D. Accordingly, a Centrally sponsored scheme of Vocationalization of Secondary Education was launched in February 1988. Under the scheme, substantial financial assistance is provided to states/UTs for introduction of vocational courses in classes XI and XII of the school system.

About 150 vocational courses have been introduced in six major areas, i.e., agriculture, business and commerce, engineering and technology, health and paramedical, home science, humanities and others and 60 vocational courses have been notified under the Apprenticeship Act. Additional 34 vocational subject fields have been identified for inclusion under the Apprenticeship Act. Collaborative arrangement has been made with National Institute of Fashion Technology (NIFT) for introducing courses in Fashion and Garment making in three identified schools at Ludhiana (Punjab), Vizag, Andhra Pradesh, Indore and Madhya Pradesh. Under the scheme, 56 voluntary organizations have also been provided assistance so far for conducting innovative and non-formal programmes of vacational education. (Annexure I gives a perview of Vocational Education in India).

A Centrally-sponsored scheme of re-vocational education was launched in 1993-94 with the objective of imparting simple marketable skills to the students of classes IX and X. So far assistance has been provided to 11 states/UTs for introduction of pre-vocational courses in 652 schools.

A Joint Council for Vocational Education (JCVE) was set up in April 1990 for policy formulation and coordination at the national level. A Standing Committee of JCVE was also set up in April 1990 to follow up on the decisions taken by the JCVE. A Central Institute of Vocational Education (CIVE) was set up at Bhopal in July 1993 to provide technical and academic support the vocational education programme in the country. The Institute has also been identified as a UNEVOC Centre and considerable network has been established with other countries of the region. During the first year of the Ninth Plan 1997-98, an amount of Rs. 60 crores was also allocated. A decision was also taken in Chief Ministers Conference and State Education Ministers' Conference during July 1996 respectively to transfer the Centrally-Sponsored Scheme of Vocationalization of Secondary Education to states without earmarking the funds.

Higher Education in India

Since independence, enrolment in higher education has increased by 30 times. Unfortunately, the same cannot be said about quality. In most cases, we have exchanged quantity for quality.

Indian higher education is now in a mess. Standards are low and finances are poor. Political interference is intolerable. Yet, every other day, a new college is springing up, even though unemployment among graduates is the highest among all categories of persons. Most of these colleges are mercenary in nature. Recently, a new threat has come in the shape of foreign universities opening up campuses on the Indian soil.

In a way, higher education is getting vocationalized with management education taking precedence over other disciplines. Sadly science education has almost collapsed. Most academics are concerned that the main function of a university—the unalloyed pursuit of knowledge, has been shoved back. A reason is science education has been cheapened far too much. Whatever be the reason, science education is on a downward slide; many who would have normally studied science are opting for engineering. At the same time, several well-to-do students from IITs have deliberately opted out of engineering and shifted to pure sciences for their research work. It is possible that as the economy progress more and more youngsters will discover the joy of pure scholarship.

The sign of increased scholarship is the awareness of becoming ignorant of an even larger store of knowledge. When Indian scholars measure scholarship, not by asking whether one knows the minimum (the minimum marks criterion), but by the vastness of the awareness of what one does not know. Indian education will prosper.[12]

The institutions of higher learning have special role to play in assisting the economies to attain the social and economic objectives. It need to be critically examined in the areas of education, research and service to the community, with a view to determining how, through these activities support could be organized to various developmental programmes. In addition, the institutions of higher learning need to make a special effort to rebuilt educational capabilities by mounting special education and research programmes for socio-economic development and by helping to evolve new approaches to meet the challenges of socio-economic development in different sectors of the economy.

These institutions should give their support both to government and public and private sector organizations and evolve problem solving approach particularly in the services they provide to the development of knowledge workers within the organization. (Annexure II gives a list of Institutes involved in imparting higher education to different Occupational Categories).

Efforts will also have to be made to bring these changes into practice since no significant improvement in the area of professional and technical education has since been adopted.

Education in general and higher education in particular is considered to be a powerful instrument for the socio-economic development of a country. It is difficult to over-emphasise its significance as an essential source of acquiring new knowledge and vocational dexterity. It has a crucial role in generating skilled manpower for national development. To keep pace with the worldwide scientific and technological advancements, continuous innovation in the higher education system is indispensable.

India operates one of the largest systems of higher education. There has been a spectacular expansion of higher education during the last 40 years. According to figures available in the documents of National Policy on Education (NPE) 1986 and Programme of Action (POA) 1992 (Government of India, 1986), at present there are about 229 universities and over 7200 colleges offering traditional academic programmes both at the under-graduate and post-graduate levels. In addition there are a number of Research and Training institutions involved in the area. A list of such institutes is given in Annexure III.

The expansion of higher education has been accompanied by several problems—growth of sub-standard institutions and deterioration in quality and standard of education among others.[13] This has equally effected the system of vocational education. Table 1 presents growth of recognized educational institutions since 1961. Table 2 provides information on number of teachers by type of institutions. These two tables provide comparative information from 1961 onwards.

TABLE 1

Number of Educational Institutions

Type	*1961*	*1971*	*1981*	*1986*	*1991*	*1996*
Pre-Primary Schools	1,909	4,174	10,281	13,951	15,877	38,510
Primary/Junior Basic Schools	330,399	408,378	494,503	528,872	560,935	590,421
Middle/Senior Basic Schools	49,663	90,621	118,555	134,846	151,456	171,216
High/Higher Secondary Schools	17,257	36,738	51,006	65,837	79,796	94,648
Universities/Institutions Deemed to be Universities/ Institutions of National importance	45	100	132	149	184	226

Degree Standard and above General Educational Institutions General Education	967	2,285	3,421	4,067	4,862	6,569
Degree standard and above Professional and Technical Institutions for:						
(a) Agriculture and Forestry	35	59	61	70	80[1]	90
(b) Engineering, Technology and Architecture	111	134	171	248	351	422
(c) Medicine	133	179	249	288	346[2]	437
(d) Veterinary Science	17	22	22	22	27[3]	46
(e) Teachers' Training	147	274	341	432	474	633
Below Degree Level Professional/Vocational and Technical Institutions	4,145	4,401	4,808	5,381	5,739	6,513

1 Relate to the year 1988 (IAMR-Working Paper)

2 DGHS - Health Information of India - 1993

3. Ayurveda and Unani Medicine includes Allopathy, Homeopathy,

Sources : 1. Ministry of Human Resource Development

(i) Education in India

(ii) A Hand Book of Educational and Allied Statistic

(iii) Selected Educational Statistics

(iv) All India Council for Technical Education

2. University Grants Commission.

The World of Work

The world of work is a broad classification of occupations which divides the entire universe of jobs of a country, based on financial considerations. These occupations have been classified in our country on the basis of work groups as under:

- Professional, Technical and Related Workers,
- Clerical and Related Workers,
- Sales Workers,
- Service Workers,
- Farmers, Fishermen, Hunters, Loggers and Related Workers,

TABLE 2

Number of Teachers by Type of Institution

Type	*1961*	*1971*	*1981*	*1986*	*1991*	*1996*	*1997*	*1998*
Pre-Primary Schools	-	8338	14535	20332	23337	NA	NA	NA
Primary Schools	741515	1059950	1363217	1495812	1616020	1740436	1789733	1871542
Middle Schools	345228	637569	851527	968348	1072911	1164734	1195845	1211803
High/Higher	296305	629200	912129	1131505	1334745	1493251	1542360	1521186*
Vocational and Other Education at School Level Secondary Schools	-	33223	105362	226325	NA	NA	NA	NA
Post-Secondary (but Below Degree Level)								
General Education**	-	9032	14306	18916	@	@	@	@
Professional/Tech. Education	-	33588	39108	44001	NA	NA	NA	NA
Graduate and Above								
General Education	36170	91297	137351	171780	204464	239488	247750	NA
Professional/Tech. Education/ Special Education	20470	39650	53201	54498	NA	NA	NA	NA

Univ. Teaching Deptt. and other National Importance Research Institutions	5589	16314	26661	37472	58661	71084	72873	NA
Grand Total	1445277	2558161	3517397	4168989	NA	NA	NA	NA

* Includes intermediate and 10+2 Stage Schools.

** Pre-Degree and Junior Colleges.

@ Includes Teachers in High/Higher Secondary Schools.

Sources: 1. Ministry of Human Resource Development:

(i) Education in India

(ii) Selected Educational Statistics.

2. University Grants Commission.

- Production and Related Workers, Transport equipment Operators and Labourers.

The pattern of employment in these occupations is changing, the like of which has never happened before. Services have become the most important sector of employment for educationally classified human resource. Further reforms have to be carried out in the educational system so as to provide the most suitable educational preparation for such employment.

It is also being realized that the present shift towards service sector employment has necessitated an expansion of certain disciplines of higher education. But it is not yet realized by the ministries concerned that it calls also for important reforms in the structure and contents of curricula, methods of enrolment and pupils and employment of teachers and the organization of educational administration.[14] The stock of higher educated persons can be studied either through "employment categories.

The following four "major occupational categories are identified below for purposes of detailed HRD.[15]

- Physical, mathematical and engineering science professionals.
- Life Science and Health Professionals
- Teaching Professionals
- Other Professionals.

Occupational Categories

Physical, Mathematical and Engineering Science Professionals

Tasks performed by workers in this category usually include: conducting research, enlarging, advising on or applying scientific knowledge obtained through the study of structures and properties of physical matter and phenomena, chemical characteristics and processes of various substances, materials and products and of mathematical, statistical and computing concepts and methods; advising on, designing and directing construction of buildings, towns and traffic systems, or civil engineering and industrial structures, as well as machines and other equipment, and advising on and applying mining methods, and ensuring their optimum use; surveying land and sea and making maps; studying and advising on technological aspects of particular materials, products and processes, and on efficiency of production and work organization: preparing scientific papers and reports. Supervision of other workers may be included.

Occupations in this category are classified into the following minor groups:

- Physicists, chemists and related professionals
- Mathematicians, statisticians and related professionals
- Computing professionals
- Architects, engineers and related professionals.

Life Science and Health Professionals

Tasks performed by workers in this category usually include: conducting research, enlarging, advising on or applying scientific knowledge obtained through the study of all forms of human, animal and plant life, including specific organs, tissues, cells and micro-organisms and the effect of environmental factors of drugs and other substances, on them, studying human, animal or plant illnesses, advising on and applying preventive, curative and nursing measures, or promoting health; preparing scientific papers and reports. Supervision of other workers may be included.

It should be noted that, depending on the specific tasks and degree of responsibility in executing them, as well as on the national educational and training requirements, it may be appropriate to classify some of the occupations that are identified here into Life Science and health associate professionals. This is particularly relevant to the occupations classified as Nursing and midwifery professionals.

Occupations in this category are classified into the following groups:

221 Life science professionals

222 Health professionals (except nursing)

223 Nursing and midwifery professionals.

Teaching Professionals

Tasks performed by workers in this category usually include conducting classes, courses, or tutorials at a particular educational level, for educational or vocational purposes, including private lessons; conducting adult literacy programmes: teaching and educating handicapped persons; designing and modifying curricula; inspecting and advising on teaching methods and aids; participating in decisions concerning the organizations of teaching and related activities at schools and universities; conducting research in their particular subjects to improve or develop concepts, theories or operational methods for application in industrial and other fields; preparing scholarly papers and books. Supervision of other workers may be included.

It should be noted that, depending on the specific tasks and degree of responsibility in executing them, as well as on the national educational and training requirements, it may be appropriate to classify some of the occupations that are identified here into teaching associate professionals. This is particularly relevant to the occupations classified into primary and pre-primary education teaching professionals, and special education training professionals.

Occupations in this category are classified into the following groups:

231 College, University and higher education teaching professionals

232 Secondary education teaching professionals

233 Primary and pre-primary education teaching professionals

234 Special education teaching professionals

235 Other teaching professionals.

Other Professionals

Tasks performed by workers in this category usually include: dealing with information dissemination and operational methods relating to organization of business; application of the law; enlarging, advising on or applying knowledge obtained through the study of individual or group behaviour, language development, and philosophical, political, economic, juridical, educational, social, religious and other doctrines, concepts, theories, systems and organizations, from a current and historical perspective; conceiving and creating or performing works of art; preparing scholarly papers and reports. Supervision of other workers may be included.

It should be noted that, depending on the specific tasks and degree of responsibility in executing them, as well as on the national educational and training requirements, it may be appropriate to classify some of the occupations that are identified here into other associate professionals. This is particularly; relevant to the occupations classified into Social Work Professionals.

Occupations in this sub-major group are classified into the following minor groups:

241 Business professionals

242 Legal professional

243 Archivists, librarians and related information professionals

244 Social Science and related professionals

245 Writers and creative or performing artists

246 Religious professionals.

The above described four occupational categories (taken together) account for 3.55 per cent of the national stock of higher educated manpower during the year 1991.

The percentage of highly educated manpower in National stock (Graduate and above) has increased from 2.7 per cent in 1981 to 4.5 per cent in 1991. Among the first three (0-1, 2, 3) occupational categories, we find a decreasing trend in highly educated manpower, where the percentage has decreased from 42.7 per cent in 1981 to 34.8 per cent in 1991 for Professional, technical and related workers and from 9.7 per cent to 8.8 per cent and 26.1 per cent to 23.5 per cent for Administrative, Executive and Managerial workers and clerical and related workers respectively. However, other occupational divisions show a increase in the percentage of highly educated manpower as can be seen from the figures given below.[16]

	1981	*1991*
Sales Worker	6.7 per cent	10.2 per cent
Service Workers	1.4 per cent	2.2 per cent
Farmers, Fishermen and Related Workers	6.4 per cent	10.25 per cent
Production and Related Workers, Transport Equipment Operators and Labourers	5.2 per cent	8.4 per cent

It is necessary to understand these representations of educated category in advance and in the right perspective. If these changes are visualized in advance, it will help the organizations in adopting the right kind of measures for bringing about human resource development. Hence is the need to study the prospect.

It need to be emphasized that the relative numerical importance of the above mentioned four occupational categories, to which attention has been drawn, has not come automatically. These have come about, as a result of the human resource planning decisions taken in advance, and given effect year after year in successive development plans.

It is very pertinent to mention here that when human resource planning and development exercise is undertaken both at the macro and micro levels on the basis of policy decisions, it need to be binding on the agencies which employ human resources—the source of requirement is organizations as well as institutions to provide the educational preparation for professional human resource required either at macro or micro level.

Professional preparation of educated persons will call on one hand for changes (emerging requirements) to be made in professional institutions in almost every aspect of the present system of educational preparation of human resources. It will also call for the study of the organizations which are responsible for recruitment, training and employing professionals. Hence is the need for HRD both at the institutional and organizational level.

Manpower planning is commonly supposed to be something to do with "Specialist" and these are sharply distinguished from other who are referred to by the queer name of "generalists".[17]

Whether or not such a view is explicitly accepted the present education system also has the arrangements for producing managerial-administrative manpower (currently used as human resource) as they are meeting the needs of sub-professional manpower. There are also some academic courses mainly at post-graduate level which purport to deal with public administration and business management at the professional level. They have begun to make a significant contribution and their utility for purposes of development of professional manpower be regarded as generally accepted.[18]

The most important and urgent reform needed in education is to transform its endeavour to the life needs and aspirations of the people and thereby make it a powerful instrument of social, economic and cultural transformations necessary for the realization of national goals.[19]

For this purpose education needs to be developed so as to increase productivity, achieve socio-economic development and accelerate the process of modernization and cultivate social, moral and spiritual values.[20]

The requirement of the modern society is knowledge worker and the knowledge in different spheres of education is increasing at a terrific pace and the socio-economic change is very rapid. This needs an introspection in the educational system.

Education[21] is no longer taken to be concerned primarily with imparting of knowledge or on the preparation of finished product but with the awakening of curiosity, the development of such essential skills i.e., social, moral and spiritual values and education about religions, among others.

There is need for rigorous and more refined studies for estimating professional, technical and related workers requirements at all levels. Opening of new training facilities and institutions should be linked to such forecasts.

In a system, where education directly or indirectly, points towards work areas, the following question among others becomes important. The most common anxieties in the minds of parents, thus are: (1) What is the better course? (2) Which career is going to be more promising and better in future? (3) How to arrive at the right decision? (4) Where and whom to look for guidance and information on this matter? These questions are of serious concern. But there is no advice on this crucial area.

There are usually four subject-options available to students at secondary school level to choose from. These are Science, Commerce, Arts and Vocational Streams. Each of these streams, leads towards some areas of occupations. For example, those in science stream have openings in the field of engineering, medicines, animal husbandry and dairying, pharmaceutical, Computer Science, among others. Those with commerce can enter the field of Accountancy, Auditing, Banking and Financial Services, etc. Those with Arts subjects have openings in General services such as Civil Services, Police, Defence forces, Mass communication, subject specialist such as economist, sociologist, etc. Those in Vocational Stream can enter engineering or Vocational fields. Thus, the choice of the subject is very crucial in career planning beginning with school education.

Careers Information

Information about careers, their job contents, the kind of persons who will fit into occupation, the distribution and spectrum of employment in occupations, are some of the important inputs which are the necessary means in the choice of careers. For analysis of each of these parameters, supporting materials are needed. These needs are met to a large extent by career information Guides. The careers information Guides give a comprehensive and upto date picture about jobs and their employment prospects, their educational and training requirements, salary scales on employment, among others.

There are several sources for getting career information. Some are specialized agencies who bring out publications on these subjects on a regular basis. Some of these are in the government sector both under the central or state governments. These are National Council of Educational Research and Training (NCERT), Directorate General of Employment and Training (DGET), Career Study Centre at Central Institute of Research and Training on Employment Services (CIRTES), Association of Indian Universities, Occupational Information Units at the State Directorate of Employment Exchanges, University Employment Information and Guidance Bureau (UEIGBX) at major Universities, State Bureau of Educational and Vocational Guidance, private publications by individual authors are also available in the market.

Vocational Guidance and Career Counsellors

There are several organizations of the Central and State Government which work in the area of educational and vocational guidance, and training of career counsellors and on development of careers literature and aptitude tests. The National Council of Educational Research and Training (NCERT), an organization under the Ministry of Human Resource Development in Central Government have a separate Department on Vocational guidance. This Council organizes full time training courses on vocational guidance for secondary school teachers. It also publishes careers literature and materials for evaluations and measurement of intelligence and aptitude. At the State level, State Bureau of Educational and Vocational Guidance, are responsible for development of facilities on career guidance in secondary schools. At the Centre, the Directorate General of Employment and Training (DGE&T) under the Ministry of Labour is responsible for the work in the area of vocational guidance, occupational and careers information and on development of aptitude test. This organization has a networking at the state level at the state Directorate of Employment. At the field level, Employment Exchanges also provide useful information on careers and labour markets. For students of the universities, facilities for vocational and educational guidance are available at the University Employment Information and Guidance Bureaux (UEIGBX).

The Employment Exchanges and the University Bureaus provide assistance to students on education and careers, and also make available published materials on careers and labour market.

Special Coaching cum Guidance Centres have also been set up by the Ministry of Labour, and State Governments for the benefit of Scheduled Caste and Scheduled Tribe persons.

Education a Vital input for National Development

Several new initiatives taken to harness the vast Human Resources by the Department of Education in the new millennium.

Elementary Education and Literacy

- A new Department of Elementary Education and Literacy created.
- Decision to launch **Sarva Shiksha Abhiyan** for universalising elementary education in a mission mode.
- To ensure that every child in the 6-14 age group is either in a school or education guarantee centre or back to school camp by 2003. By 2007 all children should complete 5 years of primary schooling and by 2010 they should cover 8 years of elementary education.
- Special initiatives for urban deprived children.
- The National Literacy Mission revamped and revitalized to provide life long learning opportunity.
- To attain sustainable 75 per cent literacy by 2005.
- Decision taken to involve Non-Governmental Organizations on a larger scale and to promote a network of rural libraries under the Continuing Education Scheme.

- New dedicated education TV channel **Gyan Darshan** operationalized through IGNOU. **Gyan Vani,** the radio channel on the anvil.

Secondary Education

- National curriculum framework on school education being developed.
- Computer Education to reach out to 10,000 schools.
- 100 Smart Schools planned.

Higher Education

- Increase in Non-Plan allocation of UGC from Rs. 640 crores to Rs. 975 crores.
- Release of Rs. 656 crores to States for revision of pay scales of University and college teachers.
- Bill for a new Central University for the State of Mizoram passed by the Rajya Sabha.
- Accreditation for all higher education institutions made mandatory.
- Guidelines for deemed university simplified.

Technical Education

- Accreditation and quality assurance made mandatory for institutions.
- Decision taken to hold Single Entrance Test for admission to technical courses to reduce burden on students.
- Rs. 2500 crore Technical Education Project III being negotiated with World Bank.

Other Important Initiatives

- Group of experts set up for introduction of education in human values.
- Malpractices prevention cells set up to stop exploitation of students.

- User friendly web-page on education sector being constantly updated at site www.education.nic.in steps taken to promote Indian education abroad.
- Copyright Act 1957 amended to make the Indian Copyright Lawfully compatible with the obligation under the Agreement on Trade-related Aspects of Intellectual Property Right, 1994.[22]

Restructuring Education to Cope with Changing Global Scenerio

Education has emerged as the only sustainable source of competitive human resource development. The primacy of education needs to be recognized and the human resource planning and development need to be reconfigured based on the primacy of education assumption.

The recent trends in advocating changes in education in its totality (nursery/pre-primary to higher education) demand a good deal of shift at the level of paradigms. There is need of identifying the paradigms which would promote/facilitate a shift away from short-term rise in productivity and income to stable levels of production and incomes, a shift away from consumerism to long-term use of resources, and a shift away from using research and development efforts for destruction and war to peace and protection of the weak and poor. This necessitates changes in beliefs and values at the individual and social levels, which are vitally dependent on the policies of educational planning among others.

Education and sustainable development are multidimensional and interdependent. One therefore, needs a multi-level and multi-dimensional analysis to understand the complex relationships and interdependencies to be able to identify the necessary paradigms/levels.

Education systems have to reconsider the issues of contents, (curricula, overt and covert, at all levels of education) context of functioning to monitor against lopsided emphasis and technologies related to delivery and many more issues. The curricula would have to incorporate a set of positive human and social values, behavioural education, environmental education, energy and health among others. The emphasis in learning and assessment would be on meaningfulness, context centeredness, and holistic development rather than marks/ grades. The research and development efforts have to be society oriented and humanistic, incorporating the possible misuse alongwith uses.

In the context of educational planning and development, education for sustainable development is differentiated here in the sense that the two take place and proceed simultaneously not sequentially. Annexure IV presents the changes to be brought in the educational system to develop it as a tool of development in the 21st Century.

Basis for Action

Education including formal education should be recognized as a process by which human beings and societies can reach their full potential. Basic education provides the underpinning for any environmental and development education, the latter needs to be incorporated as an essential part of learning. Both formal an non-formal education are indispensable for changing peoples attitude so that they have the capacity to assess and address their sustainable development concerns. It is also critical for achieving environmental and ethical awareness values and attitudes, skills and behaviour consistent with sustainable development. The following objectives and activities were proposed by UNESCO in the Conference on Environment education.[23]

(a) Education for All: Meeting Basic Learning Needs and to strive to ensure universal access to basic education, and to achieve primary education for at least 80 per cent of girls and 80 per cent of boys of primary school age through formal schooling or non-formal education and to reduce the adult illiteracy rate to atleast half of its 1990 level. Efforts should focus on reducing the high illiteracy levels and redressing the lack of basic education among women and should bring their literacy school age through adulthood to all groups of people.

(b) To promote integration of environment and development concepts, including demography, in all educational programmes, in particular the analysis of the causes of major environment and development issues in a local context, drawing on the best available scientific evidence and other appropriate sources of knowledge, and giving special emphasis to the further training of decision makers at all levels.

All countries were encouraged to endorse the recommendations and strive to ensure its Framework for Action. This would encompass the preparation of national strategies and actions for meeting basic learning needs, universalizing access and promoting equity, broadening the means and scope of education, developing a supporting policy context, mobilizing resources and strengthening international cooperation to redress existing economic, social and gender disparities which interfere with these following aims:

— Non-governmental organizations can make an important contribution in designing and implementing educational programmes and should be recognized;

—Governments should strive to update or prepare strategies aimed at integrating environment and development as a cross-cutting issue into education at all levels. This should be done in cooperation with all sectors of society. The strategies should set out policies and activities, and identify needs, cost, means and schedules for their implementation, evaluation and review. A thorough review of curricula should be undertaken to ensure a multidisciplinary approach, with environment and development issues and their socio-cultural and demographis aspects and linkages. Due respect should be given to community-defined needs and diverse knowledge systems, including science, cultural and social sensitivities;

—Countries are encouraged to set up national advisory environmental education coordinating bodies or round tables representative of various environmental, developmental, educational, gender and other interests, including non-governmental organizations, to encourage partnerships, help mobilize resources, and provide a source of information and focal point for internationalties. These bodies would help mobilize and facilitate different population groups and communities to assess their own needs and to develop the necessary skills to create and implement their own environment and development initiatives;

— Educational authorities, with the appropriate assistance from community groups or non-governmental organizations, were recommended to assist or set up pre-service and in-service training programmes for all teachers, administrators, and educational planners as well as non-formal educators in all sectors, addressing the nature and methods of environmental and development education and making use of relevant experience of non-governmental organizations;

—Relevant authorities should ensure that every school is assisted in designing environmental activity work plans with the participation of students and staff. Schools should involve school children in local and regional studies on environmental health, including safe drinking water, sanitation and food and ecosystems and in relevant activities, linking these studies with services and research in national parks, wildlife reserves, ecological heritage sites, etc.;

Educational authorities should promote proven educational methods and the development of innovative reading methods for educational settings. They should also recognize appropriate traditional education systems in local communities.

Countries could support university and other tertiary activities and networks for environmental and development education. Cross-disciplinary courses could be made available to all students. Existing regional networks and activities and national university actions which promote research and common teaching approaches on sustainable development should be built upon, and new partnerships and bridges created with the business and other independent sectors, as well as with all countries for technology, know-how and knowledge exchange.

Countries, assisted by international organizations, non-governmental organizations and other sectors, could strengthen or establish national or regional centres of excellence in interdisciplinary research and education in environmental and developmental sciences, law and the management of specific environmental problems. Such centres could be universities or existing networks in each country or region, promoting cooperative research and information sharing and dissemination. At the global level these functions should be performed by appropriate institutions.

Countries should facilitate and promote non-formal education activities at the local, regional and national levels by cooperating with and supporting the efforts of non-formal educators and other community-based organizations. The appropriate bodies of the United Nations system in cooperation with non-governmental organizations should encourage the development of an international network for the achievement of global educational aims. At the national and local levels, public and scholastic forums should discuss environmental and development issues, and suggest sustainable alternatives to policy makers.

Educational authorities, with appropriate assistance of non-governmental organizations, including women's and indigenous peoples' organizations should promote all kinds of adult education programmes for continuing education in environment and development, basing activities around elementary/secondary schools and local problems. These authorities and industry should encourage business, industrial and agricultural schools to include such topics in their curricula. The corporate sector could include sustainable development in their education and training programmes. Programmes at a post-graduate level should include specific courses aiming at the further training of decision makers.

Governments and educational authorities should foster opportunities for women in non-traditional fields and eliminate gender stereotyping in curricula. This could be done by improving enrolment opportunities, including females in advanced programmes as students and instructors, reforming entrance and teacher staffing policies and providing incentives for establishing child-care facilities, as appropriate. Priority should be given to education of young females and to programmes promoting literacy among women.

Governments should affirm the rights of indigenous people, by legislation, if necessary, to use their experience and understanding of sustainable development to play a part in education and training.

India's Case

Education as a process and educational institutions as organizations are known for their slow response to change. They operate in a system which has long gestation lags. Though this has been the style of functioning of educational system for a long time now, the pace is now beginning to be constrictive because of rapid changes in educational planning.

The fact that countries like India, still carry the liability of expansion along with the pressure for improving the quality of education, makes the task further difficult and complex. Needless to say that this puts enhanced pressure on the possible model of educational planning for the country. The situation impels that instead of treating education as a single monolithic structure, one has to treat it in terms of the different sectors. Management and investment of resources have to be in a more comprehensive and internally consistent manner.

The response of educational planning to the problem has been neither clear nor timely. So much so that, in certain quarters, there is a clear feeling that the discipline of "Educational Planning" is a non-issue. It is felt that the complexity inherent in the task is virtually forbidding in its dimensions. Hence, it is advised that educational planners should focuss their attention more on the management of micro-level educational projects.[24] To some extent the argument stems from the disappointment and consequent skepticism over the indifferent performance of the planned systems in the country.

However, this emphasis on planning for education does not necessarily imply that all the choices will have to be made as per the bureaucratic organization of the country. Unlike in the immediate post-war period, it is not any more purely ideological question. We now understand the developmental process somewhat better than in those days; particularly when it is realized that process of development has become much more complex overtime and everywhere, it is not the question of market versus the state, but it is the question of blending of the two. Where to provide for bureaucratic links and where to replace them by the market relations is the key area of choice and decision-making in the context of planning.

However, it is also clear that the problem of educational development is not confined only to fiscal stringency. It is a much broader issue. Earlier works in the area of economics of education confined their attention to only quantitative expansion. Now under changed conditions, a more complex approach to tributions to the advancement of educational planning could be made.

Some Suggestions

The essence of educational planning is to ensure that there is no mismatch between requirements of human resources skills and output of educational and training institutions. However, there are surpluses as well as critical shortages and the so called phenomenon of "credentialism". To avoid this, we need to know more about the relationships between productivity levels and occupational demand, between occupational structures and educational qualifications and between educational qualifications and earning levels. We need to continually monitor the conditions in the labour market so that right signals are thrown up for decision makers and educational planners. But there is not sufficient analysis of the labour market in respect of educational system. Similarly, there is no deferred information system and data base for analysing the framework of changing technology and environment.

What is the way-out? How can the mismatch and mal-adjustment between demand and supply of human resource for the strategic sectors of economy be removed, or at least minimized? Giving that the globalization policy would accelerate the development of the economy on the desired path, the onus for restructuring the education system rests with educational planning. Any restructuring programme of education sector should realize that:

(i) The present institutions whether under private or government sector are not capable of providing adequate educational facilities in terms of enrolment, infrastructure, investment in R&D.

(ii) Private sectors' initiative in educational development is required for meeting the requirements of the socio-economic development.

(iii) Private and public institutions should co-operate in achieving the developmental goals and lastly,

(iv) The aim of both public and private institutions should be to produce better educated, highly trained, disciplined and motivated human resource.

The following steps would help in strengthening the public sector education as well as encourage private institutions and provide better environment for cooperation between public and private sector.

1. In view of the high cost of tertiary education, especially of technical and professional manpower group, the method of distance education needs to be given priority, as there is an immediate need to have trained human resource in areas of engineering and technology including information and bio-technology, science, health and medical care, among others. (The existing educational set-up for engineering occupation is given in Annexure V.

2. There is need to establish Academic Staff Colleges in the emerging areas. This would help in education-industry linkages, besides meeting other objectives of restructuring educational system.

3. The large private corporations be encouraged to set up technical colleges or polytechnics and skill training institutes. These institutions may provide professional and technical manpower but their main function would be to train and re-train the middle level technical manpower—as per requirements of the industry.

4. How do the social returns of vocational education compare with those of general education, specially considering

that general education provides a certain flexibility to the participants in labour market. Also, how do the social rates of return for different types of vocational training compare? There are issues which need to looked into the structuring of educational system.

5. Then there are issues in equity relating to the manner in which educational resources and facilities are distributed among different human resource groups, and sectors of economy.

6. Emerging new technologies are more science and knowledge based. What should be the approaches to education, training and re-training, to entrepreneur development, to management education and to labour mobility for appropriate human resource development in different sectors of the economy.

7. Education is a unique investment in the present and for the future and is crucial for the socio-economic development. This cardinal principle is the key to the policy of equity, efficiency cost-effectiveness and excellence and has maximum impact on human resource development. It covers a wide spectrum and pertains to matters ranging from teaching-learning process to de-linking of degrees from jobs and deals with stages of education, types and nature of instruction and modes of learning. It also lays stress on universalisation of primary education, eradication of adult illiteracy, vocationalization, integration of child care with pre-primary schooling and removal of disparities in the educational system and on the overall optimal functioning.

9. The educational system needs to be so devised as to produce a labour force with requisite skills and technical/professional knowledge. In this connection human resource planning strategies assume importance for understanding the future evolution of the market for specific manpower groups.

10. To a large extent the efficacy with which education can discharge its role depends upon:

(a) availability of monetary resources;

(b) how the burden of mobilizing these resources is shared between public and private sectors; and

(c) to what extent potential beneficiaries of education can invest on their own.

With every phase of socio-economic development, the nature of these questions and their answers keep changing.

It is true that the resource constraint precludes several easier and softer options, however, one can still think of the means by which the teaching-learning process can be improvised without a proportional increase in the amount of resources committed. For such options to be viable, one requires detailed and meticulous planning at the level of implementation itself. It is in this sense that the National Policy on education has drawn our attention at micro-level planning as an important area.

In brief, the focus of the future learning, education and training, the three characteristics of a learning society, should be that in the years to come no child in India should be out-of-school, no adult illiterate and everybody is employable. To quote from the International Commission for Education (UNESCO): "Tomorrow's education must form a co-ordinated totality in which all sectors of society are structurally integrated. It will be universalized and continual. From the point of view of individual, it will be total and creative and consequently individualized and self-directed. It will be the bulwark and the driving force in culture, as well as in promoting professional activity. This movement is irresistible and irreversible. Of course it is the cultural revolution of our time."

References

1. Raza Moonis and Tilak J.B.C., "Longtime Educational Planning" in Moonis Raza (ed.) *Educational Planning,* NIEPA, Concept Publishing Company, New Delhi, 1986.
2. World Education Crises - A Systems Analysis by P. Coombs.
3. Planning and Educational Administration by C.E. Beeby P. 14.
4. Davis, R.C., *Planning Human Resource Development.* Rand Mc Nally Education Series, Chicago, 1966.
5. Brahm Prakash, "Transformation of Raw Human Capital into manpower with knowledge, skill and training necessary to meet the manpower requirements for Production of Required Economic Output", *Manpower Journal,* Vol. XXV No. 3 and 4.

6. R.V. Vaidyanatha Ayyar, "Educational Planning and Administration in India: Retrospect and Prospect", *Journal of Educational Planning and Administration,* Volume VII No. 2, April, 93, p. 203-204.

7. Extract from the Report on 'Regional Cooperation for technical and Professional, Education and Training' A.K. Dasgupta, Friedrich Elert Stiflung, New Delhi pp. 411-58

8. R.V. Vaidyanatha Ayyar, Ibid, p. 207.

9. Ayyar, Ibid, p. 208.

10. Srivastava, M.P., *Human Resource Planning, Approaches, Needs Assessment and Priorities in Manpower Planning,* Institute of Applied Manpower Research, Manak Publication, 1997.

11. Twenty Seventh Annual Report, 1989-90. Institute of Applied Manpower Research, I.P. Estate, Ringh Road, New Delhi-2 pp. 2-6 and 8

12. Extract from the article 'Indian Education: Will it move from slate to laptop' by V. Indiresan, Published in *Business India,* 27th December 1999.

13. V.D. Madan, "Vocation Based Higher Education Through Open Learning System" *Journal of Educational Planning and Administration,* Volume VII No. 2, April 1993.

14. Report of the Education Commission, 1964-66, pp. 542-43.

15. ISCO-88 International Standard Classification of Occupations, International Labour Office, Geneva.

16. IAMR: *Manpower Profile Yearbook 1999,* Percentages Calculated from data given in Table 3.2, 18, p. 263.

17. Report of the Education Commission, 1964-65, Minute of Supplement pp. 549-50.

18. Ibid page 550.

19. Ibid page 613.

20. Ibid page 613.

21. Ibid page 614

22. Department of Elementary Education & Literacy and Department of Secondary Education & Higher Education, Ministry of Human Resource Development, Government of India, Published on 30th January 2000 in the *Hindustan Times,* New Delhi.

23. Excerpts from the "Declaration and Recommendations of the Tbilisi Intergovernmental Conference on Environment education" organised by UNESCO and UNEP, held in 1977.

24. Psacharapoulous, Educational Planning at Micro Levei with reference to Rural Areas UNESCO, Bangkok, 1986.

6

THE SERVICE SECTOR AND ITS HRD

Economic theory traditionally looks at society as consisting of three main sectors:

- The primary or agricultural sector,
- The secondary or industrial sector, and
- The tertiary sector or service sector comprising activities like banking, insurance, transportation, communication, education, family welfare and health among others.

The service sector, therefore, comprises activities which provide a wide variety of services to individuals, public and private sector organizations and government establishments.

The present attempt is to examine the nature, role and importance as well as the relevance and application of HRD in the services sector. The attempt is also to examine general aspects of HRD as well as those aspects which are contextually specific to the services sector. To illustrate the HRD needs issues, experiences and problems of its implementation in the services sector, a study of three sectors viz., telecommunication, banking and railways are presented in this Chapter.

Nature and Role of the Service Sector

The service sector has a crucial socio-economic role to play in society. Services create value by providing a bridge between the producers of goods and the beneficiaries, or between the production and consumption segments of the society. That is why the growth of the service sector in modern society is linked with the increased productivity of the manufacturing sector. The value which the service sector provides to consumers may be private benefits which are paid for, or they may be public benefits which are free or subsidized, like health, education, information, etc. Similarly, an awareness campaign regarding rapid changes in society, case analysis, on the job development and training programmes seems to partly fulfil the needs.

A major characteristic of modern socio-economic development has been the increasingly dominant role of the service sector. It is a known fact that as an economy develops, the relative contribution of the primary and secondary sectors to the total economy decreases, whereas that of the service sector increases.

The Occupational Outlook Hand Book (1998-99) brought out by the US Department of Labour has made very interesting observations about the studies they have conducted.

As regards the nature of jobs being offered, production and manufacturing jobs will be on the decline making way for service-oriented jobs. The report further says that there will be fewer jobs for those who do not posses specialized skills or technosavvy. The jobs will be in medicine, nursing, counselling, lawyer and law enforcers, among others.

India is also becoming a service economy. The share of services in its GDP is almost 47 per cent against 29 per cent in industry and 24 per cent in agriculture. India has become a service economy without even realising it or striving for it.

Planning Commission estimates show that for the next decade the workforce will grow at the rate of 2.6 per cent. Therefore, job creation strategies for educated unemployed should focus on creation of employment opportunities in service sector. Tourism, media and Tele-Communication are a few areas which should be targeted.

Role of HRD in Service Sector

There are certain aspects of HRD which are universal to all organizations while there are some which are specific to the nature of the service industry. The universal aspects of HRD have been covered in detail in previous chapters. Our endeavour here will be therefore to look in detail at the critical aspects of HRD in Service Sector.

Universal Aspects

HRD is relevant to all sectors. It is at the base of all development. Other resources, like physical and financial can only be activated through the agency of human resources. HRD is an all pervasive concept, therefore, there are bound to be common aspects relevant to all the sectors of the economy.

HRD aims at developing the individual, matching him to different roles, both by developing him and the role, and catalysing individual and organizational self-renewal. A generalized model of HRD will include the following sub-systems: role analysis, selection and placement, transfer and rotation, reward and punishment, performance and potential appraisal, feedback and counselling, training and development, career planning, succession planning, participative devices, and HRD information system and data bank. Of these systems, some are essential to all organizations and for all sectors: selection and placement, transfer, rotation and reward and punishment, therefore, these sub-systems need to be designed well. If one wants to go beyond a status-quo bureaucracy, performance appraisal, potential appraisal and training and development are particularly relevant. If high level of performance is a goal, then the relevant additional sub-systems are feedback and counselling, and participative devices. Finally, if one is concerned about the long-term vitality of any institution including a service institution, the remaining sub-systems become essential namely role analysis, career planning, succession planning, and development of an HRD information system and data base.

Unique Aspects

Service industry has some special features, which call for particular emphasis in the design and implementation of HRD systems. These are:

- **Intangibility of product:** Service is the provision of value to a customer, without a physical product. This could create lack of clarity about the tasks and erosion of self-confidence. So HRD has to create appreciation of client needs, and pride in the potency of the service to meet those needs.

- **High public exposure:** The service institution is much more exposed to its clientele. Even if the institution does not promote its service, the clients may take the initiative and beat at its doors. In the case of subsidized or free services, some customers may be arrogant in their demands and misuse the service, while some others may be less literate, gullible and timid.
- **Size constraints:** To be effective, the service institution should be perceivea as a huge, slow, monolith, in the face of which the customer is anonymous and insignificant. Conceptualization of role is especially important. Examples are the bank teller and the 'single window' concept used recently by state industrial development corporations.
- **Back-room technology:** At the customer end, a service has to be simple to understand. For example, air travel should be made easy, but behind it may be complex aeronautics and computerised real-time reservation systems.

  HRD has to ensure that those at the delivery end of a service institution understand the power as well as the limitations of this back-up technology, while at the same time the technicians understand customer needs, abilities and limitations. User-friendly computer peripherals, for example, enhance the utilization of an information service.
- **Specialized Knowledge:** The level of general and specialized education tends to be relatively high in service institutions.

  The service institute tends to have a preponderance of white collar workers and executive manpower. Their motivation is more complex. Besides monetary rewards, they look more for ego satisfaction and quality of work life.
- **Propensity for disintegration:** Service institutions seem to have a higher tendency to disintegrate. This may be partly

due to low capital cost, low barrier to entry and the preference of the customer for specific resource persons. Therefore, HRD needs to provide for more participation in planning and control of the projects, as well as sharing of rewards, whether psychic satisfaction, fame, visibility; profits or upward mobility.

Human resources operate at different levels—as a citizen, as a member of the organization, as a person involved in family and community affairs and most important of all, at the level of being oneself, which psychologists call the existential level. It is at this personal level that some of the most fundamental issues of coping with and self-audit remain to be resolved fully.

Globalization, the emergence of free market and information technology, coupled with world-wide political changes in the last few years have only clouded our perceptions on the functioning of the 'self'.

The key question is how does the individual at the crossroads find 'the road less travelled' and discover the joys of the new journey. In Megatrends 2000, Naisbitt and Aburdene declared that the 1990s are characterized by a 'new respect in the individual', the doctrine of individual responsibility, they argue, is central to the New Age that heralds the Millennium (Naisbitt and Aburdene 1990).

The interaction between the human resources has also to be taken into account which can be done through intensity interaction matrices. Given sufficient data through research and field surveys, the various constituents can be forged into channels of effective delivery of expertise thus ensuring maximum degree of linkage in terms of HRD in different sectors of economy, particularly in the service sector of the economy.

Further general discussions sometimes emphasise the fact that there is virtually no aspect of economic and social development in any one sector of the economy that does not interact with that of other sectors. One such interaction is the way most developmental activities require services from the economy's infrastructure networks: roads, water, power, health and telecommunications.

Management scientists in the past have suggested that the capability requirements of employees in any organization can be grouped under three categories: technical, managerial and conceptual. Knowledge, attitudes and skills that deal with planning, organizing, coordinating, supervising, monitoring, controlling and evaluating various activities in order to accomplish organizational goals are grouped as managerial capabilities e.g. performance budgeting, designing and using management information systems. Knowledge, skills and attitudes to visualize the invisible and think in abstract terms are called conceptual capabilities, e.g., visualizing the various aspects of life 20 years from now with increased population, visualizing the impact of certain kinds of economic development on the future of the country.

This classification of management scientists is largely based on studies conducted in industrial organizations. One of the characteristics of industrial organizations is that a large number of employees (workers) deals mostly with materials, many with materials and money and some with men, materials and money. Thus, in the industrial management scheme of things 'people' formed only one of the components of management. As contrasted with this, in social services and development sectors most of the time people are required to deal with people and therefore, people management becomes the most important aspect of achieving organizational goals. For this reason, people working in organizations require behavioural capabilities besides technical, managerial and conceptual capabilities.

These capabilities are required also by the executives to design systems of recruiting, developing, motivating and utilizing the staff effectively. These are also required to provide a good interface between the organization and ensure good coordination between policy making and execution.

Another factor that influences employee motivation is career opportunities and professional growth. Employees would like to see themselves grow, earn higher salaries, higher status and have a change in responsibilities periodically.

Performance appraisal is another potential instrument available to keep the motivation of people high, help them to get guidance and counselling from their supervisors and continuously equip them with capabilities to do their jobs well. While the industrial sector has been using performance appraisals for such purposes, the public systems have not yet recognized and started using this instrument. Performance appraisals if designed efficiently can probably solve a number of problems.

In the context of the above observation and analysis, it would be appropriate if the management scientists, programme executives and policy makers pay attention to the human processes in relation to the following issues:

1. Evolve a full and thorough understanding of what is needed to change the attitudes of employees for the desired level of acceptance of organizational culture and objectives.
2. Conduct more research to understand the methods and ways of bringing this change at individual, group and at organizational level.
3. Design or redesign the HRD programmes on the basis of such an understanding.
4. Equip the organization or employer with competencies to bring about attitudinal change in the employees.
5. Give enough attention to different level of staff by evolving human resource management systems that can take care of staff motivation through role clarifications, exercises, salary structure, promotion opportunities, career planning, reward systems, training, performance appraisal and counselling.
6. Evolve and use HRD process mechanisms to bring about more collaboration between policy makers and employees.
7. Equip the programme managers to continuously generate and use management know-how that is needed by the HRD rather than simply what is available.

Momentous changes are taking place in the economy. Economy has a huge capital and human potential. The economy is rich in technical manpower and entrepreneurial skills. It also has a larger market of 970 million people pulsating with activities. The task at hand is to utilize these millions to achieve the optimum level of output especially in service sector. The developed economies have shown that ultimately it is the service sector which is highly labour intensive. This means that HRD should be the main focus of this sector.

Development in the next decade hinges upon communications technology. These are advancing rapidly. Hence, there is a dire need of not only understanding the technological developments and the future of work environment but also its implications for the society as a whole.

How will these developments effect the working environment in the organization. These are the questions which may interest many of us. The networking phenomenon carries widespread implications not just for the organization but for business and economy as a whole. The market and data communication is expanding at a tremendous rate. There is undoubtedly a kind of cultural overplay to these developments. Privatization, the emergence of multiple competing careers in service sector, financial institutions and a viable transport system. In fact the global information society is already a fact-of-life.

The chapter deals with the issues of development and utilization of human resources engaged in telecommunication, banking and railways and how far HRD interventions have effected the growth and development of the employees in these organizations.

Telecommunication Sector: Organization and Management

The telecommunication sector has a special place in India's economy and is likely to further consolidate its already important position, in the years to come.

Telecommunication has not only permeated all facets of human life but also have been responsible to an extent for changing the way we live.

Telecommunications is a rapidly evolving sector, which is experiencing significant technological change, and the availability of an increasing variety of options for new and innovative services. In addition, there is an excess demand for basic telecommunication services, Policy makers are increasingly aware that the economic development of rural areas requires access to rapid communication facilities Similarly, countywide data, fascimile, and conferencing systems hold the potential for facilitating large productivity increases in both the public and private sector organizations. This situation means that the management of telecommunications entities must increasingly be professionally disciplined as well as flexible, responsive, and alert to emerging needs and opportunities.

Earlier the provision of telecommunication services and the provision of post services were organizationally linked, but in the present context, however, there are several arguments for separating the managements of postal and telecommunications services. Such arguments include: (a) the provision of postal services is highly labour intensive, whereas the provision of telecommunications services is or at least should be capital intensive; (b) the provision of telecommunications services requires a much higher proportion of skilled labour and professionals than does the provision of postal services—qualified staff, or in staff-related regulations; (c) the contrasts between the technologically dynamic and rapidly evolving telecommunications sector and the less dynamic labour and physical transport-dominated postal sector are so great that the same organizational structure and management style cannot plan for and implement both services efficiently.

Until recently, telecommunications was based on 19th century analogue technology therefore while considering the potential of communications, a number of factors need to be taken into consideration:

In most organizations there will be a period of some years during which the existing analogue networks and new digital networks will have to co-exist in some form of hybrid structure. Interworking control and management will face obvious problems in such a case.

Along with such considerations, communications have brought a new set of potential problems, beyond those encountered in analogue counterparts.

The integration and expansion of communication services with any organization means that the network must be controlled and managed as a strategic company resource, in a similar manner to resources such as capital plant and manpower.

It is difficult to discuss the organization and management of national or international telecommunications activities without reference to the organization or functioning of all two-way communications activities and the rules and regulations under which they operate. Telephone, telegraph, telex, data and facsimile transmission, postal messages, postal packages, money transfer over distances, messenger services, and physical travel serve to varying degrees as both complement and substitute for each other.

Nevertheless, given the scope of this book, the focus here is primarily on the highly diverse two-way communication sectors—the organization and management of telecommunication services.

The telecommunications sector comprises of (a) public and leased telecommunications services; (b) various networks that meet specialized needs (armed forces, polices, railways, and public utilities); (c) several other private or quasi-public point-to-point network, which have been set up because the primary telecommunications operating company cannot provide adequate coverage or quality of service; (d) in some countries one or more industries manufacturing telecommunications equipments and cables; and (e) one or more bodies performing technical, economic, tariff and spectrum control regulatorv functions.

With relatively few exceptions, most public telecommunication services are provided by partly or wholly government-owned entities, and in a number of instances postal and telecommunication services are grouped together under the same organizational structure. The monopoly of telecommunications operating entities are organized in various ways, ranging from being part of a conventional government department to a semi-independent branch or board within a government department to regulated corporations.

In determining what role the private sector and government can play in telecommunications, some understanding of the economics of telecommunications is required. There is a growing consensus that competition in telecommunications services will lead to greater efficiency.

The profitability of any venture is based on the relationship between the price, it is able to charge for its product or service and the cost of providing it. In telecommunications, the price of service is almost universally regulated by government.

Telecommunications technology is evolving at a lightening pace. Computer and communication technologies are merging. Technological innovations have reduced the costs of major network components, such as switching equipment, test and maintenance equipment, and administrative sub-systems. New technologies have also reduced operational costs, primarily by reducing labour costs, but also the increased reliability of digital technology has sharply reduced maintenance and repair costs, and expanded usage rates among customers.

Economics of scale are derived from network efficiency as well as organizational efficiency. New technologies such as cellular, satellite, and packet-switching are reducing the minimum economic scale of entry into the service sector.

Organizational economies of scale can also reduce costs. Administrative, operations, and maintenance structures must be in place to operate telecommunications networks.

The debate and dialogue about the restructuring of the telecommunications sector has grown increasingly sophisticated and complex. What follows is not a comprehensive updating of telecommunications reforms, but an assessment of recent experience with reforms in the telecommunications sector. The perspective may be somewhat unconventional, even radical. Change begets change. Policy determinations in the telecommunications sector do not occur in a vacuum, they are a product of development.

New options for privatising and for introducing new sources of private investment into telecommunication sector are being much more freely explored in discussions about sectoral reform in Latin America, Asia and Eastern Europe than in the heart of the European Community.

Because of the rapid evolution of the telecommunications, environment, policy prescriptions must be based on new assessments of future trends. This applies particularly to the likely future evolution of telecommunications policies that have been undergoing restructuring because policies cannot be drawn merely on the patterns of past policy determinations.

Modern telecommunication systems and user flexibility have become important parameters in promoting economic development. Governments are faced with the challenge of harnessing effectively a complex array of technologies and systems, which have tremendous potential for enhancing social welfare but pose heavy demands on organizational and financial capabilities.

The high quality of telecommunication systems and services has become a critical determinant of economic competitiveness. Farsighted policy makers therefore, are increasingly focusing on telecommunications, and more broadly, on information technology not merely as an element of supporting infrastructure but as a driving force of economic growth.

National economies are becoming increasingly interdependent and telecommunications can be a catalytic factor in this development—leading to global marketing strategies. Communication services by now are acting as vital links between manufacturers, wholesalers, and retailers.

Virtually all structural reforms of some kind varying in scope and depth to enhance economic efficiency are a prerequisite towards increasing national welfare. The range and impact of telecommunications reform are intrinsically linked to this broader reform agenda.

Technological advances cast a new light on the traditional argument for a proactive government role in telecommunications. This argument rests on the assumption that telecommunication is an infrastructure with inherent externalities; that is, benefits derived from telecommunications services cannot be captured fully by their provider. It is generally agreed that the telecommunications infrastructure serves a broad public interest because its existence promotes development of the economy at large.

The telecommunications network is being used as a spearhead to promote economic activities and harness associated benefits that otherwise would have materialized only later, or not at all.

Rapid technological evolution in telecommunications has brought great opportunities for expanding, penetration, lowering costs, and upgrading services, thus affording an opportunity to leapfrog the stages of network development. At the same time these changes have added tremendous complexities to the work of designing, procuring, and managing telecommunication systems, which are likely to overtax the capabilities of governments, and domestic private sectors.

Developments in the last decade have changed this scenario drastically. On the one hand, quantum jumps in technology have rendered these presumptions largely obsolete; on the other hand, traditional government-operated telephone utilities have not performed well in the face of surging consumer demand for new, better, and faster telecommunications services.

HRD and Telecommunication

The key to building up a capable telecommunications operating entity is adequate staffing. Some telecommunications organizations have yet to develop and maintain an effective and expanding training system at different levels such as engineering, financial, and administrative.

A comprehensive HRD strategy is needed for recruitment, training, further education, and career development of staff. With such a plan the rapidly rising needs for middle-level personnel can soon be met with the recruitment of adequate local staff, who in turn can gradually take over all posts held by temporary specialists staff.

Specialist staff with in-depth knowledge of communications are increasingly more scarce than the average technicians and hence more costly.

A full service telecommunications regulatory agency includes at least five sections: engineering, accounting or auditing, tariff analysis, legal analysis and a policymaking head or advisory body which may or may not supervise the other four components. Obviously the precise form that these take and their relative size can differ greatly from country to country, depending on circumstances and on the goals being sought.

We are now confront with a rapidly changing economic and technical environment. The needed adjustments in policy and in regulatory and operational structures should not be considered in merely a static form. In a dynamic and rapidly changing world, institutions and structures that can continually respond to change are required. In other words, there is a vital need to institutionalize the policymaking process so that it can both react to and anticipate change. A dynamic telecommunications sector will be essential if they are to meet those challenges.

In the light of such considerations, what are the challenges, and what should be the future agenda for the telecommunications community with respect to these issues? The highest priority appears to be the development of a capacity to think through some of the above-mentioned policy issues and to provide a coherent environment for the sector. This is not an easy task, because specialized economic, legal, financial, banking, and regulatory skills, in addition to operating expertise, are required. Personnel with the necessary training and experience in these areas are difficult to find and recruit. It may not be any telecommunications company to succeed in building such a capacity by itself, but with joint ventures and other mechanisms, progress may be possible.

In this period of rapid change and organizational evolution, there is clearly a need to exchange views and experiences much more frequently. Policy makers and managers for telecommunication sector clearly need to visit each others' countries more frequently. In this connection, the World Bank has already provided its good offices to facilitate such exchanges. The International Telecommunications Union, the Commonwealth Telecommunications Organization, and the Center for Telecommunications Development have also been working in this direction.

Training Infrastructure

The Department of Telecom employs about 4.7 lakh personnel consisting of about 24,000 operational managers at senior and middle management levels and the rest in supervisory and operative category. There are, at present, 40 telecom training centres catering to the needs of various cadres viz., telecom professionals and engineers, supervisory and cutting edge level staff. These training centres function at three levels to meet the specific requirements of different cadres.

Eleven regional telecom training centres (RTTC) located in different regions of India cater to the training needs of supervisory staff of the Department. About 15,000 supervisory cadre personnel receive training in these training centres every year. Twenty-seven circle telecom training centres cater to the training needs of operative and technical staff. In a year about 30,000 staff receive training in these centres.

Bharat Ratna Bhim Rao Ambedkar Institute of Telecom Training, (BRBRAITT), Jabalpur is an apex training centre for training of telecom professionals and engineers. Prior to the setting up of Advanced Level Telecom Training Centre (ALTTC), this was the only training institute catering to training needs of telecom professionals.

ALTTC, Ghaziabad is another apex level training centre in DOT. It was established in 1975 with ITU/UNDP assistance primarily to meet the training needs of telecom professionals and telecom engineers of India as well as of the countries of ESCAP Region in new and emerging telecom technologies.

Training Activities

Bharat Ratna Bhim Rao Ambedkar Institute of Telecom Training, Jabalpur is imparting training in telecommunication technology, administrative and financial management to mainly Group 'A' and 'B' Officers of the Department of Telecommunications. In addition ADET Probationers which is an entry level for Group 'A' Officers of Indian Telecom Service are also imparted basic and specialization training in this Institute. Apart from the above, the Institute is also partly imparting training to Junior Telecom Officers and Junior Accounts Officers in order to augment the efforts of Regional Telecom Training Centres in meeting the huge training requirements of department in these cadres. Personnel from foreign countries and other departments of Government of India including public sector undertaking are also trained in different areas of telecom.

There are basically two types of training courses, i.e., induction courses and in-service courses. Induction courses are for imparting training to the newly recruited staff in various areas of telecom and as such these are pre-recruitment programmes. The in-service refresher training courses, both institutional as well as field training programmes are meant for upgrading the knowledge and skills of the department personnel, already working in various fields of telecom.

Planning Training Activities

As a preliminary step in planning a training programme, the following questions need specific attention.

What are the job requirements?

What past training, job experience and/or education contributes to job performance?

What performance deficiencies or problems could be attributed to a lack of knowledge and/or skills?

What related job functions would be useful to know?

In what areas is knowledge needed in order to develop potential for future assignments?

Answers to these questions should provide with sufficient information to identify training requirements. As part of the planning process, the following activities need to be identified.

1. Identify the areas in which training is needed.
2. Determine which courses address those needs.
3. Determine pre-requisites and ensure that they are met.
4. Map out the appropriate sequence of courses to be taken.
5. Document training planned and scheduled.
6. Schedule of training.

There has been considerable progress in the telecom industry after its privatization. New services such as pagers, cellulars and internet have revolutionized communication systems. But the supply of trained manpower has not kept pace with these developments.

The Telecom Industry Services Association has estimated the shortage of telecom managers in India to be around one million. Moreover, there is a demand for professionals, who can understand technology and also have the skill to analyse problems peculiar to the telecom industry.

The Symbiosis Institute of Telecom Management (SITM) has taken the lead in addressing this problem with its telecom management course.

The one of its kind in India and the SAARC countries, SITM blends technology and management to create specialized executives for the sector.

The Problems to be Tackled

The causes of inefficiency in the development of HRD in telecommunication sector are numerous. Perhaps the chief cause is the bureaucratic style of management typical of government departments. Administration of telecommunications in PTT departments is characterized by a civil service mentality. Appropriate HRD Plan and staffing, training, and investments coupled with management accountability and an adequate incentive system could do much to reduce the excessive labour costs, improve management, and increase efficiency. Trained staff shortages also contribute to the problem.

Education and training will be the key to success, education of staff at all levels and a comprehensive training of the employees who will be using the system will increase the efficiency of the system. Employees must be made aware that the office routines will change, that different ways of operating system will have to be developed and that nothing will be the same again. Jargon such as Bugs and Bytes will become commonplace.

Progress in information and communication technology has brought unprecedented changes and it has helped us in the movement towards in information age. The implication of the new technology necessitates a more global outlook, changes in leadership, pressure for the restructuring of the organization and employees.

Future Outlook

It seems likely that before the end of this century there will be a general convergence of various forms of data communication. The key to this will be the ability to support many new applications.

The process of telecommunications reform will evidently be most effective in an institutional structure that clearly defines, separate distinct roles for policymaking, regulation and management.

Banking Sector

Ministry of Finance is responsible for administration of finances of the Government. It is concerned with all economic and financial matters affecting the country, as a whole including mobilization of resources for development and other purposes. It regulates expenditure of government including transfer of resources to the states. This Ministry comprises three departments, namely, (1) Economic Affairs, (ii) Expenditure and (iii) Revenue.

The Department of Economic Affairs consists of seven main divisions namely, (i) Economic, (ii) Banking, (iii) Insurance, (iv) Budget, (v) Investment, (v) External finance and (vii) Currency and Coinage. This Department inter-alia monitors current economic trends and advises government on all matters of internal and external economic management including working of commercial banks, term-lending institutions, investment regulations, external assistance, etc. With a view to bringing commercial banks into the mainstream of economic development with definite social obligations and objectives, government issued an ordinance on 19 July 1969, acquiring ownership and control of 14 major banks in the country, with deposits exceeding Rs. 50 crore each. Later the objectives of public sector banking system were outlined on 21 July 1969. Some of them are to: (a) mobilize savings of people to the largest possible extent and utilize them for productive purposes; (b) operations of banking system should be promoted by a larger social purpose and should be subject to close public regulation; (c) cater to the legitimate credit needs of private sector industry and trade, big or small; (d) ensure that needs of productive sectors of the economy and in particular those of farmers, small scale industrialists and self-employed professional groups are met in an increasing manner; (e) nationalised banks to actively foster the growth of the new and progressive entrepreneurs and create fresh opportunities for hitherto neglected and backward areas in different parts of the country and (f) to curb the use of bank credit for speculative and other unproductive purposes.

Regional Rural Banks

Regional Rural Banks (RRBs) had been established to take the banking services to the doorsteps of rural masses especially in unbanked rural areas. As on 31 March 1994, 196 RRBs were functioning in 23 states covering 398 of the 492 districts with a network of 14,547 branches.

Banking Industry in the 1970s

No other large traditional industry in India was as much in search of an identity in the seventies as the banking industry. S. Jagannathan, Governer of the Reserve Bank puts it as follows:

> "Perhaps the banking history of the country will record seventies as the decade of momentous historical significance. More change, both quantitative and

qualitative, would not perhaps be compressed in so little a period of history, as we are witnessing today.... No other industry in India, no banking industry abroad, has so suddenly been thrust into the limelight of greatly heightened public expectations. The dimensions and limits of new banking in India are as yet undefined and there is certainly no foreign experience to guide us in our situation".

Similarly, within a month of his joining, the Punjab National Bank P.L. Tandon proposed to the Board of Directors a series of organizational measures that he expected would initiate a continuing process of change and evaluation so that the organization could keep pace with growing demands. He envisaged for the head office the role of total planning, policy formulation, and control on the principle of centralized policy and its decentralized administration.

Financial Committees

In mid 1973 the five committees were formed to look into matters related to: Executive, Personnel, Credit, Priority Sector and Lead Bank, and Financial and General Administration.

The objective was to refine, broadbase and speed up the whole process of decision-making by flattening the previous steep pyramid. Decision-making was earlier highly personalized. The need was to change it to a more consultative or participative style.

The committees were not hierarchical, but functional. Not a vertical chain but a horizontal group.

Managers at different levels were associated with these committees. Some of the younger managers were appointed on a rotational basis. The idea was to get them to interact with senior managers while getting a greater involvement in decision making. The committees were extended to the regional levels, especially for reviews.

The new system worked well, with improved interaction and speeded up decision making.

Management Service

A new interdisciplinary Management Advisory Services Division was, therefore, started in 1972. The division was to provide management at all levels with information and advice to help in its decision-making. The disciplines that were sought to be combined were economics, operational statistics and research, organization and methods, and technical, agricultural and financial services. The role of the Management Advisory Services Division was envisaged as follows:

> The eventual aim was to take away the entire burden of information collection and data processing from the operating divisions to management services division.

Personnel

In introducing the new systems and in re-organization, a major problem that was faced was 'inadequately trained management'. Several steps were taken in the personnel area which are described below.

Recruitment

In 1972, the institution of temporary clerks was abolished. Recruitment of clerks was planned on a regional basis, while recruitment of officers was made on all-India basis. The test papers and evaluation system for recruitment of clerks were standardized with the assistance of the National Institute of Bank Management (NIBM) Bombay.

A three-tiered selection board was used in recruiting management trainees. Advertisements for management trainees were placed three times a year instead of only once as was done earlier. It was explained that:

> "A regular inflow of able young men and a regular intake will mean that better attention will be paid to trainees. But a carefully planned training and a strict appraisal to knock out early the misfits is important. An important innovation that was attempted to give preference to scheduled castes and scheduled tribes.

A procedure of advertisements was set up to invite only SC-ST and general candidates. Reasonable success was made in recruiting SC-ST candidates."

Training

The objectives for training were set as: (i) to develop an employee's skill to do a better job; (ii) to attune him to the spirit of nationalization and (iii) to create in him a sensitiveness to the environment, social and economic.

The bank's Staff Training College which was moved from Faridabad back to Delhi diversified its programme to include new programmes on rural branch management, workshops on performance budgeting, and programmes for small-scale industries. A shift was attempted in the teaching style from lectures towards participative type of learning situations. The participant trainees were mostly special assistants and managers, including technical and agricultural officers. For on the job training, rotation of officers across functional areas such as between personnel and branch banking was pursued.

Promotion

In 1973 a new promotion policy for clerks and officers was introduced in agreement with the Employees' Federation and Officers' Association. A bank report indicates:

"The unique feature of this new promotion policy was the introduction of the element of merit in internal promotion. Thus, where a clerk had to wait on an average fifteen to twenty years to become an officer and an officer five years to go to the managerial cadre, under the new scheme, the period got reduced to five years and one year respectively. It infused enthusiasm in the young talented men and women and created a healty competition to rise quickly through merit."

With such promotion policies, personnel were promoted quick to take responsibility at an early age which generated more confidence and greater growth opportunity. Ad hoc appointments were stopped and eminent outsiders were associated as members and even chairmen of the selection committees.

In view of the above stated recruitment, training and promotion policies an attempt is made here to provide a useful backdrop in having a closer understanding of the problem areas in the HRD process as also the inherent strength of the mechanism.

Human Resource Development in Banks

Employees are primary resource in bank business where all the tangibles as well as intangibles are delivered through them. Therefore, it is required to manage them in the best possible way through effective resource management.

In the coming era of competition, technology and increase of network in products/services—their range, variety and price structure, the need of quality human resource becomes absolutely imperative. This can be addressed by multiskills, attitudinal/skills, training and cross training. With the basic objective of enhancing the efficiency levels and to increase the capability of all individuals where the yardstick would vary from person to person, the function of human resource becomes extremely difficult as well as critical for the success of any organization.

Human Resources department is responsible for the qualitative and `quantitative development of all the employees within the organization. The responsibility starts from interviews, selection, orientation, training, and through various benefits and continuous concern for them.

- The concept revolves around the following fundamentals:

  Empower the organization (HRD Department) to manage human resource in terms of requirement, interviews, selection, recruitment, placement and determining training needs of the employees.
- Quantify human resource like any other resource of the organization to move towards efficient management.

- To account the profit and loss incurred by measuring the activities carried by the employees and formulate profit and loss statement accordingly.

Employees being the main resource, one should treat them accordingly and quantify the productivity. As human resources is extremely critical due to its complex characteristic, the value addition need to be done through tangible, as well as intangible efforts.

In fact, the thinking is that this critical function should be called or rather feature as Human Potential Management (HPM).

Banking in India has undergone a dramatic change in the last four decades. In order to meet the development needs of the economy, many innovations have undergone during this period. Several new concepts have also come forth from planners and thinkers alike which have helped in giving a direction to work for national growth through bank services.

It has taken us very long to realize the importance of human element in bank services. Now it is conceded that much of the credit for affecting the change in the functioning of the banks would go to its vast human resources. It is also true that human resource is not a constant factor, it undergoes changes at every stage.

The banking industry has its own fascinating possibilities. No doubt, it has its share of problems too. Through a sustained effort and planned HRD function, we have to ensure that the employees who are initially good not only continue to be so but also need to undergo a process of development which would enrich their life style and subserve the interest of the organization.

As early as in 1968, the Government of India introduced 'social control' over the banks, under which commercial banks were directed to provide a large volume of credit to hitherto neglected sectors like agriculture, small industries, village artisans etc., so that bank credit may prove a more effective instrument of economic development. However, this was found inadequate. Therefore, 14 major Indian scheduled commercial banks were nationalized in 1969. This was further followed by nationalization of 6 more banks in April 1980.

Beginning of HRD

After the personnel administration and the industrial relations were professionalized in banks, the concept of HRD got attention of the bank management. It was felt that it was not enough to recruit good employees, but also to have effective personnel administration and maintain satisfactory industrial relations. It was also thought necessary to ensure that employees were treated as the most important resource in the organization and receive all the care and attention throughout their stay in the organization.

It gradually dawned upon the bank management that human resource was not only the most important resource but also the most expensive and most delicate resource which require a very humane handling. Human resource is the only resource which has feelings and a behaviour pattern which is not easy to predict. Hence is the need for special care.

Functions of HRD

When this realization dawned, the banks started setting up HRD departments. These departments were asked to frame (1) policies in regard to recruitment and training (2) to introduce manpower planning.

Banks reorganized these on the advice of the management experts and created HRD departments with senior functionaries, in many cases specialists were recruited to head these departments.

Recruitment of human resource is now streamlined. Direct recruitment in clerical and officer cadre are made by the Banking Service Recruitment Boards from the open market. As a result, banks are able to get best talent available in the market. The human resources requirements are now planned by banks in advance. Human resource 'forecast' exercises are carried out annually. Even long range forecasting is now being done.

As such, there is greater need to mould and develop the human resource, keeping in view the Organizational

Development (O.D.) requirements. Edwin B. Flippo in his book *Personnel Management* has analyzed this requirement in the introductory paragraph of the book, 'Individual and Organizational Development'.

"After the employee has been recruited, selected and inducted, he or she needs to be developed to fit in the job and the organization. No one is a perfect fit at the time of selection, and some training and education is required for efficient operation of the work. If no organized programme exists, then development will largely be self-development, i.e., learning on the job. Development would include both training to increase skill in performing a specific job and education to increase general knowledge and understanding of the total environment."

The banks are sometimes accused of setting up HRD departments merely as a institutional requirement. There is no worth-while contribution of these departments and whatever is done by them is merely an image projection exercise. That is why HRD, despite its extended setup has not been able to make a mark.

The value and importance given to human resources now could not be compared with the importance given to them in the early days of banks. The management has started to ensure that the right employees with the right attitude are asked to manage the function. There can be specialists from outside and there can be professionals from within. In fact, it is blending of the two which can bring out the best results.

The effect of the global recession has made us aware that the need in the new millennium would be an increasing attention on HRD. What is needed is a "Paradigm Shift" to ensure that the employees get all facilities to do the job on their own. "Action" is relative to both employee and his superior, it would mean giving authority to implement every day decisions to the employee with prior approval from the supervisor, entrusted with a higher level of responsibility. The impact would be enormous.

Since the employees are the ones actually working with the systems and facilities, they are probably the best qualified to make recommendations and changes. Fundamentally, the employees should be better educated, seek greater responsibility and expect more opportunity to provide inputs and be a part of the ongoing action. Similarly, employees today have greater expectations about job satisfaction, expect minimal supervision and are more keen to fit into the management of the organization.

But how do we do this? Whether, through a change of management style, communication of the goals of HRD, introduction of value system within the organization, respect of individual choice, develop individual capabilities, knowledge, skill, competencies. These are questions, which need to be answered for effective human resource planning and development.

HRD could perhaps be the cutting edge and could be used as a foundation stone for the entire organization, HRD does not stand alone, but is a part of the organization and only when HRD becomes a part of the organization and the management is able to get the best from amongst the employees. This is more relevant to banks as they serve customers which are also human beings.

HRD planners should make use of the traffic signals as a guide for the development of the organization and its employees. The three lights at traffic signals provide three dimensional approach to HRD, which is related to human, physical, operational and financial resource and convey different meanings to us.

Red-(Stop): Think about your direction,

evaluate which factor in a job

the organization values most.

Orange - (Prepare) - Bridge the gap between the employees and the organization through appropriate preparation.

Green - (Go) - Enjoy (Employee and organization) the work through proper planning of the future.

Look through the HRD signals at each turn in the career of the employee growth and development of the organization and keep reviewing your choices.

Fourthly, it recognizes that human beings are born into and live all their lives in structured social situations and, therefore, every analysis about them must take into account the potent institutions which shape and give direction to their lives. Finally, it believes that human beings, with passage of time and acquisition of experience, continually engage in a learning process whereby they can gain new understanding about themselves and the institutions to which they are bound.

The organization is neither a technical nor a social system, but a socio-technical system, and the type of inter-relationship between these two sub-systems is crucial to the effectiveness of the organization. To achieve the best result from the organization as a whole, it is desirable to design the social system jointly with the particular technology. This entails the nature or the fundamental characteristics of human beings.

The task-need, the team-need and the individual-need of human beings that continually interact in an organization have to be blended in the most desirable proportion with a view to optimising performance, production and satisfaction.

Effective Utilization of Human Resources in Banks

Human resources are a potential high yield investment and effective and optimum utilization alone will yield results coupled with quality. This has been succinctly put forward by one of our Prime Minister late Shri Rajiv Gandhi, in his foreword to the Seventh Five Year Plan document where he had pointed out that "In the final analysis, development is not just about factories, dams and roads. Development is basically about people. The goal is the people's material, cultural and spiritual fulfilment. The human factor, the human content is of supreme value...."

When we look at the issue of effective utilization of human resources in the banking industry, we have to take into account two basic variables, first the very complex nature of the banking industry and secondly the more complex human element that mans the industry.

Why Human Resources Management in the Banks?

In fact, a careful examination would reveal the following advantages:

(a) To help the banks to reach the set goals.

(b) To effectively utilize the skills and abilities of the workforce.

(c) To provide the banks with motivated and developed employee potential.

(d) To develop employee job satisfaction.

(e) To meet the self actualization needs.

(f) To develop and maintain the quality of work, rendering employment in the organization a highly merited and desirable occupation.

(g) To develop desirable behaviour patterns, to become better societal beings and to develop and maintain the quality of life itself.

(h) To effect and manage change to the advantage of the individuals, groups, the organization and the society.

There are two factors for the utilization of human resources viz. internal factors and external factors. The internal factors among others are:

(1) Development of work ethics.

(2) Development of expertise, data base and organized approach to managing the employee and the organization.

(3) Development of discipline, communication, effective participative culture training and development.

(4) Development of job satisfaction and motivation, leadership in effecting and managing changes.

The external factors relate to:

(1) Factors relating to external controls and delays.

(2) Legalistic position in matters relating to human resources, planning, development and utilization.

Banks in India are highly human resource intensive. The post-nationalization period has seen a phenomenal increase in the number of bank employees. The quantitative increase underscores the massive human resource component that characterizes the commercial banking operations in India.

Indian banking system has been unique in several respects. A product of Indian conditions, it has met the demands on it over the years. Rather than following any Western model, Indian banking has developed its own ethos, based on native imagination and innovativeness, and the overall performance of Indian banking in the post-nationalization period has drawn encomiums both from within the country and from abroad. In a country where labour supply is abundant, the banking sector has had its share in providing employment opportunities.

The growth of human resource in the banks may be attributed, inter-alia, to the large scale branch expansion, enormous quantitative increase, manifold increase in bank credit to priority sectors and weaker sections, entailing the servicing of a large number of small accounts and the substantial increase in the volume of work in reporting and submission of statements and returns.

While there can be hardly any doubt on the enormous quantitative expansion that banks have recorded in the last decade and a half, there is now a growing recognition of the fact that it is time to lay equal, if not greater, stress on the qualitative aspects of Indian banking. The tone and tenor of customer service, quality of lending, productivity, efficiency, profitability and house-keeping are presently among the areas that have been identified for greater attention. In the sphere of branch expansion which has its implications on human resource growth with the per branch population having been brought down to the desired level and the spatial gaps largely covered, the pace of branch expansion is expected to be much less than what it has been in the past. The policy for 1985-90 has stress on economic viability and operational efficiency.

In their endeavour to bring qualitative change within the vast reservoir of human potential available with the banks, the strategies relating to human resources development will have to pay greater emphasis on work measurement and improving human resource productivity, induction, training and attitudinal reorientation as well as enrichment and employee motivation. However, the basic challenge that confronts banks, in the area of human resource today, is how to improve business turnover in quantitative and qualitative terms, without adding proportionately to the staff in the banks as well as to develop suitable training programmes at different levels—managerial, technical, supervisory and clerical staff.

Training Programmes in Banks

The banks organize a number of training programmes. The details are given below:

1. Advance Training Programme in Foreign Exchange for Inspectors.

   Objective : To update the knowledge of Inspectors in Foreign Exchange for effecting Inspection of Branches.

2. Programme on Concurrent Audit for Senior Executives

   Objective : To update the knowledge of participants in critical areas relevant for concurrent Audit.

3. Credit Management

   Objective : To upgrade the skills of participants in tools and techniques of credit appraisal for efficient management of credit portfolio and ensure effective surveilance on large removal accounts.

4. Career Development Programme

   Objective : To develop a cadre of officers well versed in credit Foreign Exchange and HRD skills to enable them to handle high growth business for the bank.

5. Programme on Concurrent Audit

   Objective : To orient the newly Senior Inspectors towards inspection assignment and equip them with knowledge on important aspects of branch inspections.

6. Prevention of Frauds and Adherence to Bank's system and Procedures

   Objective : To sensitize the participants about frauds occuring in banking industry and focus on compliance of our banks systems and procedures.

7. Programme on Derivatives

   Objective : To give the participants better ideas of the changing world of the Banking Corporate Finance and to import knowledge of the new products under derivatives.

8. Managing Very Large Branches: Profitability for Senior Executives

   Objectives : To focus the attention of senior officers in managing VLBs laying focus on all aspects of profitability including management of credit portfolios, increasing Non-fuel based business, Managing NPAs, Preventing Leackage of revenue and improving productivity of manpower.

9. Project Financing and Project Appraisal

   Objectives : To develop the knowledge of the participants on tools and techniques of project coding and groom them to appraise proposals involving term financing.

10. Investment and Treasury Management

    Objectives : To make participants aware about latest developments and equip them with knowledge to handle such assignments.

11. Trends in Information Technology

    Objectives : To enhance knowledge about latest developments in the areas of information technology and how best to use them to meet organizational requirements.

12. Branch Automation Programme

    Objectives : To update the knowledge of system administrators and sharpen their skills for handling branches.

13. Managing Non-Performing Assets

    Objectives : To sensitize the participants about the vital importance of the subject and help them to thrash out effective strategies for reduction of NPAs.

14. Developing and Managing Foreign Exchange Business

    Objectives : To equip the participants with knowledge about FEB rules, regulations, schemes and procedures so as to handle such potential business.

15. Strategies for Improving Profitability, Productivity and Managing NPAs

    Objectives : To create awareness about profitability and to thrash out strategies to convert loss making branches into profit making branches.

16. Computer Application for Credit Appraisal

    Objectives : To provide knowledge and participate in various software packages which can be used in credit section.

17. Intensive Credit Management

    Objectives : To prepare a cadre of trained Managers/Senior Managers to cater to all types of credit requirements of corporate borrowers in branches and administrating offices.

18. Swift and FEB Computerization

    Objectives : To import knowledge about swift and Swift Network and Foreign Exchange Software.

19. Comprehensive Programme on Loans and Foreign Exchange for Inspectors.

    Objectives : To import latest knowledge in critical areas of credit and foreign exchange to help the inspectors effectively audit the branches.

20. Handling of Disciplinary Action Matters

    Objectives : To enrich the knowledge of participants and improve their skills in handling DAC matters

    (DAC = Disciplinary Action).

21. Managing People for Better Performance

    Objectives : To provide solid grounding in management of men to enable the participants to take charge of situations, enhance communication skills and become effective leader of the team.

22. Developing and Managing Bank Credit Portfolio

    Objectives : To have the skills of the Managers for effective marketing of Bank Credit Schemes by upgrading their skills in credit tools and techniques.

23. Comprehensive programme on Loans and Foreign Exchange

    Objectives : To impart latest knowledge in critical areas of credit and foreign exchange.

24. Faculty Development Programme

    Objectives : To enhance the teaching skills of faculty and acquaint them with the latest training technology.

25. Updating of computer knowledge through various packages.

    Objectives : To impart knowledge for developing applications as per requirements of their respective offices.

Source: Central Staff College, Punjab National Bank, 8 Under Hill Road, Delhi-110054.

Human Resource Information System in Banks

The amazing achievements of Indian banks in the post-nationalization era do not have a parallel anywhere in the world. With a prolific branch expansion of over 47,000 branches in the hitherto unbanked rural and semi-urban areas they have fulfilled the onerous objective of covering a population of more than 14,000 per branch. They have accomplished against heavy odds, the painful shift from class banking to mass banking to the beneficiaries under the priority sectors.

They have systematically deployed more and more funds into the so far neglected areas and, in the process, greatly reduced the sectoral and regional imbalances. They have introduced a number of innovative customer services which are unheard of even in the industrially developed countries. They have successfully ventured into new business areas such as leasing, merchant banking and credit cards.

Overseas, their opening of new branches at strategic locations, their steady expansion of business, their joint ventures with Asian and African Banks and their adept handling of foreign exchange business have made them a force to reckon with in the international banking circles.

What is amiss?

Men and women working in the banking sector today are amongst the best "paid and looked after" white collar employees in the country. If they are still disinterested in their assignments or not capable of handling their work efficiently then something is obviously amiss with the Human Resources Management in banks and an urgent introspection is necessary.

It has become vital for banks to exactly know what are the strengths and weaknesses of their available human resource, in what way they can be developed into a highly motivated and result oriented work force, what specialist and non-specialist human resource should be acquired through fresh recruitment and in what way the existing and the new resources should be deployed in the most profitable manner.

Developing an efficient human resource information system which can provide adequate and timely information for decision making in the sphere of human resources development, has thus, become the need of the day.

By its very nature, an HR information system would be a sub-system of the overall Management Information System of an organization. The basic concepts of MIS are by now quite well known to bank management and without going into the details, it would suffice to state that the sub-system design should take into consideration, the following:

(i) What information will be needed for decision making in the sphere of HRD?

(ii) What will be the source of this information?

(iii) Who will be responsible for collection of the information and how will it be done?

(iv) In what form the extracted information will be stored and what would be the format, coverage and periodicity of the feedback to be disseminated to the different levels of the organization?

(v) How will confidentiality of information be ensured?

Most of the banks in India have at present adopted a four-tier or five-tier organizational structure comprising of central office, circle offices, zonal offices, regional offices, and branch offices and it would not be difficult to determine the source of information and feedback requirements at the various levels of the organization. Similarly, determining the responsibility of the data collection, designing the feedback formats and ensuring information security will also depend on the individual organization structures.

Information required for HRD, can be divided into two basic segments—quantitative and qualitative. Certainly, the qualitative aspects have a much greater impact on the organization from the development point of view and will be the most sought after segment of information generated by the system. However, in view of the innumerable statistical returns banks are now-a-days required to submit to the Reserve Bank of India, the

Finance Ministry and other authorities the performance reviews, fresh recruitments or replying to Parliamentary questions, it would be necessary to first ensure that the system will adequately meet the requirements of quantitative information. This will include the data required for statutory purposes covered by the RBI Act, Banking Regulation Act, Banking Companies Act, etc. The data required by the Ministry of Labour and Employment and other Ministries for review of performance in fulfilling the social obligations such as recruitment of ex-servicemen, physically handicapped persons, minority communities, women employees, etc. data on matters related to the official language policy, data required by Banking Service Recruitment Boards, Employment Exchange etc., data on training plans, facilities available at training centres, etc. and data relating to overtime paid to staff members and remuneration to directors and first ten highest paid employees.

However, this in only the tip of an iceberg. A discerning management would like to have qualitative information also on the following aspects:

(i) What are the strengths and weaknesses of the existing manpower in terms of educational qualifications, skills, talents and behaviour which reflects, on the overall performance of the organization?

(ii) What are the motives which influence the behaviour of different categories of employees?

(iii) What are the reasons for the frustration?

(iv) In what way changes can be brought about in the behaviour of the staff?

(v) In what way the gap between organizational goals and goals of the individuals can be bridged? And in what way the task relevant to maturity of employees can be developed to ensure maximum attainment of organizational goals?

The MIS should provide qualitative information on each individual employed by the organization on the following aspects:

(i) Educational qualifications, skills and talents
(ii) Needs and motives
(iii) Frustration indicators
(iv) Task relevant maturity
(v) Individual maturity
(vi) Leadership style and abilities
(vii) Changes required in behaviour.

The sources for this information will include application forms at the time of recruitment, rating forms completed at the time of annual increments, appraisal reports, interview assessments at the time of promotions and so on. The information on individuals will not only be required to be properly recorded and indexed for quick retrieval but also collated and analyzed with a view to providing a clear picture of the organizational behaviour pattern, to identify the problem areas and required changes in and to make it more effective in achieving its goals. The system designed for this purpose should take into account the regular and ad hoc requirements of the management mode, coverage of feedback communication and the means to avoid time lags and ensure fast turn-around data.

The acute need for adequate information for human resource development at present experienced by bank managements, however, makes it imperative that such a system need to be developed and revised periodically keeping in view the needs of the employees and management as well as the technology and customers requirements.

Planning, human resources development assumes great significance in a labour intensive industry like banking. Public sector banks in our country have shown a good deal of interest in designing and using HRD systems and mechanisms for improving effectiveness of their employees. In public sector banks, the focus of human resource development (HRD) effort is to develop versatility and ensure flowering of potential of the individuals through innovations. In realization of these objectives, these banks introduced Quality Circles for team building and work life improvement, Circle Management and

Branch Management Boards as a training ground for developing analytical and decision-making skills for all levels of personnel, involvement of cross section of people in decision-making process for wider participation in policy formulation, meditation room for creative thinking and organizational renewal.

Public sector banks have given continued emphasis to capability development through study circles, brainstorming sessions purposeful staff meetings at their branches, effective job rotation by formal one year advance planning, encouragement to self-development through incentives and bringing out knowledge booklets like counselling techniques, HRD compendium, etc. The institution of welfare office adopt branches for all round development. The welfare offices set up by these banks at various centres attend to aspects relating to employee grievances and also assist in focusing faster attention to customer services.

Communication was given added focus through interface by executives at all levels of management, formal collection of feedback to gauge the effectiveness of policies and systems, publication of educative brochures to highlight various leadership aspects and special communication on productivity improvement.

By and large, banks have come to recognise that HRD is more than training programme. Training of employees is only one component of HRD. Therefore, other aspects of the HRD system like performance appraisal system, job rotation, career plan and organization development etc. have also to be given equal importance.

Indian Railways

Origin

Indian Railway has had its origin in the middle of 19th century. In fact, the beginning of railways stands out as one of the most fascinating events in the history of India.

The idea of railways in India was first conceived in 1843 by George Clark, the Chief Engineer of the then Bombay

Government, during his visit to Bhandup. Since then events had moved at a fast pace.

The administrative control of railways in India was originally in the hands of a separate branch of the Public Works Department. The committee headed by Sir Thomas Robertson (1903) criticized the adoption of the departmental type of organization for the Railways and recommended for the establishment of Railway Board for efficient administration and working of Indian Railways. In accordance with this recommendation, the Railway Board at the apex level was established in 1905, under the Department of Commerce and Industry of the Government of India.

The main reasons which contributed for the rapid expansion of railways were (i) famine prevention, (ii) development of internal and external trade, (iii) growth of more remunerative crops in tracts reached by railways, (iv) opening up of coalfields and (v) improvement in the economic conditions of the people.

The entire Indian Railway system is now owned and managed by Central Government.

The Indian Railway System

Indian Railways (IR) is the principal mode of transport in the country. In 143 years of its existence, it has successfully adapted to the changing needs of travel and transport in the country.

The development plans of IR are drawn up within the framework of National Five Year Plans.

IR has drawn up a Corporate Plan for the 15 year period 1985-2000, providing a basic frame-work for Planning. The main objectives enunciated in the Corporate Plan are to:

(a) Optimize investment and improve productivity of assets.

(b) Upgrade technology

(c) Bring down costs by reducing fuel consumption, material costs, etc.

(d) Adopt cost based tariff policy

(e) Rehabilitate and maintain assets, particularly track and rolling stock

(f) Develop human resources

(g) Divest auxiliary activities.

Human Resource Development

Organizational excellence can only be achieved through a well trained and motivated workforce for which training has to be accorded highest priority. The National Training Policy envisages a minimum 1.5 per cent of wage bill spent on training activity. At present, IR spends around 0.75 per cent of staff cost on training which will have to be enhanced to cater to the emerging training needs in the areas of:

- Increased level of customer satisfaction
- Maximizing return on investments
- Cost reduction for higher internal resource generation
- Adoption of state-of the art technologies.
- Improved reliability of assets and services.

At present, more than 42 per cent of the total manpower is unskilled. With rapid changes in technology, the balance of manpower has to shift more towards skilled workforce. For this purpose, the personnel policies have to be redesigned to suit an emerging industrial environment. The shift would also contribute to increase in human resource costs which will have to be balanced by overall reductions in the strength of the employees.

With sustained human resource planning exercises, IR have been able to reduce its staff to the extent of about 10 per cent during the last five to six years. Despite this the percentage of staff costs to ordinary working expenses has increased. Considering the present financial situation of the organization, there is an urgent need to reverse this trend.

Major initiatives are now inescapable to reduce the workforce both by improving human resource productivity in real terms through multi-skilling and mechanization, as also by outsourcing certain off-line activities, which incidentally may also help in meeting the rising customer expectations. Therefore, there is need to change the mindset as the Railways can no longer be seen as a vast reservoir for providing additional employment.

Indian Railways has traditionally been the principal mode of transportation for freight and passengers. It connects people and places in the farthest corner of the country to central places and brings them closer for business, sightseeing, pilgrimage and education (Indian Railways year book, 1991).

Performance of Indian Railways needs to be understood on multiple dimensions. The dimensions, among others are growth rate, asset formation, market share, profitability, customer satisfaction, and employee motivation. HRDs concerns among others have been discussed in this chapter.

Indian railway is one of the very few organizations in the country which have a wide range of employee benefit schemes such as medical, housing, travel for their employees and their families and various other schemes like loans and advances, sports and recreation, canteen facility, among others.

The analysis of activities of Indian Railways indicates that it has large scope for improvement. It is, therefore, important to understand the role of organizational structure, systems and processes as well as the behaviour pattern of the employees.

Organizational Characteristics: Indian Railways has a unique characteristics owing to its historical development. The brief details about organizational characteristics along strategy, structure, process, technology, culture, goals, and staffing practices are presented below.

(a) Strategy: Business strategy of the railways could be identified along the dimensions: pro-activity, cost control, analysing, and risk taking. Railways has traditionally been high cost control based organization.

(b) Structure: For an organization where the cost control is the primary concern, the automatic choice is to have department based structure. However, due to large geographical spread the organization is primarily having a department dominated matrix structure.

(1) Vertical Differentiation

(2) Horizontal Differentiation

High level of vertical and horizontal differentiation along with large geographical dispersion provides some of the unique challenges to the organization. These are:

1. Co-ordination
2. Information flow
3. Inter-departmental conflicts.

(c) Process: Processes on the Railways are highly rules and procedure bound and there is very little scope for discretion for the individual at the middle and junior management level.

The long history of the organization has created a web of rules and procedures which are complex and complicated in nature. In most of the situation, expert advice is required before arriving at solutions to the problems.

(d) Technology: The Research, Designs and Standards Organization (RDSO) is the sole Research and Development Unit of IR providing direction to the technology development in almost all the fields of railway activities. RDSO functions as the technical adviser and consultant to IR.

(e) Personnel: As on 31st March, 1997, IR had 15,83,614 regular employees as against 15,86,654 as on 31st March. 1996—decline of 3,040.

The table below gives, at a glance, the strength of Railways employees under various groups:

Number* of staff as on 31st March

Year	*Groups A and B*	*Group C*	*Group D*	*Total*
1950-51	2.3	223.5	687.5	913.6
1960-61	4.4	463.1	689.5	1,157.0
1970-71	8.1	583.2	782.9	1,374.2
1980-81	11.2	721.1	839.9	1,572.2
1990-91	14.3	891.4	746.1	1,651.8
1991-92	14.3	887.2	752.6	1,654.8
1992-93	13.8	891.5	740.2	1,645.5

1993-94	13.8	894.5	717.2	1,625.5
1994-95	13.5	895.9	693.0	1,602.0
1995-96	13.7	891.9@	681.1	1,586.7@
1996-97	**13.9**	**902.4**	**667.3**	**1,583.6**

* Includes number of Railway Protection Special Force (RPSF) personnel and their cost from 1980-81 onwards. These were not included in earlier years.

@ Revised

Source : Annual Report, 1996-97.

(f) Human Resource Development Strategy: Human Resource Development strategies aim to improve the productivity on IR. With this in view, a number of initiatives have been taken to improve the quality of the training programmes offered to railway personnel. Periodically the training needs are analysed and training modules revised/updated. This is supplemented by availing opportunities of specialized training in reputed non-railway organizations in India and abroad. Railway employees are also being encouraged for enhancing their knowledge and skills by acquiring higher qualifications through part time courses/distance learning/off campus programmes of selected Institutes. The training activity on the zonal railways is co-ordinated by the training managers of different departments.

Training of officers is conducted in the following Centralized Training Institutes (CTIs):

(i) Railway Staff College, Vadodara.

(ii) Indian Railways Institute of Civil Engineering, Pune.

(iii) Indian Railways Institute of Signal Engineering and Telecommunications, Secunderabad.

(iv) Indian Railways Institute of Mechanical and Electrical Engineering, Jamalpur.

(v) Indian Railways Institute of Electrical Engineering, Nasik.

The five centralized training institutes impart probationary training to probationers of Group 'A' services of Indian railways. Apart from this they also cater to the training needs of serving officers. Railway Staff College provides General Management, Strategic Management and function related management courses for serving railway officers. It has world wide access through internet for suitable networking with relevant international training establishments also. Other centralized training institutes conduct specialized training courses in respective functional areas. In addition 160 training centres located across the railway system cater to the training needs of non-gazetted staff.

During 1996-97 a total of 4,176 officers and 1,32,747 non-gazetted staff underwent different types of training programmes.

Traditionally, Indian Railways has emphasized on functional training due to high requirement of specialization by the management in their field of operation.

There is very little focus on training for attitude and groups skills in different programmes. This is further highlighted by having different institutes of training for employees from different streams like IRICEN, Pune for civil engineers, etc.

Further, most of the training is confined to class room training and on-the-job training. There is very little focus on conferences and seminars. Hence, training has failed, to a large extent, to create a learning organization which requires inflow of new ideas.

Extent of training in the Railways after initial training of probationary officers is one of the lowest among the service sector organizations/individuals. They are trained for about 5 days per manager per year as against the average of about 14 days per manager per year in the country.

Training: Today Indian Railway faces the major problems of attitude. The attitude of officers towards customers, bosses, peers, and subordinates needs to be modified. Today the major focus of training institutes is on functional aspects of employees. The training programmes need to be modified to have a balance of functional aspects and attitudinal training. For this following are the possible recommendations, among others.

(a) Field training of probationary officers of all the services including engineering officers need be at one place. Officers should be asked to work on projects which require inter-disciplinary inputs.

(b) Officers need to be encouraged to attend seminars and conferences from a very early stage.

(c) Trainers should be a mix of professional trainers who could be posted at training institutes for a very long tenures and field officers who could impart training for a tenure of 4-5 years. The field officers could be more for functional training while the permanent trainers could be for attitudinal training and for management themes.

(d) Training should be a co-ordinated effort of all the centralized training institutes. Today they work in isolation without any co-ordination between them.

It is clear that the staff are mostly provided for handling various selling activities and there is nothing about the marketing, i.e., trying to know the customers' problems, changes in their needs, inter-model trends of traffic, additional facilities required and the planning for future requirements.

The suggestions are only of indicative nature and details are to be worked out separately.

S.N.	*Competitive HRM policies and practices required by IR*	*Existing HRM policies and practices of IR*	*Suggestions*
1.	Review the job requirements on continuous basis as per market needs and change the job specifications accordingly	Not regularly done and even today emphasis is only on management of sales. Marketing functions.	We must stregthen market research, facility planning and market promotional functions and create new jobs in these areas. Also the concept of jobs with multiple skills to be created for optimization of manpower and integrated services.
2.	Recruit/Select and place right person on the right job.	Current recruitment/ selection and placement policy generally ignores the job profile.	Conduct psychological tests to ensure selection of persons with positive mindset, strong affiliation needs helping attitude, cool mind and strong persuasion power.
3.	Train the employees as per changing job requirements.	It is ad hoc, static and does not relates to the changing job profiles	The marketing job is mostly attitudinal and we must inculcate positive attributes. Commercial orientation and HR qualities in the commercial staff apart from routine functional

			expertise. This could be done by role play, games and psychological counselling.
4.	Have clear job descriptions	Does not exist	It should be created with clearcut mention of attributes needed in the incumbent.
5.	Appraise performance objectively with full transparency.	It is too general and subjective and serves no purpose in day to day management.	It should be largely objective, performance indices based and transparent. it should become basis of financial incentives, promotions, training, placement and termination of service.
6.	Promote only the deserving employees based on results. Seniority does not fit in the competitive era.	Promotion policy is not very transparent and objective/ performance based and it is very difficult to ignore the seniors even if they are inefficient.	We must adopt merit based promotions on totally transparent performance yard sticks and not on vague rankings like good, very good and outstanding which are sometimes given without any supporting performance indices.
7.	Terminate the services of non-performances	This is very rare.	Message has to go down that there is no room for non performers. This is only possible when we install objective and transparent performance appraisal system.
8.	Wage must recognize the differences in jobs and performances	The current policy does not distinguish between good performers and the bad.	The wage should consist of basic job element (basic + DA) and performance elements in some acceptable form.
9.	Install effective machinery for resolution of industrial disputes	It exists except that sometimes labour agreements ignore the market realities leading to deterioration in the financial performance.	No change required except for more strategic understanding of the market compulsions by the trade unions. The pay-out must bring additional benefits more than the payment agreed upon.
10.	Negative behaviour with the customers is to be penalized	No such system exists.	The penalty may be imposed depending upon the number of customer complaints against an employee based upon agreed formula.
11.	Immediate attention to customers complaints	Done but slow.	Special cell to be manned by dedicated staff and time bound disposal to be ensured by penalizing the delay beyond the target date.

12.	Ensure good amenities to staff to maintain their level of motivation	Housing problem exists.	We may consider reimbursing lease rentals and be liberal in grant of other incentives till the employee gives more than what he gets from the railways.

Source : Abhivyakti, July-September, 1998, Vol. 10. No. 3.

It is evident from the above analysis that the current HRM policies and practices for the commercial (marketing) staff require drastic changes if IR has to have a responsive team. Of course, management of change will require wide ranging consultation at various levels including trade unions or may even involve corporatization of IR.

Mandatory Courses for Group "A" Railway Serving Offficers

Group 'A' Foundation Programme

Objectives: To introduce newly selected Group 'A' officers through UPSC, to the Indian Railway System.

Group 'A' Induction Programme

Objectives: To reinforce the participants understanding of the working of Indian Railways and to enable them to become effective practising managers in their maiden Railway assignments.

Group A Refresher Course (Accounts)

Objectives: To review the short working experience of these officers and provide professional and managerial guidance to improve their effectiveness.

Civil Service Foundation Course

Objectives: To enable the newly joined Group A officers of various Central Services of Government of India to understand the background, significance and expectations of them by public.

Group A Refresher Course (Traffic, Personnel, Stores)

Objectives: To review the short working experience of these Officers and provide professional and managerial guidance to improve their effectiveness.

Management Development Programme

Objectives: To provide management inputs and help participants solve problems faced by them in the field and seek opportunities offered by technological and managerial innovations. To prepare officers to hold independent charge of their departments as Branch Officers on a Division as well as to integrate them as members of the Divisional team.

Senior Professional Course (Traffic, Stores, Personnel and Accounts)

Objectives: To prepare officers for the responsibility of coordinating work, both intra-disciplines as well as inter-disciplines and to acquaint them with the latest challenges and opportunities in their respective departments.

Advance Management Programme

Objectives: To acquaint officers with areas of strategic management and to improve organizational effectiveness through its Senior Administrative Grade.

Mandatory Course for Group 'B' Officers

Group B Foundation Programme

Objectives: To facilitate systems thinking and appreciate overall Indian Railways scenario by officers promoted from the Group 'C' cadre.

Group B Integrated Programme (Personnel, Traffice Signal and Administration)

Objectives: To give an overview of the working of the entire department to officers coming from different streams within the discipline and therefore having experience in only some of the functions of their department.

Programmes on Information Technology and Computers

Introductory Information Technology

Objectives: To introduce computer culture among the officers and to acquaint them to independently work on PC with Microsoft office.

Advanced Information Technology

Objectives: To introduce networking and database management system with a view to manage company wide database and move towards paperless office.

Strategic Management Seminars

Strategic Management Seminars for General Managers

Objectives: To provide a strategic management focus to the top managers and facilitate common understanding among senior managers.

Programmes for the Indian Railway Medical Service Officers

Medical Induction Course

Objectives: To acquaint new entrants to IRMS with Railway working rules and codes and to provide departmental inputs for effective performance.

Medical Refresher Course

Objectives: To refresh Professional and Managerial skills of Medical Officers.

Hospital Management

Objectives: To prepare Medical Officers to solve problems of managing a hospital health unit.

Chief Medical Directors Workshop

Objectives: Exchange the views of Chief Medical Directors about the common strategy for better health management and to acquaint the CMDs on Information technology.

Programmes on Functional Related Areas

Course on Discipline and Appeal Rules

Objectives: To enhance the understanding of officers to manage the problems faced in the field in the areas of D & AR.

Rajbhasha Foundation Programme

Objectives: To facilitate systems thinking by Rajbhasha Officers, awareness of computers, HRD and strategies for spreading Hindi on the Railways.

Vigilance for non-Vigilance Officers

Objectives: To inculcate awareness in the participants about the roles and procedures of vigilance department, and their roles in combating corruption.

Project Management

Objectives: To equip officers involved in projects with the current techniques of Project Management so as to complete those without cost and time overruns.

Vigilance Course for Vigilance Officers

Objectives: To improve the investigative skills of the vigilance officers and making them aware about the procedural aspects of dealing with vigilance cases.

Works and Purchase Contact Management

Objectives: To equip officers dealing with contracts for the execution of works and supply of stores to complete the same efficiently without time overrun, and financial or procedural irregularities and dealing with related disputes.

Intermodal Transport

Objectives: To acquaint the participants with current and future trends and to develop strategies for intermodal transport.

HRD for DPOs/Sr. DPOs

Objectives: To acquaint participants with new ideas and recent changes in rules in HRD, MPP and Personnel Manager.

Energy Management

Objectives: To acquaint participants with energy saving techniques in Railway traction, workshops and general areas.

Divisionalization of Stores

Objectives: To review the present problems and challenges in Divisionalization of stores and evolve means for effective working.

Mukhya Rajbhasha Adhikari Workshop

Objectives: Exchange ideas and formulating strategies for making Rajbhasha popular and common mode of communication.

Multidisciplinary Workshop on the Financial Management of Stores and Workshop

Objectives: To highlight and discuss interdisciplinary linkages and co-ordination problems and suggest solutions for improvements to prepare for challenges ahead.

Scrap Disposal

Objectives: To acquaint the officers with detailed knowledge and challenges in identification, collection, and disposal of various scraps arising on the railways.

CD's Workshop

Objectives: To acquaint the participants with the procedural aspects of inquiry arising out of vigilance investigations.

Workshop Management

Objectives: To acquaint workshop managers with correct practices for managing workshops effectively.

SRAs Workshop

Objectives: To acquaint the participants with the latest Rajbhasha Policy and evolve strategy for implementation of same.

Terminal Management

Objectives: To acquaint the participants with siding planning terminal design (both coaching and freight) computerization of terminals.

Multidisciplinary Workshop on the Management of Traffic Earnings and Support Systems

Objectives: To highlight and discuss interdisciplinary linkages coordination problems and suggest solutions for improvements to prepare for challenges ahead.

Devnagari Computing

Objectives: To acquaint the participants with the use of computers and computer software packages in Hindi (Devnagari) script.

Public Relations

Objectives: To deliberate on the problems and opportunities of public relations and discuss strategies for improvement.

Purchase Management

Objectives: To familiarize participants with latest trends in Purchase Management.

Programmes on Management Interest Areas

Managerial Effectiveness

Objectives: To develop managerial skills so as to be more effective in the organization.

Seminar on Freight Business

Objectives: To facilitate discussion on ways and means to be competitive in freight business.

Seminar on Alternate Financing

Objectives: To enable participants to understand the Alternative Financial Strategy, including lease finance, for Indian Railways in the changing economic environment.

Seminar on Manpower Planning

Objectives: To review the current policies of Manpower Planning and evolve effective means of implementation.

Marketing Management

Objectives: To develop sensitivity to the needs of marketing for the Indian Railways, to develop skills, to develop marketing strategy and marketing research.

Seminar on Safety

Objectives: To review the trends emerging on safety front and to analyse reasons behind accidents and evolve strategies for improving safety.

Strategic Human Resource Management

Objectives: To equip participants to deal with the current issues and opportunities of HRM for strategic advantage to IR covering various issues like employee relations, discipline, organizational culture, reduction in staff strength.

Computers and Communication

Objectives: To acquaint the participants with the latest communication, hardware and technology including national telecom policy.

Seminar on Materials Management

Objectives: To deliberate on the emerging scenario and generate strategies for effective materials management on Indian Railway.

Total Quality Management

Objectives: To acquaint the participants with the concepts of quality control, quality costs and Total Quality Management with special emphasis on quality in Service Organization.

Seminar on Passenger Business

Objectives: To facilitate discussion on passenger business to be competitive in passenger business.

Productivity Workship

Objectives: To review the productivity of various railway system and to acquaint the participants to productivity improvement strategies with special emphasis on productivity of workshop and production units.

Customer Care

Objectives: To renew the current scenario, including passenger amenities, catering and consumer relations and generate strategies for improvement in passenger services.

Roles, Goals and Mission

Objectives: To enable the participants to formulate their own mission/vision statements and strategy to achieve them to improve personal and organizational effectiveness.

Management of Change

Objectives: To acquaint the participants with the techniques and skills required to lead change, transformations in the organization and create necessary environment for large scale implementation of change in the Railways.

Business Planning System

Objectives: To develop skills in generating business plans and action plans in the context of Indian Railways.

Video Workshop on Communication

Objectives: To assist participants to improve communication skills presentation skill and use of computers for making presentations.

Learning Organization

Objectives: To enable participants to understand the concepts and practices for developing a learning organization and identify methods for developing that.

Creative Problem Solving

Objectives: To acquaint the participants with creative problem solving.

The course uses the tools of role-playing and sharing of experiences to bring about a change in their attitudes.

The demand for training and retraining in the railways is at its peak and growing. Several key factors that drives this need are: rapid technological change, an ever expanding customer service as well as to bring more and more avenues to facilitate travel and transportation of goods. But surprisingly training budgets are not increasing in proportion to the growth and development training at a reduced budget could de-motivate employees until they are made to accept the rationale behind it. Communication and proper motivation would help a training department to achieve this. Employees need to be enouraged to appreciate in-house training and go for learning value rather than merely a pleasure cum training tour.

Strengths of the Organization: Indian Railways has a few unique strengths which need to be capitalized for improved performance. First, it has a vast pool of skilled employees who are relatively cheaper. Secondly, Railways has developed infrastructure in different areas like telecommunication, immovable assets which can bring in high revenue, thirdly, organization has unique core competence in the transport sector, hence can take lead in the overall emerging multi-modal transportation in the country.

Fourth, it has very strong managerial process which can lead to high efficiency. Fifth, being a government run department, there is no tax liability.

Weaknesses: Indian Railway has some weaknesses which need to be addressed. First, the organization has low customer orientation due to historical reasons to achieve efficiency.

Second, market research is virtually non-existant in the organization. Third, in the over enthusiams to achieve efficiency and short-term goal, there is no long-term policy and vision for the organization at the moment. And fourth, management processes in the organization have led to a situation where the identification of people with organization is on a decline leading to lower loyalty and motivation to work.

Information Technology Areas

Information Technology has made rapid strides in recent years. Indian Railways are yet to fully realize the potential Information Technology offers in all areas of railway management and operations. The recent decision of the Indian Railways to go in for a pilot project of the European Train Control System on the Indian Railways network is a step in this direction.

Points for Introspection

By analyzing the items especially those which deal with training and development, the following points come to surface.

- Personnel policies are not very conducive for development.
- Proper training need analysis is not carried out. Selection or nomination of officers for training programmes, is sometimes, arbitrary. This results in low motivation level at the training programmes and most of the trainees take it as a break from their day to day activities. Training can be of use only when the trainees are given enough opportunity to apply what they have learnt from the training programmes.
- The performance appraisal system is not really perceived as a tool for development by the employees. The weaknesses of the employees are communicated to them more in a threatening manner. A realistic assessment of the employee will go a long way in experiencing job satisfaction and eliminating unrealistic expectations.
- The concept of career planning and development in IR is yet to catch on. The employees are not very clear about their future prospects in the organization and this leads to a fair amount of frustration in them.

Empowerment

In view of bringing in a good development oriented culture, empowering employees will definitely help. The possible gain would be (a) quicker online responses to the customer needs, (b) quicker online responses to dissatisfied customers during service recovery, (c) higher job satisfaction of employees, (d) improved inter-personal interactions, (e) generation of better ideas, (f) high publicity.

Empowerment is necessary for increasing efficiency and effectiveness in services sector particularly railways. But, Bowen and Lawler suggest that empowerment is not always desirable in the same degree for all services sector. In certain cases, production-line approach can be a better choice. It is suggested that aspects such as basic business strategy, tie to customer, technology, business environment and types of people should be taken care while determining the levels of empowerment.

References

1. Renewal, Bulletin on human and organization development for NGOs, No. 1, September 1995, Academy of Human Resources Development.
2. MS-22, Human Resource Development, Indira Gandhi National Open University, School of Management Studies, Comparative HRD Experiences.
3. Mannual on Manpower Planning, Bharat Heavy Electricals Ltd., Corporate Personnel, New Delhi.
4. Banking Century, Prakash Tandon, A Short History of Banking in India and the Pioneer: Punjab National Bank.
5. Human Resource Development in Banks, Punjab National Bank, Central Staff College, 8, Underhill Road, Delhi - 110054.
6. Course Directory 1998, Advanced Level Telecom Training Centre, Ghaziabad (India).
7. Alt Centre Course Directory 1999.
8. Course Directory 1999, Bharat Ratna Bhim Rao Ambedkar Institute of Telecom Training, Jabalpur.
9. Calendar of Courses 1988-99, Railway Staff College, Vadodara.
10. Indian Railways, Year Book 1995-96.
11. Indian Railways, Year Book 1996-97.
12. Indian Railways, Year Book 1997-98.

13. Indian Railways, Annual Report and Accounts 1995-96.
14. Indian Railways, Annual Report and Accounts 1996-97.
15. Indian Railways, Annual Report and Accounts 1997-98.
16. *Human Resource Development,* School of Management Studies, Indira Gandhi National Open University, MS22, 1996.

ROLE OF HUMAN RESOURCE DEVELOPMENT IN SERVICE SECTOR: AN INTROSPECTION

Human resource development exercise provides an opportunity for introspection and planning for the future strategies. Keeping in view the activities and inbuilt factors, it facilitates the task of reviewing performance of the current and prospective activities. The clarity of objectives, existing work methods, tools and facilities, working conditions and motivation are the main determinants of the human resource development exercise.

It has been observed very often that the actual work content of jobs is much more than the ideal work content due to a number of reasons, such as, design defects, ineffective method of working, obsolete tools and facilities, shortcoming in the organizational efforts, poor attitude of employees, among others.

Similarly, proactive personnel policies, participation, motivational schemes, achievement, behaviour modification, action research, feedback and counselling, goal-setting and others will go a long way in improving the effectiveness of human resource development.

One important HRD feature is 'Reporting'. The number and nature of the reports would depend upon the requirement which in turn is linked to the activities of the organization and specific thrust areas. The reports would help to meet the needs of monitoring and review the activities related to HRD and would also trigger necessary control and development measures having both long and short-term perspective.

It is difficult to prepare an exhaustive list of reports but the important ones are identified below:

HRD Status Report

HRD Analysis Report

Actual Data/Statistical Reports

Activity Reports.

HRD Status Report: This provides a reporting system which has a close observation on the changes of employees strength. This type of report reflects the changes in the structure at different levels, on the wastage among the employees, status of surplus manpower, (categorywise and skillwise) and also on retraining and redevelopment efforts.

HRD Analysis Report: This HRD inventory in each organization contains all important information regarding each employee. Analysis on various dimensions gives useful data indicating the salient aspects of the existing situation and also projections of the future.

Actual Data/Statistical Reports: The report inter-alia provides an analysis of the performance indices and is helpful in identifying areas requiring specific attention.

Activity Report: The main purpose of such an activity is to evaluate the effectiveness of the steps already implemented in different directions, highlight their impact in future and recommend corrective measures.

A number of HRD activities are being carried out in different organizations in the field of personnel, production, services and marketing but they need to be further integrated.

Priority areas for intensifying the above mentioned and other HRD sub-systems need to be identified for the development of the employees. Although, the HRD departments are generally responsible for such activities but the personnel department need to take the initiative in commissioning and monitoring such efforts as the various sub-systems are closely inter-related, therefore, no conclusion should be drawn in isolation. Its impact on other sub-systems is to be well understood.

To meet the above challenge the organization need to create efficient HRD system and sub-system to manage the different activities. What is expected from the organization is the organizational structures in which individual/team is given strategic responsibility for each and every activity.

In essence, this implies a matrix form of organization. However, what is key to success in a matrix is not the formal structure but the organizational processes and the organizational mind set which the organization is able to develop.

As the organizations develop there is one bottleneck that keeps coming up, i.e. need for qualified personnel. Most of the organizations have started developing a pool of multicultural managerial talent to meet the requirement of qualified personnel.

Citi Bank is one such organization, which has implemented a scheme called Global Employee Management System. This scheme involves development of a database to know who and where the talent is. The database thus, established provides a detailed description of the organizations mix of managerial skills, talents and potentials. This also helps the organization to identify the capacity and capability of the employees.

The next step is to identify the strength and skill gap of the organization in order to compare the present skills and characteristics with the ideal requirements, defined for the current position and the preferred next position. This information can be used as the basis for organizational development and training programmes.

The other issue is to provide greater importance to human values in the organization. The emphasis on human values, is not extraneous to organizations success as the new millennium will witness a greatly increased focus on basic human values.

The organizations have started developing an integrated HR strategy to bring changes in methods of evaluation. The approach will help in sustaining a high level of morale and motivation and will also synergise the intellectual potential of the employees and finally develop an effective organization.

The rapid changes in the late eighties and nineties have, among others, compelled many organizations to reengineer various functions such as manufacturing, accounts, distribution and after-sales services. The one function, that has somehow escaped attention is HRD for these activities. Though there are approaches and framework for each activity, HRD professionals appear to be blissfully ignorant about them.

Need for Insight

Traditionally, HRD functions depend on either past data or on sheer hunch. What will be needed in the future is the development of insight, using high quality data on the specific segments, being studied. Breakthrough ideas and insights will require rigorous HRD activities and willingness to question conventional approaches.

There are three key requirements for developing insights into HRD functions:

- To widen the scope of HRD definition: exhaustive mapping of activities are important:
- To assess employee dissatisfaction through understanding, and exploring their experiences in enhancing/improving the organization products and services:

While in the long run, the growth of HRD function is of key importance, but the blind adoption of such an approach can be dangerous, particularly, in developing and declining organizations. What will really matter in the future is the involvement of employees in the growth and development of the organization and the employees. The strategy of the organization, among others need to develop appropriate developmental activities through the creation of value system that is unique and sustainable.

For this to happen an organization can use the concept of human resource inventory which is really a step forward to streamline HRD practices within the organization. (Box 7.1)

Box 7.1

Human Resource Inventory Quantitative Inventory

Section 1 : Personal Data

1. Staff Number of Appraisee: ____________________
2. Man Number of Appraisee: ____________________
3. Surname: ____________ Other Names: ____________
4. Data of Birth: Date ________ Month ________ Year ________
5. Sex: Male ☐ Female ☐
6. Marital Status: Single ☐ Married ☐

   Widowed ☐ Divorced or Separated ☐
7. Nationality ☐
8. Details of entry into the Civil Service and of current appointment

Entry into Service **Current Appointment**

(i) Date of Joining____Month____ Year____ Month____ Year____

(ii) Designation____________________

(iii) Number of Persons Supervised:____________________

(iv) Name and full address of the current Ministry:__________

9. Terms of Appointment:

   Permanent and Pensionable ☐ Probation ☐

   Contract ☐ Temporary ☐

   Gross Salary per annum (Rs.)____________________

10. Retirement and Contract Particulars:

    Date of Retirement:____________________

    End of Contract:____________________

Section 2 : Education and Training Data

	Subject	Year
(1) Higher academic qualification (2) Professional qualifications (3) Technical qualifications		

2. (i) Civil Service (obligatory) Examination Passed

	Lower	Higher	Others
Year			

(ii) Departmental Examinations passed
(other than Civil Service) _____ _____ _____

3. Training Programmes/Courses/Study Tours Attended during the Appraisal Period.

Dates/ Duration	Institution and Place	Title of Programme	Grades Awarded (if any)

Section 3: Career Data

1. Position held with years during the last five years (Government and Parastatal)

Designation	Year From	Year To	Full Address of the Ministry/Province/ Department

2. Training Programmes/Courses/Study Tours attended with years during the last five years:

Dates/ Duration	Institution and Place	Title of Programme	Grades Awarded if any

(Note : Section 3, Nos. 1 and 2 need to the filled in the first year only when the present Annual Performance Evaluation Form is Introduced.)

3. Indicate help and guidance that would improve your job performance (specify a minimum of three salient points):

____

____

____

I certify that the above information is correct

Signature of Appraisee______________ Date______________

Further, for successful implementation of evaluation practices the organization will need the vision and capabilities to forge useful partnerships between employers and employees. (Box 5.2)

Box 7.2

Qualitative Inventory

Section 1 : Appraisal of Performance Against Objectives and Targets During Appraisal Period

1. Main duties of the job:

____

____

____

____

2. Key performance areas of the job:

____

____

____

3. Functions performed:

____

____

____

4. Achievements:

____

____

____

5. Appraiser's comments:

___

___

___

Certified that the above information is correct

Appraisee's Signature_______ Appraiser's Signature_______

Date :__________________Date: ______________

Section 2 : Evaluation of the Critical Attributes of the Appraisee

I. Performance Output and Productivity	Out-standing A	V.Good B	Good C	Ade quate D	In adequate E	Remarks of Reviewing Authority
1. Job responsibility						
2. Quality of work						
3. Productivity enhancement						
4. Professional Ability						
5. General Management Knowledge						
6. Commitment and self-discipline						
7. Planning and organising						
8. Participation						
9. Administrative and Executive						
10. Innovative						
11. Communication						
12. Decision-making						
13. Co-operation						

Overall Evaluation of Critical Attributes of the Appraisee by Appraiser with remarks of the Reviewing Authority. Give your evaluation by (✓) mark in the appropriate box below on the basis of A, B, C, D and E given above:

(a) Ready to meet requirements of higher responsibility ☐

(b) Expected to meet requirements of higher responsibility ☐

(c) Would not meet requirements of higher responsibility of present reckoning ☐

Signature of the Reviewing Authority__________

Signature of Appraiser__________

Date__________ Date__________

Section 3: Evaluation of Placement and Potential

To be filled in by the Appraiser and Reviewing Authority

1. Placement

1. Is the Appraisee well utilized in the present field of work taking his ability and interest into account?

   Please suggest any additional responsibility he can undertake.

____

____

____

____

2. Other than his current field of work, please suggest the field of work for which the Appraisee has shown interest and ability and where he can be better utilized

____

____

____

____

II. Potential

Is the Appraisee suitable for promotion to a higher grade? Please (✓) tick.

Most suitable ☐ Suitable ☐ Not Suitable ☐

Signature of Appraiser__________

Signature of Reviewing Officer__________

Date:__________ Date:__________

Section 4: Development and Training Needs

Development and Training needs proposed by the Appraisee	Recommendations on the needs by Appraiser in: (1) Functional Areas (2) Managerial Skill Areas	Sources : (1) Name of Institution (2) Period of Training

Signature of Appraiser________________________

Signature of Reviewing Officer____________________

Date:________________Date:________________

Section 5 : Settlement of Key Performance Areas and Targets for Next Year

To be filled by the Appraisee in consultation with the Appraiser

Key Performance Areas	Objectives/Targets to be aimed at under each Key Performance Area (Specify)
1.	
2.	
3.	
4.	
5.	

Signature of Appraiser______________________________

Signature of Reviewing Officer__________________________

Date:_______________________Date:___________________

Section 6 : Overall Evaluation

1. General Evaluation

Please give an overall evaluation of the appraisee with reference to his/her strength and shortcomings and also by drawing attention to the qualities, if any, not covered by the entries above.

____

____

____

2. Grading (circle one)

Outstanding/Very Good/Good/Inadequate
(An Appraisee should be graded excellent only when exceptional qualities have been noticed. Grounds for giving such grading should be clearly brought out.)

Full Name of the Competent Authority:______________________

Signature of the Competent Authority:______________________

(Permanent Secretary/Head of Division/Department)

Designation:____

Date:____

The future thrust has to be on HR Building and HR Management rather than just on product. For this to be successful, organizations will have to recognize the value of the employees through the development of strategic assets and capabilities within the employees.

Extrapolation of past patterns will not be adequate to predict future possibilities, be it with regard to identifying new HR practices or offering differential services. Traditional HR practices have already become outdated and the new requirement is to find employees potential and emerging needs.

Time-based HRD is the new rule and the organization has to appreciate this. Similarly, empowering organization need to respond to employees requirements, be it with regard to performance, evaluation or a drive to bring change in the system, will be critical for ensuring rapid response.

The responsibility of HRD has remained by and large with the organization. Employees generally interact with management who in turn passes on required information to other functional departments such as personnel, production, finance, etc., which then take necessary action. The "feel" for the organization is thus indirectly communicated by the management to support functions and services.

This must change, being close to the employees will not be enough, the employee need to be at the centre of the organization, and every function and department need to be accountable to meet employees requirements. In other words, discipline and responsibility must spread throughout the organization. Each employee will have to be provided with the value, he is looking for and to accomplish this, all resources of the organization available with various functional areas must be exploited to the maximum. This implies a very high level of coordination and integration, a requirement that was not given adequate attention till recently. There has to be an emphasis on core process that create value for employees and the traditional HR department need to be replaced by a network of HR specialists involved with such processes. Organizations need to be without boundaries, both within its legal structure and in relation to employer-employee relationship to create the desired value. There is thus the need for each HR professional to discard their traditional role and become "integrators", capable of marshalling all available resources and assets, within the organization.

The organizations must discuss at length the performance of the employees to enhance the productivity and efficiency. It is ironical that not many organizations are known to spend time on HR-related matters. This has to change to ensure future success.

Need for action

Victor Hugo once said, "when the time for change comes, nobody can stop it." It is said that the HR-function is now at crossroads and it must exhibit new-generation breakthrough thinking, both in terms of strategy as well as organizational structures, systems and processes. Old ways of HR must be discarded and new thinking, as spelt out above, must be put in place. HR professionals must have a broader view of the development and concentrate on satisfying the potential and emerging needs of their existing and future employees.

In the beginning of the threshold of the new millennium we can say with confidence that the future of our organizations is assured if we continue to remember that employees are the ultimate source of strength for the growth and development of an organization.

The organizations have to practise and discover the positive characteristics of the new culture. Optimism need to be the basic characteristics of a good organization and this also includes optimism about the capabilities of the employees within the organization.

The other prime characteristics are curiosity and participation. The organization and the employees both need enthusiasm and interest in looking at the way things are done in an unfamiliar/familiar environment.

The organization and the employees, among others, need to focus on the following three areas:

- The employees need a strong concern for his/her organization and where the organization is going, what the organization stands for.

- The employees need an aptitude towards work as well as the ability to communicate about the job at hand.

The maxim, "knowledge is power" is indeed true. Today the organizations are in knowledge era, where values are being created, where knowledge is work, whether it is in service organizations or infotech organizations.

In India, the emergence and awareness of knowledge and values within the organizations is very recent. This is visible in the form of learning/training initiatives for employees within the organization and its linkages to the strategic planning process. Quietly, the face of the Indian organizations are changing in just the same way as elsewhere in the world.

The organization's value system should be governed by the need for continual adaptability of the organization within its external environment. It rejects most of the suppositions which render it difficult for the organization to survive and promotes those which increases the chances of its survival and further growth. Obviously, this value system is dynamic. In the current highly competitive environment, characterized by increasing trends towards globalization, privatization and liberalization (all the buzzwords of today's business environment in India), one can see the evidence of newer value systems emerging, which would give high priority to efficiency, productivity, and quality.

Similarly, the personal value system is governed by the need for continual adaptation by the individual, the organizational culture and the culture of the society at large. While it has conceivable that there may be conflict between the two, these demands are increasingly becoming convergent, with socioeconomic and technological factors within organization.

Knowledge and Growth

The management within the organization is the custodian of the organizations legacy, and also a trustee for tomorrow. The measure of its achievement is not just sustaining present performance, but equally assuring future prospects. To secure the future, the main task of management is to realize sustainable growth and HRD.

The quest for growth is underpinned by the belief that the new millennium is the millennium of knowledge. This inevitably means that employees, as carrier of knowledge, will be an organization's most important asset.

The millennium of knowledge calls for a new paradigm-growth through employees. Growth is created not by the amorphous entity of the organization, but by its talented and knowledgeable employees.

The issue which supports this paradigm of growth through employees is knowledge development. We must complement this with an outward-looking perspective to identify, evaluate, and apply ideas and best practices from in and around, and compound this learning with the distinctive insight and skills of employees to build an unbeatable competitive edge.

Similarly, to win in the millennium of knowledge, the organization must continue to attract and excite the best talent. Today talented employees have more options available than ever before. The challenge for the organization is to create an environment in which employees can work with freedom, within a framework of empowerment and accountability, vested with parallel power to imagine, create and implement their ideas—fully supported by investments in knowledge and technology. These issues will hold together the future edifice of the organization.

Shaping Destiny

It is important to recognize that changes lead to new opportunities for growth. In India, we have already discerned some mega trends. The early years of the next millennium will be marked by major social and economic shifts. Stimulated by increased knowledge, information and HRD practice, these shifts will create aspirations for better work culture.

To realize growth, knowledge must be converted into products or services that actually offer value to the organization and employees. Today, much of this knowledge belongs to employees and to various functions within the organization. This knowledge inter-alia could also be applied at different levels within the organizations, to create opportunities through extensive sharing of the same within the organization.

It is critical for the organization to continuously build upon and refresh the knowledge it develops within. This will not only help the organization's to have continuous interface with employees, but also to strengthen growth and development within the organization by helping in the process of recruitment and retaining the best talent.

In order to develop the potential, the organization should continue to empower the employees to stretch their minds, ingenuity and abilities. In the ultimate analysis, the organization is nothing but a collective intellect. Its success is determined by the state of mind, and therefore, centres around employees attitudes. It is the positivity of mind that leads to action and it is this action which ultimately decides success or failure. Therefore, the dynamism within the organization is proportional to the dynamism unlocked in the minds of the employees.

The organization must transform the employees into sustained winners, accentuating the strengths and bridging the gaps. This in turn will influence the organization's collective entrepreneurial ability and competitiveness, ability to adopt new approaches and an abiding ability to take risks, the rewards of which would be huge, if practised.

In the model of growth, the employees need to be vested with unparalled strength to imagine, innovate and implement new ideas. This need to be fully supported by investments in technology, marketing research and employees development.

This approach within a framework of accountability will require an organizational structure that aims to drive decision-making to empower teams as close as possible to the objectives of the organization. This empowerment will breed entrepreneurship. The organization also needs to tune employees to such management system which would enhance employees strengths and bridge their skill gaps.

The over-riding theme, however, is always growth. To this end, the organization needs to develop an HRD system which would inter-alia help to analyse future trends and suggest ways and means to strengthen growth and development.

The extensive interface which the organizations are currently building with employees is adding to the understanding of the emerging needs. This understanding will further help the organization to manage the other horizons of growth such as to develop and strengthen the work culture within the organization both for the existing and potential employees.

The services sector has been growing at a phenomenal pace. Yet, very few organizations have developed focus on the issue of education and training. There are two reasons for the lack of focus on the above issue. First, most organizations believe that skills required to manage services set-up are similar to those of in other sectors. Second, is the heterogeneous nature of services sector activities, such as airlines, hotels, banks, railways, makes the task of education and training difficult.

The focus of HRD in service organizations is required to sensitize employees, to:

- Define the requirements of services sector activities.
- Identify an effective services sector strategy.
- Design performance/evaluation measures which have services sector orientation.

A programme for services sector organization needs to include a holistic perspective to implement the programme of skill development. Skill development is not an automatic process. For its effectiveness, it requires planning and management with the following important ingredients:

(1) to set-up objectives of skill development against broader organizational priority,

(2) to maintain a balance between the skill requirements of manufacturing, social and other growth inducing sectors,

(3) to acquire a good management system to plan, supervise and monitor the development and utilization of skilled persons.

Since the employees are the driving force for the development of the organization, attempts should be made to work through appropriate incentive systems and policy actions.

It is becoming increasingly fashionable to talk about building HR in the organization. The reasons are obvious. There are a number of ways through which organizations can bring change and create HR awareness to improve performance. These can be achieved by:

Identifying the most important opportunity and by introducing a practice already tested and implemented to improve operational performance.

Having put systems in place to create HR awareness, the challenge would be to implement it effectively for improving the performance of the employees.

HRD Applications in the Service Sector

There are now more sophisticated HRD applications which are being used by organizations. These among others, include preparation of the human resource inventory, human resource profile as well as human resource information system. It is of recent that human resource information system is playing an important role and creating HRI systems for different manpower groups. This has resulted in the development of various layers of human resource inventory.

To successfully, compete in new millennium, organizations need to reinvent HRD and the structure of the organization around explicit and implicit human resource information processes rather than based on traditional functions, because with globalization, it is the information system which will prove to be of paramount importance in any developmental activity.

Success will be determined by the speed with which organizations are able to study the changing scenario and their ability to introduce and implement human resource development processes and practices. The HRD methodology needs to introduce team spirit, harmonious work, integrity, accountability, visibility and a work culture. Similarly, the organization needs to develop a family environment where each employee feels equally empowered.

There are now two angles to HRD programmes. First to stop attrition and reduce rate of decay and second to win back employee loyalty through novel reward activities. This would mean that HRD intervention needs to be for each and every employee and also for the identification of individuals within the organization. There is an ancient Chinese proverb, which says "tell me and I will forget", "Show me and I will remember", "Involve me and I will understand". This should be the objective and concern of HRD planners in this new millennium.

As per the Human Development Report of UNDP, about 40 per cent GDP in India comes from services. In industrial countries this is close to 60 per cent. Therefore, we need to improve the effectiveness and efficiency of the services. The services that need to be improved come from strategic sector like Banks and Financial institutions, Insurance, Transportation (Rail, Road and Air), Telecommunications, Posts and Telegraphs, media including Radio, Television and Newspapers, Hotels, Municipal Services, Hospitals, Educational institutions, Government and the like.

Service sector in India is largely managed by the government. Generally, the railways, telecommunications and financial institutions are all managed by the government. The services sector besides being public managed is also characterized by the use of outdated technology, lack of professional management, bureaucratic structures, overstaffing, poor skill base and practically no HRD orientation.

Services Sector is one where employees are required to serve customers and the scope for influencing satisfaction both positively and negatively is high. Therefore, human relations, skill base, service orientation, positive attitudes among employee are very crucial.

What are the HRD Challenges faced by the service sector?

HRD philosophy is based on the premise that employees are the source and strength of an organization. They provide organizational intelligence and determine organization's strength and vitality. These attributes may be developed through training and job rotation, among others. Such analysis will facilitate better assessment, redesigning roles and will also fulfill accountability requirements.

Role of HRD[1]

The next question is about the role of HRD in developing the efficiency in the services sector. Taking telecommunications as example, HRD can play an important role. These are as follows:

(1) Transactional Analysis: As mentioned earlier when we deal with the services sector we are dealing with the human interfaces and here perceptions are very important. In fact, one can go to the extent of saying that where human beings are involved, perception is reality, the truth.

A Transaction Analysis exercise, specially to the employees of the telecom may be useful as a good starting point. When Mr. V. Krishnamurthy took over as the Chairman of Steel Authority of India, he conducted a series of exercises/training programmes for changing the work culture. Initially the employees took this in a very light hearted manner, but, in effect, after year or two, it was found that their mental attitudes underwent change. Therefore, the exercise in changing the work culture is a good starting point in providing the basic mind set.

(2) Training: In activities like telecom we are not only governed with the term mind set of the service provider but we are also concerned with technology. In areas like telecom, technology is changing very fast. We have a multiplicity of new technologies coming in and it is necessary that the employee is trained effectively. Today, in the telecom sector, we have 4.7 lakh employees and bulk of them were recruited and their pay scales were decided at the time when we had manual exchanges. But today electronic exchanges are in operation and a number of surplus employees are there. At the same time employee can not be retrenched as it is the government's social responsibility to provide for their career prospects. The unions have also been demanding that employee need to be given training for skill development. There is need for the restructuring of the organization. This indicates how technological changes call for the need for continuous upgradation of human resources in a services sector organization.

(3) New Technology for Better Service: May involve introduction of new technology. It is here that the HRD planners face a problem. It is a challenge for the HRD planners to face the transition.

We have seen the successful transition to computerization in the railway reservation system. At the same time we have also seen the resistance of the banking employees to computerization. So, upgrading the skills and to overcome the resistance is one of the important aspects for HRD planners. It is a means of improving the effectiveness or the efficiency of the employees, particularly in the services sector.

(4) Delegation to Encourage Initiative: Above all, there is a need for greater delegation. Without this, at the cutting edge, all HRD will have no value. Apart from the cultural aspect of the services sector a certain degree of organizational initiative to improve the characteristics of the sector is very vital.

(5) Participation: Another aspect of improving efficiency is training in better practices. In fact, an effective suggestion can be a method which would continuously involve the employees specially, at the cutting edge to think about the constructively.

(6) Incentive Schemes : Similarly, there is a need to introduce a system of incentives to the employees for efficient performance.

It is not enough to change the mind set and the organizational culture, it is not enough to increase the skills, but is necessary to provide, incentive schemes for employees to increase their efficiency.

HRD Approach for the Future

The concept of Human Development[2] (HD) as distinct from HRD looks at employees not as resource, but the target of development while HRD treats human beings primarily as an input in the production process, HD focuses on the formation of human capabilities in their own right. In this new perspective, all economic activities, including functioning of organizations, is not merely directed at economic growth but also to enable the employees to enjoy long healthy and creative lives.

Taking a cue from this paradigm shift at the macro-level, can HRD at organizational level be sooner or later transformed to HD at organizational level? This may well turn out to be a major challenge to the future of HRD interventions in organizations.

HRD approach realizes and recognizes that individual can be assisted through fitment, feedback, counselling, training as well as other appropriate organizational activities. It is a process which need to be undertaken by an organization to promote the intellectual, moral psychological, cultural and social development of the employees and also help him to achieve his potential as a resource. Such primacy of human resource over other resources is confirmed by what Johan D. Rockfeller once said; "I will pay more for the ability to deal with people than for any other commodity under the Sun". Realization of staff potential calls for use of certain techniques and skills. Principal techniques and skills are:

Role Analysis

Role analysis looks at each job not in isolation but as a part of whole set. It is an attempt to generate information/data. These attributes may be developed through training, job rotation and experience. Such role analysis will facilitate better fitment, redesigning roles and also fulfilling accountability requirements.

Goal Setting.

Every role in an organization is intended to contribute towards fulfillment of the organizational goal. Goals should be realistic and achievable.

Appraisal

Performance appraisal as the term indicates the task of assessment and evaluation of performance of an employee. This is intended to ascertain, among others, the level and quality of performance, gap and shortcomings, training needs, rewards and incentives. Commonly used instrument, confidential report can hardly serve the purpose objectively. Today, professional organizations depend on the performance appraisal system to evaluate the employees. Hence, it is necessary to understand the implications of the performance appraisal system and its dimensions. Determinants of performance are related to the following indicators:

- Determination and perseverance
- Consistency
- Expertise in analysis
- Courage of conviction
- Team work
- Responsibility
- The knowledge factor

One can carry out a self-assessment on the basis of these factors which are normally recorded in any performance appraisal. To be useful the system should provide both for performance appraisal, and potential appraisal.

Training Activities

Training is a major mechanism for development of human resource. According to Dunn and Stephens, training is the organization's efforts to improve the employees ability to perform a job or organizational goal. Many big banks have their own training arrangements. In their HRD consciousness there is a co-ordinated approach between the training institution and HRD division/department. As a result, large focus has gradually been on personality development, management development and organizational growth. Multi-tier programmes—branch, region and corporate level are also organized. Some of the banks have introduced innovations like mobile training teams which conduct spot programmes.

Sincere Approach

There is a growing appreciation about the importance of human resource as a key element in the organization. At times this finds place in the introductory part or concluding paragraph of the annual reports. Unless due opportunities are provided to the employees HRD will be contained in concept and discussions. Many a times a lot of deliberations go into HRD endeavour and action points are also made out. But implementation is half hearted. Elements which need attention in this context are:

- Human resource plan including training plan,
- Career plan and career opportunities,
- Staff welfare and participation,
- Changes in organizational culture.

Employees should have opportunities for growth and to enrich their skills. The environment should be open with accessibility to senior management.

Learning opportunities, for both the managerial and technical cadre would provide them with the requisite skills needed for building a managerial career.

Policies and Programmes for effective HRD

Personnel and HRD planners agree that organizations should have structured and well-communicated organizational policies which need to be implemented in a fair and just manner. Discretion, not discrimination should be the key factor in monitoring these policies.

In India, more often than not, the older generation was governed by the principle of loyalty to the leader and the organization, in that order. The younger generation is more inclined towards professional loyalty. This is especially true of the service industry in areas such as the hospitality industry, journalism, software, and to a certain extent accounts and personnel. They are willing to sacrifice all other goals to achieve their professional goals.

People are looking for more challenging work, more learning experiences and more money. According to Ravindran, since 9 out of 16 working hours are invested in the workplace, a little money cannot substitute for a positive work culture. Loyalty is about affiliation and being together, voluntarily.

A good work culture definitely entails high loyalty. The present generation is influenced by the work culture and environment of the organization, they work in. However, one question which faces us today is whether the current HRM policies and practices will be capable to face the future challenges?

Though we have a large personnel force, suitable personnel for undertaking specific jobs are lacking. This situation has arisen because the organizations have failed to identify new areas of specialization. Increasing reliance on consultants for many of the functions which are hitherto being done departmentally is a manifestation of this malady. Admittedly erosion of discipline is also a factor why organizations tend to throw the activities to the consultants from whom extraction of work is easier than an indisciplined employee. Non-availability of personnel having requisite skills is also a factor responsible for this shift.

To improve the situation, therefore, the first task is to identify different activities which the organization is supposed to perform, next step will be to train the employees in those activities and also streamline the system for better performance.

Do not neglect people and their strengths

The current HRM policies, among others, relate to the knowledge, skills and competencies of the personnel. When pooled together they provides unique strength to the organization which eventually provide the competitive advantage required to achieve the target. However, these competencies need to be acquired, developed and nurtured in a manner that minimizes conflicts and promotes synergy and harmony.

The strength of the organization is in its employees. If an organization pays attention to its human resource aspect, it is bound to succeed. Excellence at work due to devotion to duty would help the organization to achieve these objectives. The excellence is an inner attitude. This inner consciousness is to be enlightened by ensuring that the day to day problems of the employees are completely taken care of by the organization.

The need is therefore, to develop the role efficacy of the employees on the following dimensions:

(i) Self-suggestion: Use self-suggestion, develop expertise and learn the best possible skill to perform the role effectively, develop awareness and always be conscious of the basic contribution made by the employees to the organizational objectives.

(2) Integration: A self-revealing exercise of one's strengths, weaknesses, opportunities and threats (SWOT) needs to be conducted. It will improve performance.

(3) Pro-activity and creativity: Since the jobs to be performed are routine type of jobs, new ideas need to be developed.

(4) Inter-role linkage and helping relationships: Will identify the areas of coordination with the employees concerned and identify the kind of help required from them?

Training of Employees: As Dr. S. Radhakrishnan pointed out, "the mind that invented the atom bomb is more powerful than the atom bomb itself". So, when you look at building the organization, you should think of optimizing its human resource potential through appropriate training and in order to meet the future challenges the organization needs to take care of the employees and put them to optimal use by developing their competencies. This can be done by taking the following steps:

(1) Devote sufficient time to employees

Dr. Stephen Covey mentions in his book "7 Habits of effective people" that "of the three kinds of assets—Physical, Financial, Human, human assets are the most important and often the most neglected." This is very true of most of the organizations as they are generally bogged down by 4 Ms i.e. Materials, Machines, Money and Methods and often do not devote adequate attention to men and leave HRM completely to personnel branch forgetting that they are also the responsibility of the organization.

Thus, inadequate attention to human resource is one of the reasons for lack of discipline, interference of trade unions, low level of morale and motivation, poor quality, among others. Therefore, the organizations need to devote sufficient time for human resource planning and development.

(2) Give respect, not mere popularity

It has been observed that due to populist decisions work culture of the organizations has deteriorated. It is, therefore, time to take the right decision which may lead to unpopularity but which will earn the respect of employees within the organization.

(3) The Organization must send the message that "we care"

A very strong signal needs to be sent down the line that WE CARE. This will go a long way in creating satisfaction among employees. It has been recognized that body language conveys more than oral communication.

(4) Select employees with right attitude

The organization needs to ensure that the skills and attitude of the employee matches with the requirement of the job.

(5) Organize need based training

(i) Employees should be given Induction training.

(ii) Each employee needs to undergo refresher repromotional course once in 5 years.

(6) Today HRM is treated as

"Important, But not Urgent" HRM need to be treated as urgent. Only then the present work culture of the organization will change.

(7) The Management of Relationships is the Key of Survival

Indian people being highly emotional attach a lot of importance to this variable. This helps in bringing best out of the person. Therefore, there is need to develop true relationship of care, trust and help amongst the employees so that the organization can overcome all challenges.

(8) A Caring but Result Oriented Approach is Needed

This factor has an immense potentiality in creating human resource development but unfortunately is being ignored at all levels within the organization. This could be the root cause of failure of HRM policies.

With this background, the organizations need to introspect and identify their strength and weaknesses and suggest remedial measures.

This would entail realization that employees without motivation is not an asset rather a liability, only a resourceful and motivated employee is an asset. Therefore, the organization needs to:

Motivate the employees

It is the most important tool for encouraging human potentiality for better output but unfortunately, not effectively used.

Utilize unions creatively

Unions do play positive role by bringing out the employees problems which are mostly the result of managerial indifference as such they are to be used in positive manner.

Discipline is indispensable, maintain it at all cost

Discipline is essential. It helps in the output of the employees and helps in establishing the work culture and environment within the organization.

Plan for supervisory development

Selection and training of operational employees, who play important role in dealing with employees at different levels is almost being done casually without proper planning. This needs to be reviewed.

Change attitude

Today, organizations have an attitude of indifference at lower level, play ignorant at middle level and close eyes at higher level. This has to change and the organizations have to demonstrate that they care and are interested in the well being of the employees and the organization.

A recent study has shown that 75 per cent of senior employees have been found to be 'skill-strong but value-weak', says Rajender S. Dabas, leading management consultant and former vice-president (HRD) of Hero Honda Motors.

According to Jones the Western concept is management based on material achievement. The Indian approach to management is to first develop oneself and then strive for other goals.

However, there is yet to emerge a universal acceptance of this new form of management. Many even question the Indianness of this managerial concept.

The Japanese success is primarily motivated by nationalism and excellence to the extent that employees are regarded less as individual and more as collaborators in a project.

In the opinion of Palhan, "Everybody has skills but the ability to harness them without getting stressed is something we have to strive for."

The Western management is guided by three basic principles survival, growth and profitability. Gurus like Peter Drucker, Tom Peter or Lee Lacocca seldom lay stress on human values like honesty, integrity, truthfulness, cooperation and brotherhood. Material achievement and consumerism have resulted in social deviance in the West. Therefore, divorces, violence child abuse are rampant. Adds Prof. Narag of Delhi University's Faculty of Management, "Modern managements must address themselves to work-related problems of its employees. The technique should be value based and not merely skill based."

In fact, what was perceived as a fad just a few years ago is now turning into a reality. Many international experts are taking a second and more serious look at Indian style of management. A style not born out of lust, greed, consumption and killing competition but one which has its foundations in spiritualism and religious literature.

It is all about managing intangibles for tangible gains. In the New Knowledge Economy, value is created not by capital, land or labour, but by knowledgeable workers.

An Overview of Future Organizations

What we need today is the Western efficiency and dynamism, Japanese obsession for excellence through team spirit, and the Indian attitude of dedicated service. From this combination of western beginning and Indian ending, will emerge the future Human Resources, who can promote material progress guided by spiritual enrichment.

Tomorrow's organizations will have to manage the knowledge within their organization, capture best practices, formalize it and make it available to employees within the organizations. "Knowledge resides between the ears of the individuals and walks on a pair of legs". Physical assets, unlike knowledge assets, are replaceable. Often, people use innovation management interchangeably with knowledge management. Technically, of course, the two are different but innovation is the natural result of managing knowledge. "Knowledge management is important in industries where R and D is high, product life cycles are getting shorter and products need to be more innovative."

However, in recent years organizations have become complex. Increasing employees' demand, higher level of competition, shrinking loyalties and shortage of super-specializations have made the situation more complex.

New labour market policy (flexibility and responsiveness) has become key factors for the 1990's forcing organizations to reorient themselves with information technology (IT) acting as an enabler, it is now possible to have an integrated process about the HRD and all the allied processes related to the organization.

HRD enabled by advances in technology, aims to develop among others human resource information system linking employees with the capacity and capability of the organization.

Over a period of time HRD has moved from just a support function to an essential tool of the decision making process. It was earlier used to automate routine functions that broadly involved replacing clerical systems and administrative savings. However, the present system needs to look within the organization, i.e., the organization needs to listen to the employee, capture their ideas and make them a reality.

The first step is to explain the idea, see the benefit of this idea. Every idea needs nurturing and protection. The employee who believes in the idea will carry the idea forward.

The other aspect of HRD is open minded and forward thinking employees. Employees are to be exposed to the outside world, because without exposure, it is difficult for any employee to be brilliant. For example, there is no single artist who has lived all his life in the four walls of his house and been able to paint beautiful portraits and paintings. Artists travel, they go to the countryside, they talk to people and then they come out with ideas. The organization should try to give its employees as much exposure as possible.

At the gates of Harvard University, it is written "The Sky Is The Limit." It indicates that do not confine yourselves, do not believe that there is a barrier, and do not believe there is an end to it.

Egalitarianism, is the latest H R mantra in the corporate world. The first and most important area of thrust; is HR-related issues. "Understanding of human issues will play an extremely important role in future" and because of this realization around 40 per cent of time is being spent on HR related issues."

Appraisal systems across the organizations are being revamped to meet changing organizational environment and restructured portfolio.

Of course, every organization in this new millennium should be capable of meeting the challenges posed by the value system and environmental effect as a phenomenon. No organization can isolate itself from the development all around but the tasks of coping with the changes with all the attendant benefits and risk will remain an issue with the organizations.

The world today is characterized by its dynamism, with the constant process of change, its impact is being felt virtually on each and every organization and profession. In this environment, the task before every organization, particular with services sector organizations is to cope with the change by constantly redefining its human resource policies and visions.

The great theme at the conclusion of the 20th century is the triumph of individual and individual's responsibility. It is a westernized version of the Indian dogma KARMA, that every action generates consequences the actor will eventually face. The new responsibility of the organization is to reward the initiative of the individual through HRD practices and programmes.

"The organizational asset of the new millennium is its employee, not computers, robotics or automation", Says Dr. Kuezmaski. Fortunately, organizations in India are gradually assimilating this fact.

The performance of the organizations or employees need to be measured not only by economic outcomes but must go beyond the requisites of competence. The ethical behaviour of the employees also need to be based on an interpretation of the application of values. In industrialized countries, value-system is a part of the organizational culture. Indian organizations also need to develop value statements that should emphasize commitment, discipline, quality, openness and responsibility. This is the first step towards the organizational culture and ethos.

Further, the organizational policies and strategies need to be based on integrity, as reflected in the value and work culture as integrity is the foundation of ethical behaviour and good governance and the code of conduct is its tools. The code of ethics should serve the following purposes.

- Provide guidance to employees on ethical issues.
- Provide the basis for appraising and evaluating activities of the employees.
- Provide professional ethics.
- Provide values in action or operation.

To make services sector organizations more effective, the following suggestions are made:

A code of ethical conduct may be developed, aimed at building the organization on the basis of trust, honesty and integrity and also spell out conditions of employment at each level and make clear what the organization believes in, what the organization owes to the employees and inturn the obligations of employees to the organization. Organizations need to assess these on a continuing basis and plan human resource skills, accordingly.

Organizations also need to aim at developing employee skills at various levels within the organization. Employees need to be given proper training and also have information to take decisions on their own.

Responsibility, authority need to be clear for an organization to run smoothly. Mere restructuring will not help the organization, unless technology is harmonized with the existing human resource skills.

The human element is a factor that has always had a special place in the organization. Several management theorists have held the view that understanding human behaviour is the key to the success of the organization. Douglas McGregor was one such theorist. He argued that behind every organizational decision or action are assumptions about human nature and human behaviour. The nature of these assumptions then determines the way the organization responds to the task of managing the employees.

He is of the opinion that employees seek responsibility; that they desire achievement and have psychological need to work.

Above these requirements he placed 'social needs'. Above social needs he placed the needs relating to an individual's self-esteem, or "egoistic needs". And right on top came the need for self fulfilment, which would allow an individual to realize his full potential.

An organization that looks only at material need would be able to meet employees physiological and security needs. But it would not be adequate to meet the employees social needs or egoistic needs, let alone allow the employee to reach his full potential.

In order to address the higher needs of the employee, the organization needs an alternative set of assumptions. McGregor defined six such basic assumptions.

(1) An employee does not necessarily dislike work. Work may be a source of satisfaction or punishment.

(2) External control and the threat of punishment are not essential for performance. An employee will display self-direction and self-control if he is committed to organizational objectives.

(3) Commitment to objectives is influenced by the rewards associated with an achievement, particularly rewards such as the satisfaction of the ego and self-realization.

(4) The average employee learns to seek responsibility.

(5) The capacity to be creative in solving organizational problems is widely distributed in the organization.

(6) Under modern industrial life only a part of the intellectual potential of the employee is being utilized.[4]

As McGregor himself recognized this set of assumptions was not perfect. But he did serve to point to two broad trends that can be seen even in contemporary organization. The HRD planners need to introspect into the issues of the organization and the employees to meet the challenges of the new millennium.

References

1. Vittal, N., "Role of HRD to Improve the Efficiency and Effectiveness of the Service Sector" in T.V. Rao et. al. (ed) *HRD in the New Economic Environment.* Tata McGraw Hill Pub. Co. Ltd., New Delhi, 1996.
2. Dr. Surinder Batra, Designing HRD interventions Centre for Interative Management India, New Delhi.
3. A, Thyagarajan, "Appraise Your way-up", *The Economic Times,* 28 June, 1999.
4. Management Classics, Theory X, Theory Y by Narendar Pani, published in *The Financial Times,* New Delhi, Sunday 18 July 1999.

Annexure I

Vocationalization of Education

K.K. Khullar

Introduction

Vocationalization of education has been identified as a priority area in educational planning. Together with skill formation and technical education it is one of the strongest components of human resource development.

In India vocational education and training is being imparted through the following institutions at diploma level:

(a) Polytechnics
(b) Industrial Training Institutes (ITIs)
(c) Craft Schools
(d) Agricultural Schools
(e) Forestry Schools
(f) Nursing Schools
(g) Commercial Training Schools
(h) Within the School System at +2 level

At degree level

At the first Degree level, the University Grants Commission launched a scheme in 1994-95 for starting vocational courses in identified colleges and institutions.

The National Policy on Education—1986 as updated in 1992 accords a very high priority to vocationalization at +2 stage for enhancing individual employability, reducing mis-match between demand and supply of skilled manpower and providing an alternative to those pursuing higher education aimlessly and without any purpose. The policy has set a target of diverting 10 per cent of students at +2 level by 1995 and 25 per cent by 2000 A.D. For this purpose a centrally sponsored scheme has been launched since 1988. The scheme is in operation in about 6000 schools to enhance the employability of the students. A collaborative venture with the national institute of Fashion Technology for introduction of fashion technology courses in schools has been worked out.

The vocational courses are selected on the basis of vocational surveys, registration in the employment exchanges and a general assessment of manpower needs made under District Development plans. The curricula of the courses is generally need-based and socially relevant. Normally 70 per cent of the instructional time is devoted to vocational theory and practice. On-the-job training is a part of the curricula. The remaining time is given for learning of languages and general foundation course.

Polytechnic Education

There are at present more than a thousand (1011 in 1995) polytechnics offering diploma level courses in number of trades. Outside the school system they are, alongwith ITI's, the main institutions of vocational education. These polytechnics were thoroughly revamped recently throughout the country with the assistance of World Bank, with a view to upgrading its capacity, quality and efficiency. The main thrust of World Bank Project's is women's education by creating 9200 additional places for women in polytechnics by establishing 39 new women's polytechnics besides providing seats for women in Co-ed. polytechnics. The total in-take capacity of polytechnics in India is 1.64 lakh. These polytechnics are run by the Technical Education Department of the State Governments.

Industrial Training Institutes (ITIs)

The ITI's are under the Ministry of Labour. At present there are 2721 government and private ITI's with a seating capacity of 4.07 lakh students imparting training in 42 engineering and

22 non-engineering trades. The period of training varies from trade to trade extending between one to three years while entry qualifications vary from Class VIII to Class XII. On the completion of the course a National Trade Certificate is awarded which qualifies the candidates for subordinate jobs both in and outside the Government.

Capacity Vs Requirement

The total in-take capacity of both polytechnics and ITI's is 5.7 lakh. Added to this is the number generated by special schools and the extent of vocationalization within the education system. By the end 1996-97 the total number was 9.35 lakh students which is about 11.5 per cent while the target is diversion of 25 per cent by 2000 A.D. There are 16.24 crores (162 million) school-going children in India in the age group 6-14* drop-out before reaching class V and 60 per cent before reaching class VIII, it is open for discussion whether the school-based system of vocational education in the country being followed will meet the requirements. The answer is 'No'. Thus, it is obvious that non-formal vocational system should be resorted to. The success stories of countries like Japan, Indonesia. South Korea, China in vocationalization and skill formation at a macro-level illustrates this point.

The Tamil Nadu Experiment

In the Indian state of Tamil Nadu the system of vocational education is innovative, flexible and is distinct from terminal competency. It is based on centrally designed courses by NCERT. In 1990, the state had 24 per cent of the students at higher secondary level diverted to vocational education i.e., 96,000 students against a total of about 3.85 lakh. In 1990-91 the state had 68 vocational courses, within the school education system. Today the number is much more.

Vigyan Ashram Experiment at Pabal : Pune : Maharashtra

The centre at Pabal has developed itself into a community resource by training the students of Class IX and X to learn the technical skills required for the community in a wider context. These skills include metal work, electronical work, plumbing, auto-mechanics, construction work, pest control, vegetables, biogas, solar cooker, poultry, dairy, forestry, etc.

Earn-while you Learn Scheme

Many states in India have started this scheme where the requirements of the school are prepared in the school itself by the students itself such as ink-making, chalk-making, Tat-Pattis, cane baskets, registers, exercise books, etc. The result has been very reassuring. Student leave the school richer than when they came. The joy of having a bank account by the school students cannot be described. The scheme has given a new boost to vocationalization at all stages of education.

Minimum Vocational Competencies

The NCERT over the years has developed minimum vocational competencies based curricula for about 80 vocational courses in 6 major areas viz. Agriculture, Business and Commerce, Engineering and Technology, Home Science and Humanities. These are available to the states/UT's for adoption/ adaption or adaptation. Instructional material has been published for these courses. Several vocational packages have been supplied to the schools for implementation and even experimentation.

Vocationalization—a Distinct Stream

Another important issue which is engaging the minds of the educationists in developing countries is whether it should be adopted as a distinct stream or should continue as part of the general education. The National Policy on Education—1986 advocated a systematic, well-planned programme of vocational education which would be a distinct stream intends to prepare students for identified occupations. It envisaged that vocational courses would ordinarily be provided at +2 level but flexibility would be provided to start vocational education after class VIII. The revised policy formulations (1992) envisage students at higher secondary level being imparted generic vocational courses which cut across several occupational fields and which are not occupation-specific.

Craftsmen Training Scheme

The Craftsmen Training Scheme was started in 1950 under the National Vocational Training System with a view to imparting training in various vocational trades to meet the skilled manpower requirements. The skill training is being imparted both in engineering and non-engineering trades. For engineering trades higher secondary qualifications are necessary and for non-engineering trades middle school is elementary education qualifications are necessary. Apart from ITI's there are Industrial Training Centres (ITCs), both Government and non-government.

Apprenticeship Training

Consistent with the National Policy on Education—1986, the Apprentices Act was amended so as to provide training to the students of vocational courses at +2 level by placing them in real work situations in farms and industries. The scheme is being administered by the Ministry of Labour through four Regional Boards of Apprenticeship Training (BOAT). 20 subject fields were notified for such training initially and 40 more were approved. Despite this the number of actual trainees remained small.

Pre-vocational Courses

In view of the fact that about 80 per cent children do not go beyond class X, resulting into a large force of unskilled labourers, the government has started in 1993-94 a centrally sponsored scheme of Pre-Vocational Education Scheme at lower secondary level with the objective of imparting training to students of Class IX and X in simple markettable skills, to develop vocational interests and aptitudes, to inculcate in them the dignity of labour as a pre-entry into the world of work and to facilitate the students in choosing the desired vocational courses at +2 stage.

Vocationalization at first degree level

In 1994-95 the University Grants Commission started the scheme of vocationalization at first degree level over 700 colleges and 32 universities have so far been supported for starting vocational courses. 53 subjects have been identified out of which 1-3 subjects are recommended to be introduced. These subjects include Archaelogy, Museology, Functional Hindi, Sanskrit and English, Insurance, Tax procedures, Foreign Trade, Sales Promotion, Computer Application, Nutrition, Food Processing, Bio-technology, Micro-biology, Seed technology, Sericulture, Fishing, Office Management, Mass Communication, Industrial chemistry, Audio-visual, Rural technology, Refrigeration, Air-Conditioning, Water management, Environment, etc.

Infrastructure

A large infrastructure has been created for vocationalization of education. A Central Institute of Vocational Education has been set up at Bhopal in 1993 to provide technical and academic support to the programme in states and the centre. This has resulted into various imbalances such as irrelevance of courses lack of focus on relevant areas, lack of trained teachers, unwillingness of the industry to accept the products of vocational education and above all lack of social acceptability. In the words the vocationalization of education in India has suffered because of weak management structure, slow releases of funds to schools, inadequacy of placements even after apprenticeship. To put this vast infrastructure to proper use has engaged the attention for the Government and ways and means are being found to involve industry more fruitfully.

Issues for Discussion

The "Nationwide Debate on Vital Issues of Education" published by the Ministry of HRD (Department of Education) in 1995 lists the following issues for discussion in the context of vocationalization of education:

(1) Whether the school system of vocational education being followed in the country is suitable to meet the current requirements.

(2) Whether separate vocational institutions should be set up at each block level. These could offer two year courses

equivalent to +2 level, as well as courses of flexible duration for school drop-outs at various levels;

(3) Whether the institutions like polytechnics and ITI s should be preferred to the school-based vocational education programme being run currently;

(4) Whether presently existing vocational institutes including polytechnics/it should be "adopted" by industry;

(5) Whether the academic stature of vocational courses should be raised to the degree level instead of diplomas being awarded now".

To these, one more may be added;

(6) Whether the UGC's scheme for vocationalization at First Degree level in colleges/institutes should be continued and expanded.

Measures Facilitating Employment

These include the following:

(1) Equivalence of Certificates

(2) Amendment in Recruitment Rules

(3) Vocational Guidance

(4) Linkages with other Agencies/Departments/Industrial houses

(5) Self-employment

(6) Research Linkages

(7) Linkages between Formal and non-Formal Vocational Courses

(8) Vocational programmes for handicapped sector, minorities and other special groups;

(9) Vocational Education Programmes for Girls

(10) Vocational programmes through NGO's and Voluntary Organization

In short vocational education is the core of HRD and has to be provided not only through polytechnics and it is and Craft Schools, both within and outside the educational system but also has to cater to the needs of special groups such as the handicapped (deaf, dumb, blind, etc.) girls, women. The disabled people form a significant sector of society who have practically no means to acquire skills to make a dignified livelihood. There is also need to start and strengthen non-formal vocational training. At the same time vocational education has also to be provided through open learning system like Open Schools and Open Universities.

Involvement of Voluntary Agencies

The role of voluntary agencies in conducting innovative programmes of vocational education cannot be over-emphasized. The centrally sponsored scheme provides for assistance to selected voluntary organizations for experimental projects, short-term vocational projects and programmes in hilly areas, rural and backward areas, training of vocational teachers. The pattern of assistance ranges from 50 to 100 per cent.

Programmes for Women

Under this Programme, a National Vocational Training Institute for Women has been established at Noida as Apex body and Regional branches have been set up at Mumbai, Bangalore, Thiruvananthapuram, Hissar, Calcutta, Tura, Allahabad, Indore, Vadodara and Jaipur. The objective is to provide equal or comparable facilities in vocational education and skill formation to women. Thousands of women have been benefitted as a result of such training. Besides regular training there are ad-hoc and short-term training programmes as well. At present more than 200 recognized technical institutions in the country at the first degree level and more than a thousand at diploma level with admission capacity of 40,000 and one and a half lakh students respectively (1.64 lakh to be exact). Facilities for Master and Doctoral Programmes in Engineering and Technology have been created in 140 institutions with an in-take capacity of more than 10,000 per year. This network includes IIT's (Indian Institutes of Technology), REC (Regional Engineering and Technology), specialized institutions in Mining, Architecture, Industrial Engineering, Foundary and IIM's (Indian Institutes of Managements).

The National Policy on Education - 1986 as updated in 1992 accords a very high priority to improving the standard of technical education. 15 new schemes have been started for this purpose. The All India Council of Technical Education which is the apex body has been given a statutory status to ensure standards of technical education in the country. It has been vested with legal powers to grant recognition to technical education institutions and accreditation. Some of the issues requiring attention in the field of technical education are:

(a) Mis-match between the demand and supply, between the requirements of the industry and traditional curriculum leading to under employment and unemployment of graduates;

(b) Brain Drain (about 20 per cent)

(c) Wastage (between 20 and 30 per cent)

(d) Weak linkages between industry and education

(e) Modernization and removal of obsolescence and upgrading the infrastructural facilities

(f) Low budget support

Various steps have been taken in regard to the national development and the challenges of the 21st century.

Annexure II

Institutes Imparting Higher Education

(Listed on the basis of Occupational Categories)

Division 01 Professional, Technical and Related Workers

Groups 02 Architects, Engineers, Technologists and Surveyors

- Institute of Development Studies (IDS) (Mysore)

  Ph.D. and Masters degree in Urban Planning and regional planning, development planning, agricultural marketing and management, Diploma in environmental planning and other non-degree courses.

- Bureau of Public Enterprises (BPE) New Delhi.

  In-Service training programmes for managerial personnel at all levels in collaboration with the premier training institutes.

05 Life Scientists

- Afro-Asian Rural Reconstruction Organization (AARRO), New Delhi.

  Specialized training programme in rural development, agriculture, land reform and rural industry.

- Agricultural Economics Research Centre (Delhi).

- Agro-Economic Research Centre in Jorhat (Assam).
- Bisbhum, (West.Bengal).
- Agro-Economic Research Centre (Vallabh Vidyanagar).
- Asian Institute for Rural Development (AIRD) (Bangalore)
  Training in agrarian reform and rural development in tropical sericulture, training in silkworm seed production.
- Birla Institute of Technology and Science (BITS) (Rajasthan)
  Ph.D. Masters and Certificate training programmes in the field of science and technology, public administration, business economics and industry.
- Central Food Technological Research Institute (Mysore)
  Ph.D. and M.Sc. in food technology, short-term orientation course in various areas of food science and technology.
- Chandra Sekhar Azad University of Agriculture and Technology (Kanpur)
  Ph.D. in agriculture, veterinary science and home science.
- Department of Agricultural Economics (Rajasthan)
  Ph.D. programme with course on micro-economic theory, farm management, production economics, agricultural markets, agricultural development and policy, operation research methods and econometrics, M.Sc. Programme and basic course for undergraduates.
- Faculty of Agricultural Economics and Cooperation, (Nainital)

Agricultural marketing, farm management and production economics, agricultural finance, rural sociology.

- Faculty of Agriculture (Annamalai Nagar) Undertake Postgraduate level teaching on agricultural economics, B.Sc., M.Sc., and Ph.D. in agriculture.
- Indian Agricultural Statistics Research Institute (IASR), New Delhi
  Ph.D. and M.Sc. in agricultural statistics; M.Sc. in Computer Application in agriculture, full time training course on use of computers in agricultural research, short-term refresher courses in agricultural statistics.

09 Scientific, Medical and Technical Persons and Others

- National Institute of Health and Family Welfare (NIHFW) (New Delhi)
  Conducts two-year postgraduate degree course in community health administration, refresher courses for IAS officers, in-service training courses for various categories of health services personnel, e.g., hospital management, health and medical care management, materials management in hospital and nursing leadership, educational technology.

10 Mathematicians, Statisticians and Related Workers

- Chatrapati Shahu Central Institute of Business Education and Research (Kolhapur). Courses offered include graduate and M.Com day programme, graduate MBA, MCM, MSN and MEM day programmes, graduate evening programmes in computer programming, M.Phil and Ph.D. programmes and management development programmes.

11 Economists and Related Workers

- Delhi School of Economics (Delhi).
  M.A., M. Phil and Ph.D. in Economics.
- Department of Business and Industrial Management (Surat)
  Master's Degree in Business Administration/ Business Management.
- Department of Economics and Sociology (Punjab)
- Faculty of Commerce and Management Studies (Shimla)
  Courses offered include MBA, M.Com. and M. in Philosophy, day programmes and graduate RGDM & IW evening programmes.
- Gokhale Institute of Politics and Economics (Pune)
  Ph.D. and M.A. Economics, M. Phil and conducts refresher courses in economics for college and university teachers in the Western Region of India.

13 Social Scientists and Related Workers

- A.N. Sinha Institute of Social Studies (Patna).
  Methodological Courses in Social Sciences, Management Courses, refresher courses, research tools and quantitative analysis.
- Afro-Asian Rural Reconstruction Organization (AARRO)
- Bharatiasan Institute of Management (Tiruchirapalli)
  Offers graduate MBA day programme and management development programmes.
- Biotechnology Centre (New Delhi)
  Training manpower on plant molecular bio-technology, bio-engineering.

- Department of Business Administration (Guwahati)
  Courses offered include graduate MBA day and evening programmes.
- Department of Humanities and Social Sciences (Kanpur)
  Ph.D. Programmes in Economics, English language, English literature, philosophy, psychology and sociology.
- Department of Sociology (Chandigarh)
  Post Graduate Programme in Sociology, M. Phil, Ph.D. programmes in development studies, population studies, stratification, education, peasantry entrepreneurship.
- Faculty of Economics (Haryana)
  M.A., M. Phil, and Ph.D. in Economics
- Giri Institute of Development Studies (Lucknow)
  Doctoral programmes in economics, political science and sociology and training programmes on methodological and development subjects.
- Gokhale Institute of Politics and Economics (Pune)
  Ph.D. and M.A. Economics, M. Phil and conducts refresher courses in economics for college and university teachers in the Western Region of India
- Indian Institute of Education (Pune)
  Offers Post-graduate M. Phil and Ph.D. Degrees in education and conducts adult education classes.

14 Exporters and Foreign Trade Experts

Indian Institute of Foreign Trade (New Delhi). Offers two-years Master programme in international business, one year post-graduate diploma programme in international trade, certificate course in export marketing and import management for Mongolian Republic, workshop on framework conditions for Indian exports in collaboration with Indo-German Chamber of Commerce, executive development programme on different aspects of foreign trade for Indian exporting community, and tailor made programmes for economic ministries and Ministry of External Affairs.

- Institute of Management Studies (Indore) Courses offered include a graduate MBA day programme, a graduate evening MBA programme, a graduate evening diploma programme in marketing management and management development programme for sponsored company executives.
- Institute of Social Sciences (Uttar Pradesh) M.A., M. Phil, in Sociology, M. in Social Work, M.A and M. Phil in Statistics, Computer application.
- International Institute for Population Sciences (Mumbai)
  Ph.D., M.Phil, Master and Certificate Courses in population studies.
- Kausali Institute of Management Studies (Dharwad).
  Offers a graduate MBA day programme.
- Management Development Institute (New Delhi)
  Training programmes for general participation in company and sponsored, main areas of activity in the field of industrial management of industry and development banks, Offer part-time diploma courses in management

and certificate courses in development banking and hotel management.

- National Institute of Personnel Management (NIPM) (Calcutta)
  Conduct Post-graduate diploma examination in personnel management.
- Population Studies Centre (Tirupati)
  Provides post-graduate teaching on population, population education leading to M.Phil and Ph.D.
- Prin. L.N. Wellington Institute of Management Development and Research (Mumbai)
  Courses offered include MMS day programmes, graduate evening programme leading to MMM and MAM degrees.
- School of International Studies (New Delhi)
  M.A. and Ph.D.

15 Managers

- Symbosis Institute of Engineers Management (Pune)
  Courses offered include under-graduate evening programme leading to a DMM Diploma for undergraduates/graduates and graduate MBA and MPM day programmes as well as graduate evening programmes leading to DBM and MMS Degrees.
- TA PAI Management Institute (Manipal)
  Graduate PGDM day programme and management development programmes.
- Tata Institute of Social Sciences (TISS) (Mumbai)
  M.A. in Social Work, Personnel Management, Industrial Relations and Labour Relations, Post-graduate certificate in research methodology, Master of Philosophy in Social

Work and Social Sciences, Ph.D. in Social Work and Social Sciences.

Xavier Institute of Management (Bhubaneswar)

Courses offered include graduate MBA day and evening programmes, and management development programmes. Two years full-time courses in personnel management and industrial relations, labour relations, two and three years courses in business management and management development programmes.

Annexure III

Research and Training Institutes General

- Central Electrochemical Research Institute, Karaikudi
- Central Electronics Engineering Research Institute, Rajasthan
- Central Food Technological Research Institute, Mysore.
- Central Fuel Research Institute, Bihar
- Central Glass and Ceramic Research Institute, Calcutta
- Central Institute of Medicinal and Aromatic Plants, Lucknow
- Central Leather Research Institute, Chennai
- Central Mechanical Engineering Research Institute, Durgapur
- Central Mining Research Institute, Bihar
- Central Road Research Institute, Delhi
- Central Salt and Marine Chemicals Research Institute, Bhavnagar
- Central Scientific Instruments Organization, Chandigarh
- Centre for Biochemicals Technology, Delhi
- Centre for Cellular and Molecular Biology, Hyderabad
- Indian Institute of Chemical Biology, Calcutta
- Indian Institute of Chemical Technology, Hyderabad
- Indian Institute of Petroleum, Dehra Dun
- Industrial Toxicology Research Centre, Lucknow

- Institute of Microbial Technology, Chandigarh
- National Aerospace Laboratories, Bangalore
- National Botanical Research Institute, Lucknow
- National Chemical Laboratory, Pune
- National Environmental Engineering Research Institute, Maharashtra
- National Geophysical Research Institute, Hyderabad
- National Institute of Oceanography, Goa
- National Institute of Science, Technology and Development Studies, New Delhi
- National Metallurgical Laboratory, Jamshedpur
- National Physical Laboratory, New Delhi
- Regional Research Laboratory, Orissa
- Regional Research Laboratory, Jammu & Kashmir
- Regional Research Laboratory, Jorhat
- Regional Research Laboratory, Bhopal
- Regional Research Laboratory, Trivandrum
- Structural Engineering Research Centre, Ghaziabad

Agriculture, Fisheries and Veterinary Sciences

- Agro-Economic Research Centre, West Bengal
- Central Arid Zone Research Institute, Jodhpur
- Central Inland Capture Fisheries Research Institute, West Bengal
- Central Rice Research Institute, Orissa
- Central Tobacco Research Institute, Andhra Pradesh
- Forest Research Institute, Dehra Dun
- Indian Agricultural Statistics Research Institute, New Delhi
- Indian Council of Agricultural Research (ICAR), New Delhi
- Indian Plywood Industries Research Institute, Bangalore
- Indian Veterinary Research Institute, Izatnagar (U.P.)
- National Dairy Research Institute, Haryana

- National Sugar Institute, UP
- Rubber Research Institute of India, Kerala
- Vasantdada Sugar Institute, Maharashtra

Education

- Indian Institute of Advanced Study, Shimla
- Indian Psychometric and Educational Research Association, Patna
- To promote and develop the study of, and undertake research into, psychology, education, statistics, etc.
- National Council of Educational Research and Training with the aim of improving school education, academic adviser to the Ministry of Human Resource Development: Co-ordinates research and development in all branches of education; organizes pre- and in-service training; publishes school textbooks; six constituent units: National Institute of Education, Central Institute of Educational Technology and 4 regional colleges of education in Ajmer, Bhopal, Bhubaneswar and Mysore.

Medicine

- B.M. Institute of Mental Health, Ahmedabad
- Cancer Research Institute, Mumbai
- Central Jalma Institute for Leprosy, Agra
- Central Leprosy Teaching and Research Institute, Tamil Nadu
- Central Research Institute, Himachal Pradesh, Medical Research graduate and post-graduate training, manufacture of biological products;
- Haffkine Institute for Training Research and Testing, Mumbai, Principal Centre of Research in Communicable Diseases, Biomedical and allied sciences in India.
- Indian Brain Research Association, Calcutta
- Indian Council of Medical Research, New Delhi

- Institute of Child Health, Calcutta
- King Institute of Preventive Medicine, Chennai Postgraduate Training in Microbiology
- National Institute of Communicable Diseases, Delhi, Research and training centre in field of communicable and water-borne diseases
- National Institute of Nutrition, Hyderabad
- Pasteur Institute and Medical Research Institute, Assam
- Pasteur Institute of India, Tamil Nadu
- Vallabhbai Patel Chest Institute, Delhi, Post-graduate teaching and research in respiratory diseases and allied biomedical sciences
- Vector Control Research Centre, Pondicherry

Natural Sciences (General)

- Bose Institute, Calcutta
- Indian Association for the Cultivation of Science, Calcutta Research in theoretical physics, spectroscopy, material science, solid state physics, physical chemistry, biological chemistry, energy research unit, polymer science unit, organic and inorganic chemistry
- Raman Research Institute, Bangalore
- Tata Institute of Fundamental Research, Mumbai, Fundamental Research in pure and applied mathematics, physics and astro-physics, cosmic rays and solar physics, nuclear physics, chemical physics, solid state physics, low temperature physics, radio-astronomy and space astronomy, molecular biology, solid state electronics, computer science, speech recognition.
- UNESCO Regional Office for Science and Technology for South and Central Asia, Vasant Vihar, Co-operates with national and regional organizations; activities in three main areas: science and technology for development, science for progress and the environment, environment and natural resources management.

Biological Sciences

- Birbal Sahni Institute of Palaeobotany, Lucknow, Scientific Research on the fundamental and applied aspects of fossil plants and their bearing on the origins of life; evolutionary linkages; biostratigraphy; fossil fuel exploration, phytogeography and biodignosis; repository of fossil plants
- Botanical Survey of India, Calcutta
- Indian Association of Systematic Zoologists, Calcutta
- Institute of Plant Industry, Madhya Pradesh
- Tropical Botanic Garden and Research Institute, Kerala
- Zoological Survey of India, Calcutta.

Mathematical Sciences

- Indian Statistical Institute, Calcutta, To promote knowledge of and research on statistics and other subjects relating to national development and social welfare and to provide for, and undertake the collection of information, investigations, projects and operational research for planning and the improvement of the efficiency of management and production, departments of theoretical statistics, applied statistics and computing, social sciences, physical and earth sciences, statistical quality control and operational research, biological sciences, library, documentation and information sciences; maintains research units, laboratories; conducts courses leading to the Bachelor's Master's and Doctorate Degrees;
- Institute of Mathematical Sciences, Chennai.

Physical Sciences

- Alipore Observatory and Meteorological Office, Calcutta
- Astronomical Observatory of St Xavier's College, Calcutta
- Bhabha Atomic Research Centre, Mumbai, National Centre for research in and development of nuclear energy for peaceful purposes; facilities include: three research reactors; Van de Graaff accelerator, laboratories at

Srinagar, Gulmarg and Gauribidanur; isotope production unit; central workshops; pilot plants for production of heavy water, ziroconium titanium, etc.: uranium metal plant; food irradiation and processing laboratory; reactor engineering laboratory and test facilities.

- Central Seismological Observatory, Shillong
- Geodetic and Research Branch, Survey of India, Dehra Dun
- Geological Survey of India, Calcutta, Devoted to study of geology, geophysics, engineering geology, mineral resources, exploration and research
- Indian Meteorological Department, New Delhi
- Indian Bureau of Mines, Nagpur
- Indian Institute of Astrophysics, Bangalore, Specializes in the study of solar physics, stellar physics, sollar system objects, theoretical astrophysics including ionosphere, cosmology, solar-terrestrial relationship and instrumentation
- Indian Institute of Geomagnetism, Mumbai
- Indian Space Research Organization (ISRO), Bangalore
- Indira Gandhi Centre for Atomic Research, Tamil Nadu
- Institute for Plasma Research, Gandhi Nagar
- Inter-University Centre for Astronomy and Astrophysics, Pune, Fundamental research and training in all aspects of astronomy and astrophysics; MSc and Ph.D, refresher courses, research workshops, etc.
- Mining, Geological and Metallurgical Institute of India, Calcutta
- National Institute of Rock Mechanic, Karnataka
- Nizamiah and Japal-Rangapur Observatories and Centre of Advanced Study in Astronomy, Hyderabad
- Physical Research Laboratory, Ahmedabad, Centre for space research and post-graduate studies leading to Ph.D. degree; research in atmospheric sciences and

planetary aeronomy, optical, infrared and radio astronomy (interplanetary scintillations), astrophysics, atomic and molecular physics, nuclear and particle physics, laser physics and quantum optics, plasma theory and experiment, oceanography and climate studies, solar system and geochronology

- Saha Institute of Nuclear Physics, Calcutta

Technology

- Ahmedabad Textile Industry's Research Association, Ahmedabad
- Atomotive Research Association of India, Pune
- Birla Research Institute for Applied Sciences, MP
- Bombay Textile Research Association, Mumbai, Research in all aspects of processing cotton, silk and other natural and man-made fibres; training/communication and library services, seminars, etc.; recognized for post-graduate studies by University of Mumbai.
- Bureau of Indian Standards (BIS), 9 Bahadur Shah Zafar Marg, New Delhi
- Central Institute for Research on Cotton Technology, Mumbai
- Central Water and Power Research Station, Pune
- Indian Lac Research Institute, Ranchi
- Indian Rubber Manufacturers Research Association, Maharashtra
- Institute of Hydraulics and Hydrology, Tamil Nadu
- Irrigation and Power Research Station, Amritsar
- National Council for Cement and Building Materials
- National Institute of Hydrology, UP
- Pulp and Paper Research Institute, Orissa
- Research Designs and Standards Organization, Lucknow
- Silk and Art Silk Mills' Research Association, Mumbai
- Telecommunications Research Centre, New Delhi

- Birla Institute of Technology, Mesra, Ranchi
- Birla Institute of Technology and Science, Rajasthan.

Institutes with University Status

- All-India Institute of Medical Sciences, New Delhi, undergraduate and postgraduate training, research in all brands of medicine
- Indian Agricultural Research Institute, New Delhi
- Indian Institute of Science, Karnataka
- Indian Institute of Technology, Mumbai
- Indian Institute of Technology, Delhi
- Indian Institute of Technology, Kanpur
- Indian Institute of Technology, Kharagpur
- Indian Institute of Technology, Chennai
- Indian School of Mines, Bihar, Degree Courses, postgraduate and research degrees
- International Institute for Population Sciences, Mumbai
- National Law School of India University, Bangalore
- School of Planning and Architecture, New Delhi
- Sree Chitra Tirunal Institute for Medical Sciences and Technology, Kerala
- Tata Institute of Social Sciences, Mumbai

Colleges

- Administrative Staff College of India, Hyderabad, conducts post-experience management development programmes in general management and in specific fields; specialized programmes for education, hospital and government administrators and R & D Managers.
- Indian Institute of Management, Ahmedabad, 2-year postgraduate, 4-year doctoral programme in management, general and functional management programmes for practising managers, and special programmes for government officials, university teachers, trade union leaders and sectors such as agriculture, public

systems; undertakes project research and consulting in the field of management.

- Indian Institute of Management, Bangalore
- Indian Institute of Management, Calcutta
- Indian Institute of Management, Lucknow

National Institute of Educational Planning and Administration, New Delhi, Diploma courses for education personnel of developing countries and district education officers, other in-service training courses; research in various aspects of educational planning and management; consultancy service for developing countries, State Governments and other organizations; collaboration with UNESCO and other foreign agencies

- All India Institute of Hygiene and Public Health, Calcutta
- National Institute of Health and Family Welfare (NIHFW), New Delhi, In-service training, MD course in community health administration, biomedical research, research and consultancy regional centre for health management documentation and reprographic services
- Institute of Radiophysics and Electronics, Calcutta, Houses postgraduate teaching and research department of University of Calcutta Faculty of Technology; 3-year post-BSc integrated course leading to B.Tech. Degree, and 1½ year post-B. Tech/BE course leading to M.Tech. degree in radiophysics and electronics conducts training programmes; research facilities in radio wave propagation, radio astronomy, solid state and microwave electronics, millimetre wave technology, solid state devices, plasma and quantum electronics, optoelectronics, control systems and micro-computers, communication theory and systems, micro electronics and VLSI technology, maintains ionosphere field station at Haringhata and radio astronomy field station at Kalyani, National Institute of Fashion Technology, New Delhi, Undergraduate and postgraduate diploma courses relevant to the textiles and clothing industries.

- Seshasayee Institute of Technology, Tiruchirapalli, Training to diploma level in civil, mechanical and electrical engineering, computer science and engineering, instrumentation technology, pulp and paper technology, post-diploma course in plant maintenance.

Institutes Involved in Educational Research

- **Type of research :** Basic and action research related to education and rural development, non-formal education, educational planning and administration.
- **Functional objectives of research :** Full-fledged research, research for partial fulfilment of M.Phil and Ph.D. degrees; to evolve alternatives to the formal education system to discover and evolve linkages between education and development, to experiment and innovate in all aspects of the educational process with a view to benefiting the disadvantaged sections of society.
- **Central Institute of Educational Technology, New Delhi**

  Type of research : Formative and developmental summative planning and research.

  Functional objectives of research: To improve the quality of instructional packages; to assess effectiveness and achievement; to evaluate the programmes.
- **National Council of Educational Research and Training, New Delhi**

  Type of research: Basic, applied and developmental research.

  Functional objectives of research: Preparation of courses, servicing the educational administration; undertake help and coordinate research in all branches of education, organize perspective and in-service training in the field of education (advanced level); organize extension programmes and clearing house activities.
- **National Institute of Educational Planning and Administration, New Delhi**

  Type of research: Applied research

Functional objectives of research: Improvement of educational planning and administration; preparation and enrichment of training courses; seminars and workshops.

- **Directorate of Adult Education, New Delhi**

  Type of research: Applied research; action-oriented research having relevance to improvement of on-going adult education programme.

  Functional objectives of research: To emanate useful and high quality research; to coordinate research activities; to disseminate research findings in a manner that would comprehensible and practical for the improvement of the on-going programmes of adult education.

- **Regional College of Education, Ajmer**

  Type of research: Partial fulfilment of degree requirements; servicing the educational administration.

- **Regional College of Education, Bhopal**

  Type of research: Basic and applied research

  Functional objectives of research: Creation of modalities of integrated teacher training programme; undertake pilot studies and research projects on curricula, teaching methods, teacher education, elementary and secondary education.

- **Regional College of Education, Mysore**

  Type of research: Applied research

  Functional objectives of research: To improve the quality of education in secondary schools in the southern region of India.

- **Regional College of Education, Orissa**

  Type of research: Applied research and development

  Functional objectives of research: Partial fulfilment of degree requirements; preparation of materials; advanced research.

Annexure IV

Education for Development in Twenty First Century*

P.V. Indireasen

It is widely accepted that the coming age will be the Information Age where every nation's prosperity will depend on its ability to process information. It is a fact that technological progress is so rapid that professional skills get obsolete very fast, so fast that they no longer last a life time. So to remain prosperous, one and all have to go back to school again and again to learn new skills from time to time. This phenomenon may be explained in terms of what may be described as half-life skills: the period over which half of existing skills are liable to be superseded by better ones. In the medieval agricultural age, the half-life skills extended over centuries; in the industrial age, over a period of few generations; these days that has already become less than a career length—that is why we need refresher courses. In the coming age skills are liable to become truly impermanent; require innovation every few years. For instance, even today, the half-life of technology in some areas of computers is barely two-three years.

There is another economic issue, which too is likely to become major problem in the coming years: in the agricultural age, the economic ambitions were centered on inheriting ancestral land; in the machine age, the concern shifted to high-wage, life long employment. For the coming years indication

* Extract from "Monograph on Educational Planning Human Resource Planning and Development International Post Graduate Course of Institute of Applied Manpower Research, New Delhi (Restricted Circulation)

are that the pressure will be on for continuous career advancement—the economy and the society is expected to offer career advancement year after year. People will be getting obsolete day after day, yet, they will be so ambitious as to demand personal advancement all the time.

In addition to these economic problem, the twentieth century is likely to throw up certain difficult social problems too. The world has become a global village so now no nation can remain an island and shall have to become an integral part of the world at large. In the coming age cultural invasions will be unavoidable, so much so, it will become increasingly impractical to preserve and protect one's own traditions. In this global village, cultural tensions are more likely to increase than decrease. As a result, there is a danger that people in search of identity may turn to religious fundamentalization and make that a deadly issue. Thus, as we are already witnessing, the twenty-first century may throw up a paradox by which people in the antipodes may become close (and friendly) neighbours, but people next door may be deemed deadly enemies.

Finally, there is an issue which has already assumed significant proportions—the question of environment and its counterpart, sustainable development.

In brief, as indicated in Table 1, in the twenty-first century, all countries will have to prepare themselves to face major development shifts. These will create new problems before educators: they will have to educate not only the youth, but the entire population; the education they offer will have to prepare one and all to become, socially responsible citizens of the world, and at the same time, good neighbours too. Also people will have to be trained to prosper in an environment, which is ever changing in a kaleidoscopic fashion.

TABLE 1

Shift of Paradigms between the Past and the Future

Item	*The Past*	*The Present*	*The Future*
Tools of Production	Agriculture	Machinery	Information
Half-life of skills	Generations	Decades	Less than a decade
Economic ambitions	Inheritance	Salaries	Competitive careers

International linkages	Few	Limited	Overwhelming
Cultural privacy	Extensive	Limited	Virtually non-existent
Cultural identity	Local tribe	Nation	Fundamentalist religion
Environmental	Preservation	Development	Sustainable development

Growth and Development

Even economists are often confused about the meaning and significance of the concept of development. Hence, it is worthwhile to refresh ourselves about the meaning of development. Often the terms growth and development are used interchangeably as though the two mean the same. As a matter of fact, there is a subtle distinction between the two. Growth is a matter of quantitative change only, but development involves a qualitative change as well. The Oxford Dictionary describes development as: "to bring out, what is latent and to make it active". In other words, development is a chemical, innovative change which leads to the formation of a new compound quite different from the mixture of its original ingredients.

Growth is an objective of development and is quite distinct from development—an undeveloped or underdeveloped community may be growing while a developed one may actually be declining. At the same time, even in such a case, further development can occur only when where is growth. In other words, there could be growth without development, but there can be no development without growth in some form or other.

Another feature of development is its multi-dimensional character. As Caircross (1962) puts it, "Development is not just a matter of having plenty of money nor is it purely an economic phenomenon. It embraces all aspects of social behaviour; the establishment of law and order, including dealings with the revenue authorities; relationships between the family, literacy, familiarity with mechanical gadgets and so on."

Finally, development involves a discontinuity whereas growth is a continuous process. In the words of Schumpeter (1961), "Development is a discontinuous and spontaneous change in the stationary state which forever alters and displaces the equilibrium state previously existing. Growth is a gradual and steady change which comes about by a general increase in the rate of savings and in population."

An understanding of these features of development is important for future educators: what they should plan for, is not growth; not marginal additions and subtractions here and there, but radical paradigm shifts.

Sustainable Development

For some years now, there has been a deep concern among thoughtful people regarding the manner in which development is sought to be obtained. The problem is best expressed in Schumacher's (1973) words:

"One of the most fateful errors of our age is the belief that the problem of production has been solved. To use the language of the economist, it lives on irreplaceable capital which it cheerfully treats as income. I specified three categories of such capital; fossil fuels, the tolerance margins of nature, and the human substance."

These issues of sustainable development impose on educators usual responsibilities: it is not enough for them to dispense knowledge; they have to alert students (who, as explained above, will soon constitute the entire population) about the limitations of knowledge as much as they will normally do about its utility.

The Future Challenge of Education

Putting together expected development changes in the coming age and the fundamental requirements of sustainable development, the future challenges of education may be described as:

1. Training youngsters in logic, the manipulation of abstract symbols and increasingly language skills too.
2. Ensuring flexibility in syllabus, and installing a management structure which accommodates change with ease.
3. Re-training the entire population frequently.

4. Cultivating a spirit of tolerance, and inculcating a positive appreciation of cultural difference.
5. Imparting training in social skills and inoculating minds against xenophobia.
6. Imparting knowledge of religion other than one's own, and training students to tolerate, if not appreciate multiplicity of religious experiences.
7. Sensitizing students to the issue of the critical balance between environment preservation and economic progress.

All these issues creating complex philosophical problems, raise difficult policy issues. Instead of expanding further on these controversial issues, we shall now concentrate on one topic, and use it as an illustration of the meaning of paradigm shift in resolving ticklish issues. The topic chosen for this purpose is the conflict between merit and social justice in the admission of students in higher educational institutions.

Merit and Social Justice

As mentioned above, globalization is a development shift that is already with us. It would appear that, as a consequence, there will be greater social harmony in the world, but the prospects are distinctly otherwise: just as there is greater de-humanization and more violence in large cities than in small towns, we should expect increased conflicts when more and more people are brought close together in a global metropolis. (It is fashionable to talk of a "global village", but that is native romanticism; the truth is likely to be closer to a global metropolitan jungle). The deeper the people get immersed in the global community, the greater the risk that they will suffer from xenophobia.

This problem is liable to get further exacerbated because no matter how carefully a community is organized, social differences will not vanish: after all, half the people have to be below average, and only a few can occupy the commanding heights of society. Inevitably, populist politicians will exploit such societal differences for their own selfish purposes, and the educational system will become an inescapable victim. More specially, access to higher education will become a matter of controversy with demagogues ever eager to advocate ethic cleansing of academia. In Bosnia lives are being destroyed; in many universities minds are being destroyed with no less ferocity. How do we protect academia from such dangers? That is a question for which we will have to find a answer.

In searching for a solution, we should first of all enquire who needs higher education? Table 2 gives the percentage in each age group that has enrolled at the primary, secondary and tertiary levels of education in selected countries of the world. Two points are worthy of note. First successful countries have all near 100 per cent enrolment right up to secondary level; second, United States with 57 per cent enrolment at the tertiary level, has done no better than Japan with only a 30 per cent enrolment. Sri Lanka has a paltry 4 per cent enrolment at the tertiary level, but that has not prevented her from exhibiting the highest Development Quality Factor in the world—numerical superiority in international ranking according to Human Development Index (HDI) compared to ranking by GNP China's case is even more starting: only 2 per cent enrolled at the tertiary level; yet China is one of the fastest growing economies in the world. Hence, the case frequently made in favour of virtually universal tertiary education does not stand proven.

It that be so, two questions follow: First, the quantitative one—what percentage of youth should be entertained for higher education? Second, the qualitative one—who should be entitled to such education?

Let us consider the qualitative question first. In India and in countries like Malaysia the view is that the socially backward communities should be given preference over more meritorious students from forward communities. In contrast, in China, selection is strictly by merit; even scholarships are for merit only; the poor can only aspire for loans to meet the cost of tertiary education. Further, even though there is not much difference in purchasing power between the two countries, engineering education fees in China is $3000 per year while it is barely $60 in India. Both countries claim to socialistic; yet, there are gross differences in their educational policies.

TABLE 2

Per Capita Educational Enrolment Q Factor*

Country	*GNP*	*Secondary*	*Tertiary*	*HDI*	*Primary*	
Japan	5049	96	30	.983	102	2
USA	5075	99	57	.976	101	4
Costa Rica	4542	42	26	.852	87	34
Brazil	4718	39	12	.730	88	-17
Sri Lanka	2405	74	4	.663	100	44
China	1990	48	2	.566	100	41
Pakistan	1862	22	3	.311	?	3
India	1072	44	7	.309	?	12

(*GNP ranking minus HDI ranking)

(*Source* : Human Development Report, UNDP, New York, 1993)

Non-academic Pressures

This problem has been mentioned to highlight the fact that education is not merely an academic problem; it has important socio-political dimensions too. The Chinese argue that those who get engineering education get a substantial private economic return in the form of high salaries and status. Hence, they see no reason why such education should be subsidized. The Indian government argues that backward classes have suffered for centuries, and it is but proper that they should be compensated for the loss their forefathers suffered at the hands of the forward castes. It is also contended that without such benefits, the backward castes will remain permanently crippled. This is a controversy that is not going to be settled by an intellectual debate, but yet will critically affect the intellectual climate. Here, we shall attempt to tackle the issue by considering a novel policy which promises to indicate intrinsically both how many should be trained and who should be trained—by means of, what economists call, *Revealed Preference.*

In this connection, the primary problem is that not enough candidates are available from backward castes; yet their quotas must be filled. Inevitably that leads to lowering of standards. Ideally, selections should be made to satisfy all without interfering with standards. Unfortunately, it is common practice to measure standards not by ability, but by academic paper qualifications. Further, over the years entry barriers for various jobs have been raised well above acceptable levels. For instance, a tenth standard pass was once adequate to become a clerk; now, even with an MA degree such positions are difficult to obtain. As a result, there is an artificial pressure for higher education far beyond what the economy can support or needs. In this process, only backward classes will suffer most. First, as backward classes have higher dropout rates, smaller and smaller number of them become eligible; second, their dropout rate by itself increases as proper people are deterred by the larger duration of the minimum education needed for entry.

In consequence, higher education comes under attack on two fronts: first, because backward class students are fewer, pressures are mounted to lower standards to admit more of them; secondly, more students join though, strictly speaking, the education imparted has no relevance to their future careers. That is, higher education treated as a mechanism for short-listing, and not as a preparation for a profession, let alone as a venture in learning. Then we need a mechanism which steers higher education towards real needs, and at the same time offers a fair chance to backward classes. Either way, a critical part of the problem is differential dropout rates—the higher dropout rates among backward classes causing distortion in the final outcome.

Poor children drop out of schools early for three main reasons: (a) Schools are unattractive with uninspiring teachers, (b) parents need the earning of their children at an early age and (c) little economic value in schooling is seen—unemployment levels in India among the educated (high school and above) is (according to the 1981 Census figures) four times more than that among the uneducated. Even in Japan, unemployment amongst the Ph.Ds is reported to be high. In fact, as of today, the prospects of employment, appropriate to qualifications secured get bleaker and bleaker as the level of education increases. The rich can afford to remain unemployed, or under-employed, but the poor cannot afford to speculate on educational investment.

Selection with Revealed Preference

In this connection, it is interesting to observe that— as differences in dropout rates increases as the level of education increases— the lower the educational standard prescribed, the lower will be the disparities in dropout rates between different communities. Then, the poor will benefit most if selection is based on minimum qualification necessary. Instead, the present practice is to select the maximally qualified—who will naturally be largely from forward communities, and relatively few from backward ones.

In India, it is even now accepted that high school certificate is sufficient to recruit army officers (who can even become Field Marshals). Yet, a person may not be accepted as a bus conductor, even if he flaunts a university degree. Probably, over 95 per cent of jobs will require no more academic expertise than what can be obtained in a primary school, at the most in a secondary school. Therefore, for all but very specialized jobs, academic qualifications need only be modest. Then in order to ensure better and increased employment opportunities for the poor, (a) entry qualifications may be reduced to the barest minimum needed, (b) no extra value, exactly zero credit, be accorded for all qualifications and expertly as in a queue, on a first come, first served basis.

This scheme (Indirasen, 1990) may be called admission (as opposed to selection) by Queuing with Minimum Qualifications (QMQ). As operates on the basis of a queue, the selection is open, each candidate knows where he or she stands. As the process is one of admission and not of selection, much of the suspicions and trauma associated with present day procedures are avoided. Also once in the queue, admission is guaranteed sometime or other. Most important because admission is on the basis of minimum qualifications, and higher academic qualifications have zero value, many more among the poor can qualify than at present. What is more, the guarantee of admission provides a powerful inducement not to dropout until and unless the applicant is personally convinced that the minimum requirement is beyond his, or her, capability. That is, we get self-rejection in place of external, official rejection. In this case, as dropout rates tend to get equalized, all communities are likely to get near-equal opportunities.

There can be an apprehension that QMQ may be misused, and the poor deprived of their rights through discriminatory test procedures. Such misuse may still be minimized by adopting as far as possible open procedures, that may be done through, what is called, the mastery mode (MM) of training and selection.

At the present time, all tests are based on, what may be best described as the grace marks mode. If 35 per cent is accepted as the pass level, if implies that the balance of 65 marks are allowed as grace. Then, the candidates may not know worse still, may know wrongly this large proportion of knowledge or skill. This makes the whole exercise a matter of dispute, because it can be quite legitimately asked why the number of grace marks should be 65 and not 68 or 70 or whatever else. In consequence, it introduces an ever increasing pressure to reduce educational standards. Further, the secrecy that shrouds examinations makes the exercise highly suspect.

A better alternative is the mastery mode. This is like a high jump contest, where one either passes the test or one does not. In such a test, the level is openly preset, there is no dispute about success or failure. The result is apparent to all including the candidate. Likewise, in the mastery mode, questions are disclosed to all candidates beforehand; there is no secrecy either about the questions or about the evaluation. Candidates take the test whenever ready. Once, they qualify, they get into the queue and when their turn comes, automatically get admitted.

Here is a system which inherently indicates Revealed Preference for education, both for buyers (employers) and suppliers (students) of academic skills employers indicate what is their minimum need because anything higher will curtail their profits; students too reveal their true preference because they will attempt only where they hope to succeed and will dropout only when skills needed become too high. Some may, of course, go on trying, but there is the waiting list to help them decide what to attempt, and what not to attempt. In fact, the length of the waiting list reveals how keen a candidate is.

Further, because test levels are preset and are no surprises and no secrecy. So, ideally there is no scope to manipulate; that should inspire confidence in the fairness of the system.

The Development Approach

This solution has been presented here as an example of "development" thinking, how one may find interesting solutions by attempting paradigm shifts instead of clinging to conventional wisdom. It is immaterial whether any particular solution finds favour or not, it is our intellectual responsibility to ever attempt novel solutions even if it hurts us personally. In the example quoted there, the higher education cake will inevitably shrink, but if that is proper, we as intellectuals, should not only accept it, but even propose it ourselves.

This example highlights three important aspects of education: First, education cannot survive exclusively in an ivory tower; it has to face political interference. Secondly, for most aspirants, education is not an end in itself, but is the means for economic advancement and no more than what they deserve, they will have to pay for it through excessive political interference, and ultimately, suffer the consequences themselves.

Ivory Towers

Does this mean, we cannot have an ivory tower educational all? Not having ivory towers will be a pity, because in such a case, who will write papers like mine? Ivory tower education is needed, but only to the extent the economy will support such a venture, and the students are keen to attempt it. Today, in most countries, the quantum of higher education is largely delinked from economic needs. That appears good for college teachers—they get more career opportunities. But that is like selling one's soul to the devil; it makes students disgruntled, and invites dangerous interference from politicians.

The classical tradition of liberal education should continue, but even in the coming years, it will genuinely interest a tiny minority only; for others, education is essentially a commodity. The QMQ and MM procedures described above can reveal what is that genuine need. They can help to check the current tendency of exchanging quantity for quality. Then only will ivory towers, whose sustenance is quality become respectable.

It may be thought that problems of this nature are peculiarly Indian. That is not necessarily true. As globalization proceeds, and competition becomes increasingly severe, competitive selection will gradually exacerbate differences between advanced communities and backward ones. As a result, tensions are liable to increase inducing backward communities to resist with increasing violence selection based purely on merit. Hence, it is incumbent on the academic community to generate techniques by which inherent disparities do not translate to social conflicts. That is no doubt a political problem, but one that is too critical to be left to politicians, alone.

Conclusion

There is a view that the real change the twenty-first century will bring is to replace blue collar worker by white collar ones. If that is the only problem, modernizing the syllabus alone will suffice. However, that is too simplistic a view. As of now, education and professional occupations form a sequence; in the future, they will continue to alternate all through one's life. Universities and the society will have to accept that a degree is not a life-long endowment; instead, that it is a fast depreciating asset, which needs to be replenished periodically to remain valid.

Globalization is in, and it will prove to be a double-edged sword. It will bring people together and it will also increase opportunities for conflict. A static game like chess may be played without a referee, but a "contact" game like basket ball even a friendly practice game, needs a referee who will be blowing the whistle all the time. Globalization is rather like a basket ball game with the added complication that the number of players will increase beyond count. That is how globalization is likely to accentuate rather than diminish cultural tensions. As action and reaction are equal and opposite, increasing globalization is liable to increase rivalism to an equal degree. To keep such risks in check, new administrative solutions will have to be found, and new education responsibilities— to train students to be global citizens—will have to be shouldered. Hence, globalization will demand new kinds of personality development and social skills; the ability to interact with different cultures and tolerate such differences. The education system will be a failure if it does not prepare students to face these new challenges. In fact, the fastest growth area for higher education will be to train impartial referees whose numbers are liable to explode in a global jungle.

Increasing religious fundamentalism is a possible consequence of globalization. The solution is not to deny religion, but to make people appreciate different kinds of religious experiences. For instance, training people to respect other beliefs and faiths, and yet be capable of remaining faithful to their own inheritance; to be good Muslims, or Christians or Buddhists or Hindus, without feeling threatened by any of the others. In the last century, academia abandoned religion. Bosnia, Kashmir and if I may be permitted to say, LTTE too are as much failures of academia as those of politicians. In the new century academia will have to learn how to bring different peoples and their faiths together; train them to handle conflict, to live happily in an increasingly competitive, multi-cultural village.

More important academics have to do some soul searching. Have they over-sold the importance of higher education? Have more students been inveigled into universities than what the universities can usefully train? Have universities been repositories of wisdom or have they themselves been adding fuel to flames that are burning down our societies? After all, ethnic cleansing is not confined to Bosnia alone; it is happening even inside academia, and academics are not free from blame.

The organizational challenge of education in the twenty-first century is to make education an exercise in quality, with quantity matched to what the economy can absorb in each and every discipline; to make education a fast-response process which can keep pace with the expected rapid changes in technology, and further provide the full range of skills a modern economy needs. Further, in spite of such a materialistic approach, the education system should ensure that there is always a corner where people like you and I can play and dream, and think esoteric ideas.

References

1. Indiresan, P.V. (1990), Managing Development: Decentralization. Geographical Socialism and Urban Replication, New Delhi, SAGE.
2. Schumacher, E.F. (1973), Small is Beautiful, London, Blond and Briggs.
3. Schumpeter, J.A. (1961), The Theory of Economic Development, New York, Oxford University Press.

Annexure V

Engineering Occupation and Education

Engineering Panorama

In the present era of scientific revolution, the fields of engineering and technology are also expanding fast. There are now about twenty five broad engineering disciplines and an equal number of technologies at the degree level. At the diploma level their number is around eighty.

Engineering Education

Engineering education at the following four levels is now available in the country:-

Level of Courses	Type of Institutions
1. Doctorate/Post Graduate Level	These courses are available at most of the engineering institutes such as IITs, Birla Institute of Technology, Institute of Science, Roorke University, Regional Engineering Colleges and most of the Government and renowned private colleges.
2. Degree Courses in Engineering	Available at all Engineering and Technology Colleges and in some departments of the universities.

3. Diploma level courses in Engineering and Technology	Available at all Polytechnics.
4. Craftsmen Courses	Available at Industrial Training Institutes ITIs and through apprenticeship programme under the Apprenticeship Act. 1961

Over and above these levels of engineering education, which are through recognized channels, there are also unrecognized or informal system, for such education. Privately run engineering institutions, which are neither affiliated to any university nor government or All India or state councils of Technical Education also prepare students in this field. These institutes generally prepare students for self-employment or assist them in acquiring qualification under distance learning programmes of open university or for affiliate membership of Institution of Engineers such as AMIE, etc. Of recent, a large network of computer training institutes have also come up all over the country to provide education in computer fields such as for Data Entry Operators, Supervisors, Software professionals, etc. Some of these institutes have made arrangements with foreign institutes for award of certificates/ Diploma on completion of different levels of training. In a few cases, courses run by private computer training institutes have been approved by the department of Electronics, Government of India as being a recognized qualification for employment. For example, UPTRON,. DDE, ACE Course has been recognized by Department of Electronics, and other government organization. Similarly, APTECH have also arrangement with Indira Gandhi National Open University (IGNOU) for a Bachelor level education under the distance learning programme of the university.

The following Tables illustrates the growth of Postgraduate engineering education in the country.

TABLE

Growth of Post-Graduate Engineering Education

Year	*No. of Engineering Colleges having Post-Graduate Courses*	*Total No. of Post-Graduate Specialities/ Disciplines*	*Total Outturn of Post-Graduate Engineers*
1947	3	2	13
1960	27	48	512
1970	62	94	1970
1980	94	137	2661
1989	143	301	5160
1992	144	323	7060

Engineering Courses run by the Department of the Universities.

Apart from engineering colleges/institutions, several universities also run engineering and technology courses through their individual departments. For example, Department of Electronics and Communication, Institute of Applied Physics and Technology, Allahabad University, provide degree level education in Electronics and Telecommunication Engineering. The Department of Chemical Technology of the Bombay University provides degree level education in Chemical Engineering and Technology courses. Admissions to these courses are made as per the rules of the university concerned.

Departmental Institutions

There are also some Government Departments which run their own engineering institutions. Most of such internal courses are affiliated to some university. Admissions to these institutions are made by the department concerned. Some of such Institutions set up by the Central Government are:

Organization	*Institutions*	*Scope*
1. Ministry of Railways	Government Engineering Institution, Jamalpur	The scope of this Institute is to train engineers for the Indian Railways who are recruited through UPSC as special class Railway apprentices. The selection for this made on All India basis through a competitive examination.

2. Ministry of Defence	1. College of Military Engineering, Pune.	The Scope of this Institutes is to train Officers of the Defence forces as engineers in different branches.
	2. Military College of Electronics and Mechanical Engineering., Secundrabad.	-do-
	3. Military College of Telecommunication Engineering, Mhow	-do-
	4. Naval College of Engineering (INS Shivaji). Lona Vala	-do-
3. Ministry of Transport		
1. Directorate General of Shipping Mumbai	1. TS Chanakaya, Mumbai, (90 Seats)	The scope of these is to train Navigators and Engineers for Merchant Navy
	2. Marine Engineering and Research Institute Calcutta. (120 Seats)	Admissions to these are made on all India basis through Joint Entrance Examination (JEE) of IITs. The age limit for these courses is higher upto 20 years (As on 1st October) for general candidates and 25 years for SC/ST candidates.

Apart from the above, there are also several other streams of education avenues open to students to qualify as degree engineers. These are identified below:

(a) Institute of Engineers

(b) Institute of Electronic And Telecommunication Engineers (IETE)

(c) Associate Membership of the Aeronautical Society of India

(d) Distance Learning Programme of Open Universities

(e) Continuing Education

(f) Diploma Level Engineering Education

(g) Other Courses.

Bibliography

1. Ashok Chandra, Human Resources Planning, Some Concerns from the Technical and Vocational Education Sector, Indian Journal of Training and Development, 15(2), April-June, 1985.
2. B.L. Mathur (ed) Human Resources Development Strategic Approaches and Experiences.
3. Colin Clark, The Conditions of Economic Progress (Third ed.) McMillan & Co. Ltd., New York, 1960.
4. C.W. Mills, White Collar, New York, Oxford University Press, 1953.
5. Course Directory 1998, Advanced Level Telecom Training Centre, Ghaziabad, India.
6. Daniel Bell, The Coming of the Post-Industrial Society: A Venture in Social Forecasting, New York, Basic Books, 1973.
7. Dale S. Beach, (ed.), Managing People at Work, McMillan Publishing Co. Inc., New York, 1980.
8. Dorothy Riddle, Service-led Growth: The Role of the Service Sector in World Development, Praeger, New York, 1986.
9. D. Reisman, The Lonely Crowd, New Haven; Yale University Press, 1950.
10. E.M. Rao, Human Resource Management: Fact, Fiction and Fallacy.
11. Edwin B. Flippo, Personnel Management, McGraw-Hill Kogakusha Ltd., Tokyo, 1980.
12. Emile Durkheim, Division of Labour in Society. Trans with an introduction by Simpson George, New York, The Free Press of Glencoe, McMillan and Co., 1933.

13. E.P. Hawthorn, The Management and Technology, London, Mc-Graw Hill, 1978.
14. Ferris Gerald, Manual of Human Resource Management.
15. F. Tonnies, Community and Society, Trans. and Ed. by Charles Loomis, East Laming, The Michigan Estate University Press, 1957.
16. G. Hollinshead and Leat Mike, Human Resource Management: An International and Comparative Perspective, London, Pitman, 1995.
17. Gangadhar Rao, Human Resource Management in Indian Railways.
18. Gangadhar Rao and P. Subba Rao, Human Resource Management in Indian Railways.
19. Greetfield Hany 1, Allied Health Manpower: Trends and Prospects.
20. G. Venkatswamy, Training and Development in Public Enterprises in India.
21. Growth, April-October, 1991, Vol. 19, No. 2.
22. Growth, April-September, 1994, Vol. 22, No. 1.
23. Growth, July-September, 1996, Vol. 24, No. 2.
24. Growth, April-June, 1998, Vol. 26, No. 1.
25. G. Hollinshead and Leat Mike, Human Resource Management An International and Comparative Perspective, London, Pitman, 1995.
26. IJTD, April-June, 1995, Vol. XXV, No. 2.
27. IJTD, Jan-March, 1997, Vol. XXVII, No. 1.
28. Indian Railways, Year Book 1995-96.
29. Indian Railways, Year Book 1996-97.
30. Indian Railways, Year Book 1997-98.
31. Indian Railways, Annual Report and Accounts, 1995-96.
32. Indian Railways, Annual Report and Accounts, 1996-97.
33. Indian Railways, Annual Report and Accounts, 1997-98.

34. Joachin Singelmanu, From Agriculture to Services: The Transformation of Industrial Employment.

35. Kutti Vijaya, Services Sector and Employment, Yojana.

36. K. Barham and D. Marion, The Quest for the International Manager: A Survey of Global Human Resource Strategies, London: Business International Press, 1991.

37. Manpower Journal, 1989-90, Vol. 25.

38. Manpower Journal, 1990-91, Vol. 26.

39. Management Journal, January 1995, Vol. 8, No. 1.

40. MDI, Management Journal, July 1990, Vol. 3, No. 2.

41. MDI, Management Journal, Jan, 1995, Vol. 8, No. 1.

42. Max Weber, The Theory of Social and Economic Organization, Trans, by A.M. Henderson and Talcolt Parsons, New York. Oxford University Press, 1947.

43. M.P. Bansal, Human Resource Development in Public Enterprises.

44. Paradigm, The Journal of Institute of Management Technology, Ghaziabad, July 1988, Vol. 2, No. 1.

45. Prashashika, April-Sept, 1994, Vol. 22, No. 1.

46. Productivity, New Age International (P) Ltd. Publishers. July-Sept, 1997, Vol. 38, No, 2.

47. Productivity, Oct-Dec. 1997, Vol. 38, No. 3.

48. Public Enterprises Survey, 1990-91, Vol. 1.

49. Seventh Five Year Plan 1985-90, Vol. 2.

50. T.L. Hall and A. Mejia (ed.) Health Manpower Planning: Principles, Methods and Issues, Geneva, World Health Organization, 1948.

51. W.F. Whyte, The Organizational Man, New York, Doubleday, 1956.

52. W. Bussink and Others, Poverty and the Development of Human Resources: Regional Perspectives, Washington, D.C. IBRD, 1980.

53. W. Anthony and A.N. Elward, Management of Human Resources; A System Approach to Personnel Management, Columbus, Ohioand, 1977.

54. W.W. Burke, Organization Development: Reading, Addison Wesley, 1987.

55. WHO, Co-ordinated Health and Human Resource Development.

56. Y.P. Aggarwal, Education and Human Resource Development.

INDEX